THE COMPLETE IDIOT'S GUIDE® TO

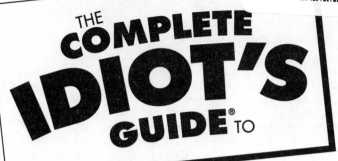

Wicca Craft

by Miria Liguana and Nina Metzner

ALPHA

A member of Penguin Group (USA) Inc.

For Paladin

Publisher: *Marie Butler-Knight*
Product Manager: *Phil Kitchel*
Senior Managing Editor: *Jennifer Chisholm*
Senior Acquisitions Editor: *Randy Ladenheim-Gil*
Book Producer: *Lee Ann Chearney/Amaranth Illuminare*
Development Editor: *Lynn Northrup*
Production Editor: *Janette Lynn*
Copy Editor: *Amy Borrelli*
Illustrator: *Kathleen Edwards*
Cartoonist: *Jody Schaeffer*
Cover/Book Designer: *Trina Wurst*
Indexer: *Tonya Heard*
Layout/Proofreading: *Angela Calvert, Mary Hunt*

Contents at a Glance

Contents

Foreword

Questions: When is a branch not just a stick? When is a rock not just a stone? When is bowl of leftovers not just a mess to be disposed of?

Answer: When it is in the hands of a Witch, where any item can be used as a tool for magical change.

I'm not an idiot. In fact, not meaning to boast, my I.Q. is above average ... considerably higher than some politicians of recent years. Yet here in this book, *The Complete Idiot's Guide to Wicca Craft*, I found many useful, interesting, and unusual projects that I never previously put thought to. For example, this book includes a variety of fascinating and unique ways to decorate a Book of Shadows, both inside and out, to make it more distinctive. For those who are devotees of the Goddess of arts and crafts, steps are even given on the process to make paper and how to bind the pages into a book. You can't get more personalized than that!

We of the Wicca walk between the worlds of spirit and form, knowing that each realm can affect the other. We consciously create bridges, links between these two domains for the purpose of creating magical transformation and deepening our connection with the Gods. Our altars are a personal microcosm, a reflection of the macrocosm of the universe. Our tools, whether it is a wand or amulet, are physical props that assist us in opening our inner awareness to the elemental forces, aiding us in visualizing our intentions and directing our energies toward change.

While *The Complete Idiot's Guide to Wicca Craft* includes tidbits of Craft (with a big "C"), lore, and wisdom, it is not just another book on Wicca. It is a craft (with a little "c") cookbook—a cauldron filled with useful information and witchy ideas. Most books on Wicca tell the reader what tools modern Witches should have in their collections. This book does not send you to the local occult store to find them ... unless it is to buy a crystal to top off your handcrafted wand. It encourages the reader to use her or his creative magical sense to fashion unique and personal magical instruments.

We practice an Earth-based religion. The earth is a living thing. It is a dirty, sticky, stinky, slimy, soft, hard, beautiful, ugly, wonderful place. Everything upon it, from concrete to moldy bread, can be used as a magical tool. Handling and transforming an object, giving it a name and purpose, creates a deep personal connection within the creator's psyche between the object and its intended purpose. Whether our hands are covered with flour from kneading dough or intuitively finding the right place on a staff to adhere a stone, we make an intimate connection with gifts of the earth. Tools fashioned with our own hands, self-defined and empowered with our own creative sweat and blood, hold the greatest power.

But *The Complete Idiot's Guide to Wicca Craft* is not only a book on crafting Wiccan tools. It is a treasure trove of ideas for both individual and group Sabbat activities. As a coven leader, I am always looking for innovative ways to open the members of my circle to the deeper mysteries of the Sabbats. Working with crafts, getting your hands dirty, and becoming immersed within the textures, scents, and sounds of the season, is a wonderful way to help connect with the energies of the Wheel.

I thoroughly enjoyed the projects and suggestions in this book, and I think you will, too. It has even encouraged me to take on a few new projects. I'm seeing hardware stores in a brand new light of possibilities. Now my only question is, how does one consecrate a miter saw?

—Laura A. Wildman, HPs

Laura Wildman is one of the original founders of the Pagan Networking organization New Moon New York. She is the Administrative Dean and an Instructor at Cherry Hill Seminary, a virtual Pagan seminary (see www.CherryHillSeminary.org), and an author. Her books include *What's Your Wicca I.Q.?* and *Wiccan Meditations: A Witch's Way to Personal Transformation*. Her latest book, *Magic in My Life: Celebrating the Pagan Soul* will be released by Citadel Press in May 2005.

Introduction

Let's start right here by saying that the most important and unique tool for walking the path of Wicca Craftworking is *you!* One of the most beautiful and enduring truths about practicing Wicca is that this is a nature-based religion that encourages you to connect in an active and positive way with the divine energy of the source of creation: the All. This pursuit, whether done in group practice, or on your own as a solitaire, is a path of personal enlightenment, discovery, and harmony with all that is human, nature, and spirit. When practicing Wicca, you are always *making and doing*, learning and growing in the Craft.

In *The Complete Idiot's Guide to Wicca Craft*, we give you projects on all aspects of Wicca that we hope will deepen and enhance your personal pathworking. We wish you the blessings of the Lord and Lady as you experience the beauty and joy of Wicca's many rituals, holidays, and magickal traditions by making and doing the projects in this book. *So mote it be!*

How to Use This Book

Okay, so it is time to start *making* magick. The way to use this book is to *use this book!* By the time you've completed the Craftworking projects, you'll kneel before your handcrafted altar, in personalized robes, with a crystal wand, an attracting energy potion, a pentagram Oracle … or, well … there are *so many possibilities*. With dozens of projects to choose from, you can make just about any tool of ritual, as well as learn how to use and direct its magickal energies. At the end of this journey we guarantee you'll stand in the center of your circle as a well-appointed witch! Here's what you can make and do with the projects in *The Complete Idiot's Guide to Wicca Craft*.

This book is divided into six parts:

Part 1, "The Art and Craft of Wicca," introduces you to Craftworking. Every religion has the spiritual tenets and beliefs of its practice, as well as the sacred items used to celebrate those tenets and beliefs. This part explores projects to help you start on the Wiccan path, dedicate yourself to the Craft, and make your own Book of Shadows.

Part 2, "Celebrating the Craft: Esbats and Sabbats," gives you projects, for both group ritual and solitaire practice, that enhance esbat Moon Magick, enrich the celebration of each of the Wiccan holidays on the Wheel of the Year, and help you connect to the divine natural energy of the Goddess and God as you honor the All.

Part 3, "For Every Magickal Purpose," details how to build altars, make magick circles, and create lovely pentagrams and pentacles. Using the projects in this part, you'll find fresh and practical ideas and suggestions to make your rituals, circle casting, and spellwork even more meaningful and powerful.

Part 4, "Make Your Own Ritual Tools and Talismans," tells you how to make all the ritual tools for your magickal closet—from athames to cauldrons to ritual robes and more. The experience of making and using your own ritual tools cannot be underestimated—handcrafted tools are infused with your deeply personal magickal energy and become the perfect reflection of your commitment and practice of the Craft. You'll also find tools for connecting to and working with allies such as faeries, elves, familiars, and more.

Part 5, "Get 'Crafty' and Make Magick," gives you projects to make tools used in various magickal traditions, including incense, candles, mirrors, poppets, cords, paper, flowers, and more. You'll also get lots of good advice for casting spells using these traditions. Using personally crafted tools can greatly enhance your magick.

Part 6, "Witches' Brew: Notions, Potions, and Powders," gives you lots of recipes for magickal compounds to use to purify and consecrate, to attract positive energy and dispel negative energy, potable (drinkable) potions for ritual and celebratory use, as well as creams and lotions you can use on your body to enhance your spiritual glow!

You'll also find two useful appendixes: a glossary of Craftworking terms and a resources listing for further exploration of Wicca and the Craft.

Extras

Throughout this book we've added four types of boxes containing definitions, tips, anecdotes and related information, and cautions to help you learn even more about Wicca and Craftworking.

Summon and Stir

Here, Liguana shares with you her experiences as a priestess on the Wiccan path, and gives personal advice for everything the projects in this book invite you to make and do for a deeper, richer understanding of the Craft.

CAUTION

Widdershins

You might know that the widdershins motion (anti-sunwise, which in the Northern Hemisphere is counterclockwise) dispels negative energy. Take heed with these warnings that help keep you moving unhindered on your path.

Magickal Properties

You'll discover the meanings of Wiccan and Craft-working terms you might not already know. And if you *do* already know them, perhaps you'll find a new magickal property for the term that you can put to good use! There's always room to learn and grow on the path.

Craftworking

These boxes contain handy and "Crafty" tips to help make your projects, spells, and rituals turn out a great success!

Acknowledgments

From Liguana:

I would like to thank Nina Metzner, of course, for all the hard work and warm words while we worked together. What a lovely way to meet a friend. I also want to thank Lee Ann Chearney of Amaranth Illuminare for giving me the opportunity to start this book and the moral support to finish it. A special thank-you and I love you to Theresa Fulton for her help with fashion designing and stitch-witchery. Finally, I send a warm thank-you and a grateful hug to Thaddeus Jurczynski for days upon days of technical support and computer know-how. I love all four of you.

From Nina:

I would like to thank Liguana for all of her great stories, her sound advice, and her incredibly good nature through it all. Thanks to Lee Ann Chearney for giving me this opportunity and trusting me to get it done, and to Kathy Edwards who created amazing illustrations to help it all make sense. To my dear friend and business colleague, Molly Forster, thank you, thank you, and thank you for picking up the slack while I was preoccupied with this project, for the happy-hour down times, and for never badgering me with "you shoulds." Thanks to Jim Nockunas, who keeps my world working smoothly in all kinds of ways. And finally, this is dedicated to my lost animal spirit, Paladin, who let me love him for a while and is surely in a better place now.

A Special Thanks to Our Editors at Alpha Books

Together we'd particularly like to thank senior acquisitions editor Randy Ladenheim-Gil of Alpha Books, a magickal and special person of boundless spirit and optimism;

we so appreciate her belief in us. Randy and the team at Alpha—publisher Marie Butler-Knight, senior managing editor Jen Chisholm, development editor Lynn Northrup, and production editor Janette Lynn—all gave their best energy to this book. Working with this team is a synergy that makes magick. We hope you feel the high vibration of positive energy as you turn the pages of this book and infuse it with your own positive magickal energy, too!

Trademarks

All terms mentioned in this book that are known to be or are suspected of being trademarks or service marks have been appropriately capitalized. Alpha Books and Penguin Group (USA) Inc. cannot attest to the accuracy of this information. Use of a term in this book should not be regarded as affecting the validity of any trademark or service.

Part 1

The Art and Craft of Wicca

The word *craft* has a double meaning in this book. Not only does it refer to practicing the Wiccan Craft, it also means handcrafting ritual tools, accessories, and magickal items. We'll even show you not only how to make your own Books of Shadows, but its paper, too! Here are some projects to get you started on learning the Wiccan path, dedicating yourself to your practice, and keeping a record of your journey.

Chapter 1

Learning Wicca

In This Chapter

◆ It's all about "doing"

◆ Live aware with a simple daily meditation

◆ Connecting with the natural world

◆ Host a garden party to celebrate nature and Wicca

◆ Turning the mundane into the sacred

This is a book about doing. Choosing and practicing a religion is—at first, anyway—a chance to embark on a new spiritual journey. However, once you've chosen to head down a particular spiritual path, engaging in outward rituals and projects that enhance that journey makes you much more committed to the practice of your religion. Our practice is the pathworking of Wicca.

In this book, you will find activities for every kind of witch—carpenters, gardeners, seamstresses, cooks, artists, hobbyists, and more. There are projects to share with friends and projects to work on alone. There are even projects suitable to share with children. Some activities require a little talent, but most require nothing but your willingness to participate and experiment. *The Complete Idiot's Guide to Wicca Craft* is not a primer on the basics of Wicca but more about how to enjoy and deepen your spirituality through making and doing projects. (For a good introduction to Wicca, see *The Complete Idiot's Guide to Wicca and Witchcraft, Second Edition;* see Appendix B for details.) Each project in this book engages your Wiccan practice, encourages a full understanding of Wiccan ritual and tools, and furthers your progress on the Wiccan path. In other words, as you work on these "crafts," you're also working on your "Craft." Pretty wonderful idea, isn't it?

Get Started "Doing"

There is no correct order to use in approaching the activities in this book. Neophytes as well as advanced Wiccan practitioners will find something here that will resonate with their particular interests or skills. But, whether you've already dedicated yourself to the Craft, or are just starting to explore the Wiccan path, let's start with a couple of easy projects to get you and your friends into the Wiccan spirit.

Craftworking

While any of the projects in this book can be done by a solitary practitioner, sometimes a group's energy makes for strong magick as well as more fun! Don't feel as though the group has to be a formal coven or even all practicing Wiccans. The laughter and camaraderie will produce its own magick.

A Simple Meditation

For the next month, go outside twice a day and listen to the world for a few minutes. It doesn't matter if you're in a big city or on a farm. Breathe deeply in through your nose and out through your mouth. Write down in your journal or Book of Shadows (see Chapter 3 for more about making your own Book of Shadows, a Wiccan diary and record-keeping book) what kind of weather the earth is experiencing. Feel yourself relax into the arms of the Goddess or the strong embrace of the God. Banish negative thinking with a chant:

I possess everything I need and more; my life and my world are filled with abundance.

Fill yourself with positive energy and make a note in your Book of Shadows about one special thing you saw or one thing you are especially grateful for that day. Don't discount noticing the small miracles and successes, like the sight of a red cardinal against the snow or the fact that your ginger cake turned out well and your headache is gone. The point is to live aware. Be in the moment and in the world. Then revel in it!

Bringing the Outside World In

Wicca is a nature-based religion built around seasonal changes that witches call the Wheel of the Year. Wiccan pathworking means following the turning of the wheel and celebrating the holidays that mark the seasons. The religion recognizes a divine source of all things, often called the Goddess or the Lady. It also recognizes a male aspect of divine energy and creativity, often called the God or the Lord. Many Wiccan rituals are meant to connect you to the earth and to the power of the Lady and Lord.

Making a Flower Chain

Flower chains are a great way to connect to the earth's bounty and beauty and to honor the Goddess at the same time. Flower chains can be part of many different Wiccan celebrations, especially those that celebrate spring or summer. Or use them as party favors at a children's party. Be creative with your newfound flower power!

You'll need a grocery bag full of flowers such as daisies, dandelions, clover, or other common flowers with long, flexible stems. Daisies symbolize innocence, gentleness, and loyal love, making them especially appropriate to weave into a crown or a necklace for a special friend. Clover brings good luck and hope, so those flowers are also a good choice. Although most people look at dandelions as weeds, Wiccans believe they protect family members from accidents and keep them healthy. They also symbolize money. (Aren't you sorry you've been digging them out of your yard?) Once you've chosen the flowers that strengthen your intent, follow these steps:

1. Make a cross with two flower stems as shown in the following illustration.

2. Bend the stem of the top flower around the stem of the bottom flower. Tie a knot with the flower stem and pull lightly to tighten.

3. Lay another flower over the joined stems and tie another knot.

Continue with these steps until the chain is as long as you like. Tie the very last stem around the first one to form a ring. Wear your flowers as a crown or a necklace.

Making a flower chain.

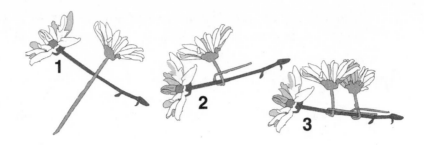

Making a Lavender Potpourri Sachet

Imagine the world without the natural smells of flowers and herbs, wonderfully embodied in potpourri. For hundreds of years, Mother Nature (a.k.a. the Goddess) has provided us with her bounty to keep away disease, improve our home environment, and embellish our gardens. Witches know scents can relieve depression, encourage sleep, and even arouse passion.

In the spiritual world lavender symbolizes devotion and trust. On a physical plane it soothes and relaxes jangled nerves. It's the perfect flower to scent a warm bath, fill an herb pillow, or tuck into a lingerie drawer.

Magickal Properties

Still rooms were a very important part of every Wise Woman's home during medieval times. (A Wise Woman is the Wiccan counterpart of the Crone aspect of the Goddess.) This was a place to dry the harvest of flowers and herbs, readying them for future use as scented waters, tonics, salves, teas, tinctures, and what we know today as potpourri.

Here's what you'll need:

- A 6-inch square or circle of material (cotton or muslin fabric is best)

- $1/4$ cup or more of dried lavender flowers (see the following instructions if you're drying it yourself)

- 12 inches of ribbon to match material

When harvesting lavender flowers to make your sachet, do so on a dry day and in the morning when the flowers on the lavender plant are not quite open. Cut the bloom stock 3 to 4 inches below the flower heads.

To dry the lavender, make small bunches of 8 to 12 stocks, fastening them together with a rubber band. Hang upside down in a dry place out of direct sunlight. If you don't have a *still room*, an extra bedroom will work. If you use a basement, shed, or attic to dry your flowers, make sure the humidity is low or your lavender will mold rather than dry. The drying process will take two to three weeks. Once dry, remove the flowers by stripping the stems through your fingers. Store them in a glass container with a lid in a cool dark place until you are ready to finish the sachet.

To make the sachet, place the lavender in the middle of your 6-inch square of material. Gather the material around the lavender and tie the top with the ribbon. Hang the sachet in your closet or put it in with your linens for a soothing fragrance next time you make your bed.

Planting a Windowsill Basil Garden

Another way to bring the outdoors into your Wiccan home is to plant an herbal garden that fits on your windowsill. Basil is an herb that does well indoors and adds a yummy touch to your spaghetti sauce! Medicinally, basil soothes an upset stomach; spiritually, it symbolizes love, although some say it is love washed with tears. Beginning any Wiccan project with love—whether stormy or calm—is bound to be a great start.

Like most herbs, basil does best in soil that is very well-drained and more poor than rich (poor soil concentrates the essential oils that give the lovely flavor).

Basil germinates easily. Place the seed on the soil, barely cover it with some sifted soil or sand, water, and wait. Keep it warm and sunny (it doesn't like cold at all) and pretty soon, you'll have a basil plant. As the plants grow, be sure to keep them well watered. Keep the plants in full sunlight and do not fertilize them.

To promote bushy growth, pinch the basil plants off at the growing tip as soon as 6 pairs of leaves have formed (usually at about 8 inches in plant height). When flowering starts, pinch off each flowering shoot, along with the leaf pair directly below (which should be used at once). The flower buds are as flavorful as or even more flavorful than the leaves, and should also be used in cooking. Toss them into your sauce as well.

Craftworking

Much of basil's tasty quality is lost in cooking, so for dishes containing basil, it is best—unless a recipe specifically says otherwise—to add it, preferably fresh-cut, shortly before serving.

Host a Garden Party

Now, take all the activities you've read about so far in this chapter and turn them all into a garden party for your coven or for your friends and family. You can make the preparations part of your pre-party plans, or wait until your guests arrive and have everyone work on the projects together.

Buy some small clay pots, some acrylic paint, and a variety of brushes, and let your guests decorate their own herb pot. Or provide beads, buttons, shells, and charms to use as decorations with enough glue to pass around. Then, let each guest take home a basil plant ready for potting (be sure to start your plants about 4 to 6 weeks before the party), a newly decorated pot, and a small bag of soil.

Or make flower chains together and take a meditation moment. Ask everyone to bring their Book of Shadows or provide each guest with paper and pens. Once everyone has taken a moment, ask them to don their flower chain one by one and share their thoughts with each other if they feel comfortable doing so. (Flower chains also make lovely centerpieces strewn down the middle of your dinner table.)

End the party with a flourish by serving a custard-filled gingerbread cake topped with fresh seasonal fruit.

For the cake:

- 1 egg
- 1 cup milk
- $^1/_2$ TB. almond extract
- 3 cups sifted flour
- 1 TB. baking powder
- $^1/_2$ tsp. salt

- 3 TB. ginger
- $^1/_2$ cup sugar
- $^1/_2$ cup (1 stick) butter
- Fresh seasonal fruit (peaches or nectarines are good choices)
- Powdered sugar

For the topping:

- 3 TB. butter
- 3 TB. flour

- $^1/_4$ cup sugar
- $^1/_2$ cup sliced almonds

For the custard filling:

- 1 cup light cream
- 2 egg yolks
- 1 TB. sugar

- 2 tsp. cornstarch
- 1 TB. vanilla

Preheat the oven to 400°F. Grease a round 9-inch cake pan. In a small bowl, beat together the egg, milk, and almond extract. In a large mixing bowl, combine the flour, baking powder, salt, ginger, and sugar. Cut the butter into the dry ingredients until crumbly. Add the milk mixture and stir quickly just until dry ingredients are moistened—don't over mix. Pour the batter into the prepared pan.

For the topping: Cut the butter into the flour and sugar. Add the almonds and spread the mixture evenly over the top of the batter. Bake for about 20 minutes.

For the custard filling: In a saucepan, whisk together the cream, egg yolks, sugar, and cornstarch. Bring to a simmer, stirring constantly until thickened. Let cool (covered), then stir in vanilla.

Split the cake into two even layers. Spread one layer with the custard filling. Top the custard with any fresh fruit (peaches are especially good with ginger) and then add the second layer. Dust the top lightly with powdered sugar.

Add small cucumber sandwiches to the menu or fresh crudités with a zesty dip if you want your guests to have something a little more than just "sweet." A variety of breads with flavored olive oil for dipping is also a nice addition. (See Chapter 20 for some sample recipes.)

Connecting with the Divine

One of the ways Wiccans connect with the Lord and Lady is through the use of symbols. Old Hermetic occult wisdom says, *As above, so below.* To many people practicing the Craft, this is interpreted to mean that what is grand and sacred and ethereal has something that corresponds to it in the mundane world. Nothing has ever existed in all of creation that was not first prefigured in the patterns of the spiritual world. A simpler way of thinking about it might be, "The microcosm reflects the macrocosm, and vice versa."

Summon and Stir

During the Middle Ages and later, a series of scripts attributed to Hermes Trismegistus known as the Hermetica were popular. "As above, so below" is an abridgement of an opening line, which says, "That which is above is like to that which is below, and that which is below is like to that which is above." The Hermetic scriptures enjoyed great credit and were popular among men of alchemy. The "Hermetic tradition" therefore refers to alchemy, magic, astrology, and related subjects.

In Wicca, we look for and work with these correspondences. We connect with the Divine by working with its mundane counterparts: the trappings, tools, and symbols of our magickal practice. Cauldrons, wands, brooms, and cloaks are all symbols of other divine objects.

Wiccans use a wide variety of working tools. While these tools are essential, they are just tools and have no power in and of themselves. Their purpose is to focus and refine our own internal power. Think of them as visual and manual aids to help your mind work the magick you desire. Ultimately, the success of your magick is in the belief, emotion, and discipline you bring to the ritual, not in the tools you use.

Making a Ritual Besom

Some Wiccans insist that a *besom* be made only out of broom plants of which there are several types, but this isn't necessarily true. In fact, it is said that fairies hate the scent of broom and good witches don't want to scare them off! Scotch broom also has a tendency to spread like wildfire, so be cautious about how much and where you plant it or it might take over your whole garden.

Here's what you'll need:

◆ A tree branch that is roughly the same thickness and length as a broom handle (or choose a branch that is a little shorter, but be prepared to have to stoop if you want to use it to sweep a magick circle)

◆ Straw, grass, hay, or any other long strands of decorative grasses to use as bristles (long stalks of herbs can be included for a fragrant touch)

◆ Twine or heavy string

Magickal Properties

A **besom** is a broom meant to be used on a spiritual plane to eliminate negative energy.

Widdershins

Just because this book gives a symbol a particular meaning, it doesn't mean you can't have your own ideas about meanings and correspondences. There is no definitive Holy Book in Wicca, and nothing is carved in stone. Always follow your own intuition. If it feels right, it probably is.

Lay the branch on a flat surface and bunch the bristle material around one end. Secure it to the branch by wrapping the twine around the grasses and branch nine times and tying a firm knot. In numerology, 9 represents one of life's luckiest numbers, and it is also the number of spiritual completion.

You can prop your besom next to your altar if you have room, or drill a hole in the top, thread a length of twine through the hole, and tie a knot in the ends. This allows you to hang the broom on a hook like a wall hanging until you need it.

Tools Don't Make the Witch

Don't feel as though you have to make all of the tools and embellishments in these chapters at once. You'll know when it's time to create a tool or to refurbish a "found" object to turn it into a tool. Truthfully, you can work magick without any tools, but these props keep your conscious mind occupied while the subconscious carries out your magickal intentions.

As you work through the projects in this book and handcraft the tools to use in your own rituals, remember their bigger meaning. A tool can be a symbol for the God or Goddess you are invoking. Or it might represent one of the four quarters—East, South, West, or North. Or it might represent an animal guide that has meaning for you. Even a simple task like sweeping can have a larger, symbolic meaning as you sweep negative energy out of your magick circle. A popular Wiccan chant goes as follows:

> *One thing turns into another,*
> *In the Mother, in the Mother.*

Invite Positive Creative Energy into Your Life

To find and connect to the energy within, we each have to choose a path that makes us active participants in our lives rather than passive observers. Take a minute to think about how happy you are with your life right this minute. Are you proud of the contributions you're making in the world? Is your household a safe and comforting place for your family, friends, and animal companions? If you aren't happy and satisfied with what you see when you take stock of your life, then perhaps Wicca is a path you should consider walking down. Or maybe you've started down that path already and are feeling largely in harmony with the world, but would like to deepen your enjoyment and practice of the craft through new projects and activities.

In the upcoming chapters, you will be given exercises and instructions for making and using many of the tools of the Wiccan path—from altars to robes to pentagrams and more. A smart witch (and aren't we all?) will tap into the talents and interests of friends to complete some of these projects. Other smart witches will find comfort in taking some "me" time and working on a project alone. With each activity, you'll learn not just the context of how it applies to Wicca, but also how to apply the ritual or the resulting object to deepen and strengthen your practice of the Craft.

Use this book to spark your own creative energies. Think of our directions as suggestions for ways to get started but always remember to let your own ideas and creativity shine through each project. Don't hesitate to add your own special touches. After all, the most magickal magick comes from deep inside each of us.

The Least You Need to Know

◆ You will feel much more committed to the Wiccan religion if you engage in activities that require "doing" and not just "being."

◆ Connect to the Goddess by using her natural gifts to make flower chains, sachets, and windowsill herb gardens.

◆ Every tool that exists in the mundane world has its counterpart in the spiritual world.

◆ Be sure to incorporate your own ideas into each project to enhance your innate witch's creativity.

Chapter 2

Projects to Enhance Your Dedication Ceremony

In This Chapter

- ◆ Ready, set, fly: a simple dedication ceremony for solitaires
- ◆ An easy recipe for holy water
- ◆ A more formal dedication ceremony to share with friends
- ◆ Creating a Goddess and God statue for your altar
- ◆ How to make a simple wand
- ◆ A little kitchen witchery

The projects in this chapter are designed to help you dedicate yourself to the Craft. Committing yourself to your religion means to actively involve yourself in its practices. Here we offer you some creative and spiritually enriching opportunities to help you to begin to do just that.

Remember that everything you do, even mundane tasks like cooking and cleaning, can become spiritual acts when you offer them up to the Lord and Lady. Whether you intend to be a solitary practitioner or work in a coven, there is an activity here for you to deepen your practice of Wiccan ritual.

A Simple Dedication Ceremony for Solitaires

So, you're ready to dedicate yourself to the Lady and Lord to confirm and honor your practice of Wicca, but you're a sole practitioner. Or maybe you just feel like this spiritual moment should be a private one. Not to worry! There is a very simple ceremony that you can perform by yourself which is just as satisfying and spiritual as a more formal group ceremony for dedication. We'll give you the details on performing the ceremony, followed by some simple Wicca projects you do to make the event even more special.

Begin by picking a day for your dedication ceremony when you are feeling especially energized and at peace with the world. You don't want to try concentrating on dedicating yourself to the Goddess and God when you're feeling stressed or irritable. Only good thoughts allowed here! (By the way, Liguana claims to be the queen of the 10-minute ritual, so if you have an especially busy life—and who doesn't?—using her ritual suggestions will allow you plenty of time during the day to practice magick and still take care of your everyday responsibilities.)

Next, pick a private place where you won't be disturbed. If you choose an indoor spot, unplug the phone and turn off the computer so you won't be interrupted with ringing or those annoying gleeping noises from your computer. If you live in a house with other people, explain to them that you need a few minutes of privacy and, if possible, go into a room where you can close a door. Or—and this might be especially true if you live with people who don't understand your choice of religion—wait until you have the house or apartment to yourself.

If you would rather perform the dedication outdoors, that's fine, too. Maybe you have a flower garden that you've planted where you feel especially peaceful. Some witches feel most connected to the earth near a vegetable or herb garden. Maybe there is a meadow, a beach, or a stand of trees that speaks to you. Orchards are especially fertile places to embrace the Goddess. If you're lucky enough to live near a river or a lake, the sound of moving water can provide a soothing background for your ceremony. Using just your apartment balcony or your own backyard is also perfectly acceptable. Whatever spot you pick, though, be sure that it's private enough so that you won't be disturbed.

Because there is no right or wrong time of day to perform a dedication ceremony, pick a time that works best for you. If you're a morning person, dawn can be an inspiring time of day, especially if you can position yourself to actually see the sun rise. If you like the idea of performing the ceremony by candlelight, wait until evening. (This might be an especially good time if you have children or roommates who are sleeping so you won't be disturbed.) Maybe you just have a free half hour in the middle of the day. Pick a time when you are feeling relaxed and unrushed, but remember, Liguana promises this will only take a few minutes.

Create a Sacred Space for Your Ceremony

Once you have the time and place picked out for your dedication ritual and you know you won't be interrupted, you can begin. It's perfectly fine to just wear your street clothes for the ceremony; always keeping in mind that comfort is the issue, not fashion. If you're comfortable working skyclad (nude) that's okay, too, but it's not required. Nudity takes a little getting used to. You shouldn't push other people to go that route if they are embarrassed in any way.

At the very least, take your shoes off. Then, create a sacred space in whatever way feels right to you. For example, you might want to cast a *magick circle* using your *athame*. (You'll find Wicca projects related to casting magick circles in Chapter 8.)

Magickal Properties

An **athame** (pronounced *A-tha-may*) is a two-edged knife, usually with a wooden or silver handle, which is used both as a symbol of God and in various rituals; for example, casting a **magick circle,** which is a formal sacred space for doing Wiccan ritual, and also for performing some spellwork. Most Wiccans reserve their athames for magickal purposes only. An athame cuts on a spiritual plane, not on a physical one.

However, as we've promised simple and quick, if you're indoors you might just opt for lighting some incense or candles. Some Wiccans like to sprinkle the area with a little holy water they've made prior to the dedication. (See our recipe in the next section.) Or bring a special comfy rug or blanket into the space. If you're outdoors, scattering a few flower petals or making a small cairn using stones or shells might feel right. Keep the sacred space you create for your ceremony as simple as you want it to be.

A Simple Recipe for Holy Water

Here's a simple recipe for holy water that can be used for your dedication ceremony, or in many of the different rituals in this book. Sprinkling a few drops can help consecrate a sacred space. And, in the more formal dedication ceremony, this holy water can be used as the anointing water. You'll want to prepare your holy water before the day you intend to perform your dedication ceremony or other ritual, as there is a short waiting period involved before the water is ready to be used.

Here's what you'll need:

- ◆ Small bowl of spring water (see the following note)
- ◆ 1 tsp. rose or lavender water (optional, but lovely)
- ◆ 2 TB. sea salt
- ◆ Small storage bottle

If you have access to river, lake, or ocean water, you're lucky! Rainwater works very well, too, or melted snow, but you might want to collect the water as it falls, if possible, rather than having it run off the roof. However, if you are dry-docked, bottled spring water works just fine. And, if necessary, plain old tap water is sufficient. If you use tap water, letting it sit in an open container for 24 hours eliminates some of the artificial chemicals that are added to most city water systems.

Pour the water into your ceremonial bowl. Add the rose or lavender water if you're using it, and a sprinkle of salt. Place your hands over the bowl, palms down, and say the following out loud:

> *On this day and in this hour,*
> *I call upon the Ancient Power,*
> *I seek the presence of the Lady and Lord,*
> *To bless this water that I will pour.*

Place the bowl on a windowsill or porch where it can catch the light of the moon. Full moons are best, but any bright moonlight will do. The following morning at dawn, pour your holy water into the storage bottle (as fancy or plain as you prefer!) and use as needed.

The Dedication Ritual

Spend a few moments touching base with your own feelings. Sprinkle your sacred space with holy water. Take several deep breaths. Listen to the sounds around you. Once you're sure you are in touch with yourself and aware of your surroundings, kneel down on your left knee. Put your right hand under your right heel and your left hand on your head. Then, say out loud:

> *All that is between my two hands I dedicate to Lady and Lord and to my growth*
> *in the Craft.*

Presto! You are dedicated to the practice and launched on the Wiccan path.

A More Formal Dedication Ceremony

Our simple dedication ceremony may not sound very witchy to some of our readers who want to see something a bit more elaborate. Where is all the pomp and ceremony? Where are all of the Wiccan symbols and tools? Can a Wiccan dedication ceremony possibly be *that* simple? Well, it *can* be just that simple, but if you want a more formal dedication ceremony with more elaborate projects, keep reading.

Create a Goddess and God Statue for Your Altar

For the more formal ceremony, you will need a symbol of the Goddess and God for your altar. Some simple suggestions for appropriate symbols include a round stone, shell, bell, small cauldron, or a picture cut from a magazine and laminated for the Goddess; and a forked piece of wood, sword or athame, staff, or a picture cut from a magazine and laminated for the God. However, if you want a more challenging project, making your own statues can be a fun activity. This project takes a bit of time and talent to pull off, but it is very rewarding.

Sculpting your altar symbols can be done as a solitary project, or throw a Lady and Lord party and have everyone make their own statues. Divide up the various pieces of this project if there are timid people in your group who insist they aren't talented enough to make a statue. Give them the job of sanding and staining the bases while the artists in the group mold the statues. First, though, try to encourage everyone to make their sacred statues. The statues are meant to be representational, not lifelike replicas, so free-form creativity is welcomed!

Here's what you'll need:

- Box of Sculpey modeling compound
- Sheet of wax paper
- Set of sculpting tools (pencils, letter openers, etc., will do just fine)
- Wooden base (or other type of base, such as stone)
- Fine-grained sandpaper
- Can of wood stain—the size depends on the size of the statue you plan to make
- Brush or cloth suitable for staining wood
- Paint to decorate the finished statues
- Small brush

- Three or four pieces of sponge
- Container of Sculpey glaze
- Adhesive
- Lots of newspapers … how messy are you?

For this sort of project, Sculpey modeling compound works very well and can be purchased in most hobby shops or ordered online. It is fairly inexpensive (about $10 dollars for a 2-pound box, which is plenty of clay to make two small statues with some clay left over) and doesn't air dry. This makes it ideal for inexperienced modelers because it allows you to take your time with the creative process.

Now that you have all your supplies you are ready to begin. Start by preparing a work area. Put down a sheet of wax paper to work on (the Sculpey won't stick to it). Place a picture of a Goddess or God symbol that you like nearby for inspiration, or sketch out your own designs and experiment as you go. Lay out your tools and then follow these steps:

1. Start sculpting! Keep the statues fairly simple. If you add arms, keep them as close to the body as possible to add strength to your finished statue. (Very thin pieces make the statues more fragile and because you might have occasion to carry them from place to place, you want to avoid potential disaster.)

   Once the body and head are sculpted, consider using your sculpting tools to add small details like a spiral over the Goddess' womb, a pentagram, or a rune symbol that has meaning for you. Texture will really pop out when you paint them (see step 4). Once you have your statues the way you want them, you're ready to bake!

2. Follow the directions for baking on the back of the Sculpey box carefully. Big warning: Don't leave the statues unattended; it only takes about 15 minutes to bake, depending on the thickness of the statues. Any longer and you risk burning them. Trust us! There's no potion in the world powerful enough to remove the stink of charred modeling compound!

3. Once your statues are baked, you can start on the bases (unless you've divvied up the pieces of the project and the bases are already finished). Using wood is a nice touch; however, you can also sculpt a base from the clay (even the nonartists can handle that), or use a flat stone. A variety of wooden bases are available at most craft shops. It might take some light sanding to smooth the wood, and then stain or paint each base as you prefer.

4. Now, you're ready to paint your statue. While you are at the craft shop buying your Sculpey and wooden bases, take a look at the paint supplies. Although many

different varieties of paint will work, look for the *faux* stone and marble paints. Here's a suggestion: Heavenly Hues Transparent Wash "Brush-On, Wipe-Off" is available in a variety of colors and is fairly easy to find. You apply it evenly with a small brush and then wipe off the excess with a damp sponge. It gets into all the small recesses of the statue and brings out the details very effectively. It is likely a group will only need one bottle to do all the statues unless a variety of colors is preferred.

Although the paint washes off your hands with soap and water, you should definitely put down newspaper to protect your workspace. Fill small dishes with water to rinse out your sponges.

> **Craftworking**
>
> Liguana suggests painting your statues with nail polish as a cheap alternative. Nowadays a bottle of 99-cent drugstore nail polish comes in so many colors, it's mind-boggling. She encourages you to spiritually cleanse and bless it before use.

5. Now that your statues are painted, you will want to protect them. Sculpey glaze is effective, but any quick-dry lacquer will work. There are several spray-on brands, or you can use a paint brush method. If you use spray-on, be sure to use it in a well-ventilated room.

6. Attach your statues to your bases. Loctite Handyman's Choice Adhesive and Sealant is an excellent choice for this part of the project. It does a good job of bonding the wood and the clay together, but most hobby shops will have a variety of adhesives from which to choose. Just be sure to read the directions carefully to make certain you're purchasing an adhesive that will permanently bond different mediums.

Goddess/God sculptures.

You're done—add the Goddess and God to your altar!

What Else Do You Need?

Now that you're ready for a more formal dedication ceremony, you'll need a few more things. Use this list as a starting point, but add or subtract items as it seems appropriate:

◆ Your portable altar box

◆ A 27-foot length of rope

◆ Five candles: yellow, red, blue, green, and white

◆ A symbol to represent the Goddess—use the statue you just made, or a round stone, shell, bell, small cauldron, or a picture cut from a magazine and laminated

◆ A symbol to represent the God—use the statue you just made, or a forked piece of wood, sword or athame, staff, or a picture cut from a magazine and laminated

◆ Incense

◆ Small candle (a tea light, for example)

◆ Two small bowls or cups

◆ Salt—kosher salt, sea salt, or gray salt is preferred, but, in a pinch, table salt will do

◆ Spring water (or the holy water you've prepared in advance)

◆ A mixture of flour and barley, or just flour, enough to make a large circle by sprinkling it on the ground

◆ A symbol for yourself—for example, a wand, a pentacle/pentagram, or a piece of jewelry you intend to wear only when you are practicing the Craft

◆ A magickal robe or cloak

Take your portable altar box filled with all the goodies you will use in your ritual to your sacred place. As this is a dedication ceremony you will most likely want to share with a group of people, it may be fun and empowering to send out formal invitations indicating the time and place you intend to dedicate yourself to the Craft. You might ask each guest to bring a symbol of themselves to add to the power of the ceremony. If you're planning to wear a ritualistic robe, be sure to tell your guests to dress appropriately so no one feels underdressed.

Before your guests arrive, set the stage. Form a circle with the rope—don't worry if it isn't a perfect circle—and place your portable altar box in the center. This circle is for you. If you want to include all of your guests inside a larger circle, you may draw a circle on the ground with flour or flour and barley. Make the bigger circle as large as it needs to be to include everyone. Place yourself inside the circle of rope that lies within the larger grain circle. Obviously, flour and barley circles are best done outside. Once your guests arrive, these circles will define the sacred space for your ceremony and for the boundaries of the magick circle you will cast for it.

Summon and Stir

Grain such as barley is often used to represent the God because it is harvested, used to give strength to people, and sown again in the spring to renew our store of sustenance— the cycle of birth and death. Flour is often used to represent the Goddess because it is the primary ingredient in bread, a food common to almost all cultures, and is generally made by mothers and grandmothers to nourish their families.

On your portable altar box at the center of the rope circle, mark the four corners, the directions, with the candles you've brought. It's a good idea to make sure you know which direction east is prior to the big day, especially if "right" and "left" normally have more directional meaning for you than "east" and "west." Place the yellow candle toward the east, the red candle toward the south, the blue candle toward the west, and the green candle toward the north. If you have trouble remembering which color represents which direction, it might help to remember that each direction corresponds to one of the four elements. North represents the "green" Earth; west represents the "blue" Water; south represents "red" Fire, and east represents … well, think of "yellow" as smoggy air, perhaps. The white candle goes in the center.

Summon and Stir

If a different candle color speaks to you, by all means substitute your own preference. A friend of Liguana's loves the fog and thinks of it as "walking in the clouds"; she uses a gray or silver candle to represent Air on her altar because it seems more appropriate to her. Always listen to your own wisdom.

Next, place the symbols for each element next to its representative candle. Use incense next to the yellow candle to symbolize Air. Light a small candle (in addition to the red candle) to symbolize Fire. Fill a small bowl or cup with water to symbolize … well, Water. Fill another small bowl or cup with salt to represent Earth. Place the symbols for the Goddess, God, and yourself on the altar.

Once the altar is prepared and your guests have arrived, wearing your magickal robe and cloak, step barefoot into your circle of rope. Cast your magick circle by walking *deosil* around the edges of the rope, starting in the east then moving south to west to north. Use your athame to trace a protective circle in the etheric realm as you walk your circle three times. (If you've included a circle of flour for your guests, you'll have to cast that one first, and then cast your own special inner circle for yourself.)

Magickal Properties

Deosil means clockwise; **widdershins** means counterclockwise. The **quarters** often refer to the elements of nature that are forces honored by pagans and witches. They are named many things, but you will often hear them referred to as corners, quarters, watchtowers, elements, or elementals.

Once you've traced your circle, welcome the four *quarters* into the circle by lighting the candles that represent each one, again starting with the east and moving clockwise. Next, welcome the Goddess and God into your circle and light the white central candle.

Say out loud: *I am* (insert your magickal or mundane name here); *I come into this sacred space before all witnesses to dedicate myself to Goddess and God and to my own growth in Wicca, the craft of the wise.*

Take a pinch of salt and put it into the water. Dip two fingers into the water and anoint yourself as you say a self-blessing. Here is Liguana's suggestion for a blessing, but if you feel like writing your own, she says, "Have at it!"

> *Bless me, mother, for I am a child of yours.* (Anoint your forehead with water.)
>
> *Blessed be my eyes that I may see the correct path before me.* (Anoint your eyelids.)
>
> *Blessed be my nose that I may breathe your holy essence.* (Anoint your nose.)
>
> *Blessed be my mouth that I may always speak with wisdom.* (Anoint your lips.)
>
> *Blessed be my heart that I may be faithful in my workings.* (Anoint your chest.)
>
> *Blessed be my loins that I may know I can create each day in beauty.* (Anoint your genitals or womb area.)
>
> *Blessed be my knees that I may kneel at your sacred altars.* (Anoint your knees.)
>
> *Blessed be my feet that have brought me this day to your path.* (Anoint your feet.)
>
> *Bless me, mother, for I am a child of yours.* (Anoint your forehead again.)

Take a few minutes to meditate on your intentions and how you feel about them. Thank the Goddess and God for their attention and blessings. Something simple will do, for example: *Thank you, Lady and Lord, for your presence and for your blessings as I begin my journey on the Wiccan path.*

Blow out the central white candle and then blow out the directional colored candles while thanking and dismissing the entities and elementals of each. This time, proceed *widdershins*, beginning in the north and moving to the west, to the south, and ending with the east. Finally, using your athame, open your circle, walking widdershins and, visualizing the circle, erase it with your blade.

Craftworking

Some practitioners of the Craft believe it's best to use a candle snuffer to extinguish candles because using your breath scatters and dissipates the magickal energy you have invoked. Other witches pooh-pooh that idea. As always, do what feels right to you.

Make a Simple Wand

A witch's wand is most often associated with the element of Air and is aligned with the east. The wand represents magickal knowledge; therefore, it makes a perfect symbol to represent *you* on your dedication altar.

A wand is generally made of wood and is most powerful if it is made by the person who will use it. However, if someone makes it for you, it's possible to fill the wand with your own magickal vibrations before using it. This is easily done by handling it often and deliberately sending your own positive thoughts through your hand down to the tip of the wand and out into the universe.

Here's what you'll need to make a wand:

◆ A tree branch or wooden dowel approximately 5 to 10 inches long and as thick as you want your wand to be

◆ Super glue or craft glue

◆ Paint, stain, or varnish if desired

◆ A variety of small crystals, stones, wooden beads, buttons, shells, or whatever else tickles your fancy

◆ Silver or gold wire or thread, thin ribbon, feathers, thin leather strips or shoelaces (optional)

If you are using a tree branch, you may strip the bark off or leave it on, whichever you prefer. If you are using a wooden dowel, it may be left natural or stained, varnished, or painted if you desire. The length of the wand depends on what feels comfortable to you, but tradition states that is should be no longer than your forearm. Liguana prefers measuring from the crook of the elbow to the tip of the longest finger to determine the length. She believes this personalizes the wand and binds it to the practitioner. Likewise, use whatever diameter width seems most comfortable and wandlike to you. It should be small enough to lay on your altar without taking up too much room. Don't worry if your tree branch isn't perfectly straight, a crook or two adds character.

If you stain or varnish your wand, be sure to let it dry thoroughly before continuing. An alternative is to paint decorations on the wand. Keep them simple, especially if the wand's diameter is small. Try spirals, half moons, stars, flowers, herbs, or whatever seems right to you.

CAUTION

Widdershins

Never use someone else's tools without spiritually cleansing them first, or at least having a good idea what they have previously been used for.

The next step is gluing on whatever crystals, stones, beads, or shells you find appealing. One tip is to leave the center of the wand free from decoration so you have a handhold unencumbered by bulky objects that could distract you during a ritual. Clustering small stones at the top or bottom of the wand works very well. If you have a larger crystal, you can glue it to the top of the wand as the magickal tip, then cover the "seam" between the tip and the wand with other, smaller rocks or crystals.

If you like, finish the wand by tying a ribbon, thread, or thin leather lace to the top of the wand and crisscrossing the ends, braiding them down the length of the wand. This adds color to your wand; you might use purple ribbon or gold thread, for example. Tie the ends in a knot at the bottom and trim the ends, or leave them long to add a "tail" to your wand. Glue decorative beads, shells, or feathers to the ends.

Cooking Up a Little Kitchen Witchery

Now that you've dedicated yourself to the Lady and Lord, why not end your dedication ceremony with a feast for your friends? Are you a kitchen witch? A witch's cauldron can just as easily be a soup pot or a wok. Serve whatever fruits and vegetables are currently in season. Think about each friend and family member (don't forget your animal companions) and what she or he means to you as you peel, chop, or cube the food. Bake some homemade bread and thank the Goddess and God for their bounty as you knead. Serve up a warm dish of couscous or *quinoa* on the side (see the recipe in the next section).

Magickal Properties _____

One of the most sacred foods of the ancient Incas of South America is **quinoa** (pronounced *KEEN-wa*), a plant so nourishing, delicious, and vital they called it *chesiya mama*, the Mother Grain. Each year the Incan emperor, using a golden spade, planted the first quinoa seeds of the season, and at the solstice, priests bearing golden vessels filled with quinoa made offerings to Inti, the Sun. Most all health food stores and some grocery stores carry quinoa.

Herbed Quinoa

Here is a particularly good quinoa recipe, but you can substitute quinoa in any of your favorite rice recipes whether the resulting dish is savory, spicy, or sweet. If you use dried herbs instead of fresh, the dish will be just as tasty. If you're using dried herbs, use less than if you are using fresh. Just experiment with quantity and remember, it's easier to add spices than it is to take some out!

♦ 1 cup quinoa, thoroughly rinsed

♦ 2 cups water

♦ 1 tsp. salt

♦ ¼ cup olive oil

♦ 1 or 2 cloves minced garlic

♦ Black pepper to taste

♦ ½ cup fresh basil, *or* ¼ cup fresh tarragon, *or* 2 TB. fresh thyme, *or* choose any favorite herb—rosemary, oregano, sage, or dill, for example

Put the quinoa, water, and salt into a medium-size saucepan, cover, and bring to a boil over medium-high heat. Reduce heat to medium, and simmer until tender, 12 to 15 minutes. (It's a lot like cooking rice, so just follow your witch's instincts.) If necessary, continue cooking, uncovered, until all the liquid has been absorbed or has evaporated, which may take one more minute.

While the quinoa is cooking, combine olive oil, garlic, and a generous amount of pepper in a warmed medium-size bowl. Just before the quinoa is cooked, coarsely chop the herb leaves and mix them into the olive oil mixture. When the quinoa is ready, add it still hot to the olive oil mixture, tossing until it is thoroughly combined. Check seasonings and serve immediately.

It's easy to add seasonal vegetables to extend this dish. In the summer, try adding fresh, chopped tomatoes with basil (this helps use up those surplus tomatoes that accumulate when your favorite garden witch has worked overtime!). In the spring, a handful of fresh baby peas with tarragon is light and yet filling. In the fall and winter, try adding winter squash or cubes of fresh pumpkin with rosemary or sage.

Everyone Can Join In

If you're a klutz in the kitchen, let your talented friends pitch in to bake the bread or bring the chocolate brownies. Liguana professes to fall back on tribal connections inherent in Wiccan covens whenever projects feel too complex or just aren't up her witch's alley. Her sister Ariel is a seamstress and a graphic artist. Her brother Samash is a carpenter. We should all be so lucky! Oh, wait! I'll bet we are. Ask your friends where their talents lie. You'll be pleasantly surprised at the diversity.

The Least You Need to Know

- ◆ Dedicating yourself to the Craft can be a simple, solitary ceremony or a more formal one you share with friends.

- ◆ Creating a Goddess and God symbol for your altar is a good activity to share with friends.

- ◆ A simple-to-make wand can be a good symbol for yourself and your practice of the Craft to use on your altar.

- ◆ Encourage each member of your group to use his or her strongest Goddess-given talents to participate in group activities.

Making Your Book of Shadows

In This Chapter

- ♦ Journaling—an easy beginning
- ♦ Scrapbooking techniques—collage, calligraphy, stamping, and computer graphics
- ♦ Making your own paper
- ♦ Making a mini spell book
- ♦ Folding or binding your own Book of Shadows

A Book of Shadows is the journal a witch keeps. Your book reflects where you are spiritually as well as chronicling your continuing growth in the Craft. It may contain favorite recipes, spells you've written, personal musings, descriptions of rituals or dinner parties you've hosted, or just an account of your day.

A witch's Book of Shadows is as personal as a toothbrush. This means you don't want to share your Book of Shadows with just anyone. You want to be careful not to share your magickal recipes, spells, and musings with casual acquaintances or even with other Wiccans whom you don't know very well.

Of course, you can share your book freely with loved ones or coven members if you choose to do so. Liguana has a good rule, consistent with the Wiccan Rule of Three: Think about it three times before showing your Book of Shadows to someone else. (The Rule of Three says that whatever you do will come back to you threefold.)

There are many ways to create a Book of Shadows, from buying a blank journal to binding your own book. This chapter offers several projects to help you get started creating your own Book of Shadows. Although writing in your book is most likely a solitary activity, some of these projects lend themselves to a fun group get-together.

Journaling: A Simple Way to Get Started

The easiest way to create your first Book of Shadows is to buy a blank book. You can find these at book stores and in office supply stores in a variety of sizes. Some of them are lined, others are unlined. Look through several of them before you decide which one you want. Weigh the size and shape in your hands to see if it feels right. Decide whether the book will lay flat enough for you to utilize it the way you will need to. Spiral-bound blank books are available but may not appeal to your aesthetic self. Or maybe a spiral-bound notebook is exactly what speaks to you.

Some witches prefer to keep two different kinds of books—a *Book of Shadows* and a *Grimoire*. A Grimoire is a book of just spells and rituals. The Grimoire is like your Betty Crocker cookbook, while your Book of Shadows is more like your diary. For example, you might have a favorite magick cookie recipe in both books, but your Book of Shadows might also include an account of when you first made the cookies, why you like them, and how others in your coven reacted to your kitchen witchery. Whether you want to keep one book or two is your choice, but if most of your important phone numbers and reminders are on sticky notes and scraps of paper, start with one.

> **Magickal Properties**
>
> A **Book of Shadows** should contain personal revelations as well as a record of what has worked for you in your practice of Wicca. You should also include some "not trying *that* again" reminders. Less successful experiments teach lessons, too. Your **Grimoire** is a record of your spell and rituals, which can be a separate book, or simply a section of your Book of Shadows.

Treat yourself to some special colored pens, pencils, or markers. (Liguana has a friend who loves to use crayons.) Consider putting different types of text in different colors. For example, recipes can be in red, spells in blue, personal observations in green. Or color-code your moods—mellow thoughts in green, frustration in red, happiness in gold. Or maybe use whatever color feels right for the day. Feel free to draw sketches in your book—and stop worrying that you aren't a good enough artist! Remember, this book is just for you, so you're the only person you have to please.

More Than Just a Diary

If you've kept a journal or diary before and want your Book of Shadows to feel like something more special, here's a simple project to get you started. Take a nature walk, even if the closest you can get to nature is down a city street. Take your Book of Shadows with you and sketch the flowers, trees, buildings, and birds you see along the way. Describe the color of the sky, the smells in the air, the sounds you're hearing. Adding pressed flowers and leaves to your book can help you remember the walk even more vividly.

Here's what you'll need:

◆ Simple flowers, leaves, or herbs

◆ Plain absorbent paper (unprinted newsprint works well, or use white paper towels)

◆ A heavy book (such as a phone book or dictionary)

◆ White glue (such as Elmer's glue)

◆ Small bowl of water

◆ Tweezers

◆ Toothpicks

◆ Small brush

◆ Clear contact paper

Choose flowers and greenery that are simple with few petals such as pansies, daisies, impatiens, ferns, Queen Anne's lace, or violets. Pick the flowers after the dew has dried, usually late morning or early afternoon.

Remove all the stems from the flowers. Spread the blossoms or leaves in a single layer on the absorbent paper or the paper towels. Place a second sheet of absorbent paper on top. Place the sandwiched flowers inside the heavy book you've chosen. Place heavy objects on top of that—other books or bricks, for example. Try to use about 20 pounds of weight. (You can buy a commercial flower press if you'd rather, but this works just as well.)

> **Craftworking**
>
> It's a good idea to note the date, phase of the moon, and what astrological sign the moon is in whenever you make an entry in your book. That way you can watch how you are affected and what you are moved to write about under different astrological influences.

Leave your flowers or herbs for two to three weeks but check occasionally to make sure they aren't molding. Change the absorbent paper if it seems too damp.

Once the flowers are dried, mix one part white glue to one part water in your small bowl. Pick up each flower carefully using the tweezers and brush a light coating of the glue mixture on the back of your flower. Place it in the book, using a toothpick to nudge it into place if necessary. Once you have your arrangement the way you want it, brush another light coat of the glue mixture over the top of the flowers to set them. The glue will be invisible once it dries. Or use the clear contact paper to cover your flowers. The contact paper will keep your dried flowers from crumbling as you use your book.

Decorating a Cover for Your Book

Another easy way to create your first Book of Shadows is to buy a three-ring notebook. This approach lets you add or subtract pages as you go, which is especially helpful if you like to organize your book by topics rather than by days. You can insert rituals, observations, recipes, or spells in any order that makes sense to you.

Decorating the cover is a way to make the book seem more your own. Find the right material to cover your Book of Shadows. Buying a $1/2$ yard at a time gives you a little extra to work with, and is fairly inexpensive. You will also need 2 yards of $5/8$-inch-wide ribbon to match. Lay the material down, wrong side up, and lay the cover, right side down, on top of the material. You might have to play with the positioning, depending on the design; if the material has a print, like the face of a moon, you'll want to make sure the design is centered. Next, pull the material over the edges of the album cover. Trim the material down to about $1 1/4$ inches over the edge, and then glue the material down.

At the corners, trim a little away so when they're folded, it won't be lumpy. Finish it off by gluing the ribbon on the inside of the album to cover the edges of the material and give it a finished look. Let the album dry thoroughly.

Ideas for the Inside

Once you've chosen your book and have decorated the cover (or not, as you prefer), you're ready to start filling the pages. You can add your own special touch to the pages in a variety of ways.

Collage: Cut and Tear Your Way to Creativity

Collage is one of the easiest of all art forms to get started with, and magazine collage is a good place to begin because everyone has most of the materials within easy reach. Here is a project using collage to decorate a page or two in your Book of Shadows.

Here's what you'll need:

- Colorful magazines (if you like to haunt flea markets and garage sales, look for old books, too; often you can find interesting old illustrations to use, and large blocks of text can provide an interesting background)

- Scissors

- White glue, acrylic medium, or glue stick

Decide whether you want to make a realistic or abstract collage. For a realistic collage, decide on a theme. The time of year or a sabbat party you've attended might give you a theme. Liguana recently attended a Middle-Earth Ball, providing a wonderful opportunity for a couple of theme pages in her Book of Shadows.

For an abstract collage you will work with colors and shapes. The technique itself couldn't be easier. You simply cut or tear pictures or shapes from magazines and arrange them on the book's pages. Repeat colors and patterns to make an interesting design. When you have an arrangement you like, use the glue to adhere the pieces. Be sure to cover the entire back of each piece before you apply it and gently wipe off excess glue with a damp paper towel as you pat the piece gently into place.

Avoid using newspaper clippings because they become yellowed and brittle over time. If you want to add a story that appeared in a newspaper, it's best to photocopy the story and paste it in your book.

Calligraphy

Another fun project is to try hand printing some headlines, recipes, and titles. First, buy some inexpensive calligraphy pens. Practice holding your pen tip at a constant angle—a 45-degree angle is best, but right now it really doesn't matter which angle, just the practice of keeping the pen constant is what you are trying for. Try vertical lines about $1/2$-inch long and try to keep them straight. Don't be discouraged if the lines don't all come out perfectly.

Next, try horizontal lines. If you are working with a 45-degree angle, notice there is little difference between the width of the horizontal and vertical lines. (You *are* remembering to keep the pen at a constant angle, aren't you?) Next, do a few of the letter *X*. It is a great letter to practice the 45-degree angle on, because when properly done it has one line as thick as your pen will allow and one the thinnest.

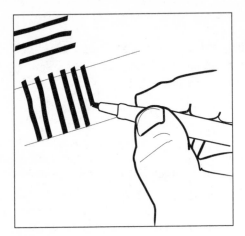

Calligraphy lines.

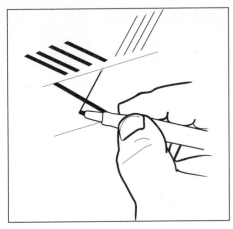

Calligraphy X's.

Now try a circle. Start with your pen at the 11:00 position, remember to keep your angle constant, and draw down in a gentle counterclockwise curve to the 5:00 position. Finish the circle by starting again at the 11:00 position and move clockwise to the 5:00 position. If you were using a 45-degree angle you should have thin spots at the 11:00 and 5:00 position and thick in the 2:00 and 8:00 positions. Draw a few more until it gets comfortable.

Calligraphy circles.

How's your angle? Are you keeping it constant? Practice these few exercises until you can keep the angle constant and your straight lines straight.

Now practice a few Theban or Runic alphabets.

As always, don't worry if it doesn't look perfect. "Perfect" in this case means readable.

Theban Script

The Theban alphabet.

Feoh or Fehu
Energy, power, wealth, good fortune, sexual passion

Ur or Uruz
Quick change, strength, determination, good health

Thorn or Thurisaz
Fate, protection, overcoming, obstacles, unfortunate events

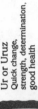

Ansur or Ansuz
Communication, wisdom, learning, social magnetism, divine inspiration

Rad or Raido
Travel, discovering inner wisdom, change

Ken or Kano or Kenaz
Creative energy, music, protection, movement, change

Geofu or Gebo
Giving and receiving gifts, generosity

Wynn or Wunjo
Happiness, especially in love, success, control, celebration

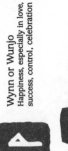

Hagall or Hagalaz
Change due to outside forces, frustration, disruption, destruction

Nied or Nauthiz
Need, obstructions, success in the future, overcoming difficulties

Is or Isa
Wait, take a break, stand still

Jara or Jera
Cyclical return, harvesting, success in legal actions, birth, new beginnings, gradual change, fulfillments

Yr or Eihwaz
Remover of obstacles, protection, access to spirit world, endurance

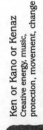

Peorth or Perth
Success in gambling or investments, finding the lost or hidden, mysteries soon revealed, magick

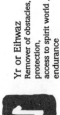

Eolh or Algiz
Protection, friendship, success, luck

Sigel or Sowolu
The life force, health, vitality, luck, success

Tir or Teiwaz
Facing difficulties, victory, bravery, return to health, honorable conduct

Beorc or Berkana
Women, Mother Earth, protection, nurturing, fertility, new beginnings

Eoh or Ehwaz
Change, adjustment, improvement, partnership, psychic ability

Mann or Mannaz
Relationships, cooperation, learning, communication, personal potential

Lagu or Laguz
Creativity, intuition, imagination, psychic awareness, sensitivity

Ing or Inguz
Power, fertility, happy conclusion, success, limitless possibilities

Daeg or Dagaz
Security, truth revealed, matters brought into the light, change for the better, enlightenment

Othel or Othila
Family, grounding, money, tradition, care of the elderly, property, home

Wyrd
Some people believe that this rune is a new addition to the ancient symbols and will not use it. Others see it to mean mystery, acceptance of what is to come, fate.

Rune symbols.

Masking: A Simple Stamping Project

Using stamps to decorate book pages could be a whole book in itself. There are a gazillion ways to use stamps. It can be as simple as stamping directly onto your page and coloring the image with pens or markers; there are thousands of stamp images available. Here is one stamping technique called masking that looks complicated, but is really very simple. Masking is a technique that makes images look like they are behind other images. This gives the image a three-dimensional look.

Here's what you'll need:

- ◆ Two or more related stamps, for example, flowers and leaves, moon and clouds, or mortar and pestle and herbs

- ◆ Quality ink pad in the color(s) of your choice

- ◆ Some sheets of practice paper—if you're bold, stamp the image directly into your book, and remember that "perfect" isn't a requirement

First, stamp the image that you want to appear in the "front." Next, stamp the same image on scrap paper—Post-it Notes work well if they're big enough. Be sure to stamp the image so that the sticky edge is included. Cut out the scrap image right on the edges of the image. Place the scrap image, also called the mask, over the original image. Use the sticky edge to hold in mask in place. Then stamp the second image (which you want to appear behind the first image) so that part of it is stamped onto the mask.

When you remove the mask it appears that the second image you stamped is behind the first.

Computer Graphics

For us less artistic witches, using computer graphics to enhance *journaling* in your Book of Shadows is easy! You will, of course, need a computer, a printer, and some basic software.

The kind of printer you have will, to some degree, dictate the kinds of things you can do. With a black-and-white inkjet or laser printer you can do journaling and headline text. You can also use black-and-white clip art (art that looks a little like a child's coloring book) that

Magickal Properties

Journaling just means adding words to your Book of Shadows. Be sure to include not just spells, recipes, and incantations, but personal history and observations on the day. If you're having particularly strong emotions, try to capture them so you can tap into them again if you need to remember that feeling.

can be colored after it is printed. Don't rule this out! Coloring in clip art can give it a very personal touch. Another option for black-and-white printers is to print out text or clip art, then trace over it directly onto your scrapbook pages.

Magickal Properties

A **font** means a set of letters, numerals, symbols, and punctuation marks all the same style and size. For example, all of the letters on your keyboard are the same font. Fonts are measured in points; 72-point type is approximately 1 inch high. If you use your computer to create titles or headlines for your book, keep in mind the space you have when you're choosing a point size.

With a color inkjet printer, you can do all of the things you can do with a black-and-white printer, plus you have the option of printing colored text, using colored clip art, and printing colored backgrounds and photo frames. Most of the newer color inkjet printers also do a great job of printing digital photographs.

Although using a basic word processor program to create graphics is fine, a layout program will be much, much easier to work with. All you need is a card-making software program. It doesn't need to say "scrapbook" anywhere on the box. If the program says it will do cards, flyers, and banners, that's what you're looking for. These programs will come with a variety of decorative *fonts* and clip art, too.

Before you start working on a page, familiarize yourself with the program and learn what it can do. After you have gone through the software program's tutorials, make sure that you experiment with and understand about using different fonts, changing font colors, and changing font sizes. How big can you make a font? How small can you make it? Become familiar with importing clip art into a page, changing the sizes of images, and so on. Play around with any special effects your program might have, too.

"So," you're thinking, "I'm supposed to fill my book with Halloween graphics of broomsticks and cauldrons?" Well, maybe sometimes. If you've thrown a Samhain party (see Chapter 5) and you want to keep a record of the day in pictures and memories, traditional pictures and borders can add a touch of whimsy. But don't stop there! Graphics of Goddesses, moons, suns, cacti, herbs, bells, leaves, animals, or even kitchen utensils can create some fun in your Book of Shadows. Decorative borders and fun fonts can spice up your pages, too. Bottom line: Always use what appeals to you.

Scrapbooking

Creating a Book of Shadows should be as much fun as a hobby, not a chore. Get out your pens, your scissors, and your glue and have at it. Use any of the techniques we've suggested or make up your own as you go along. If you think of your book as a Wiccan scrapbook, here are a couple more ideas to spark your own creativity.

Here's what you'll need:

◆ Scrapbook album—some standard sizes are 12 by 12 inches and 8 by 10 inches, but use whatever size works for you

◆ Adhesives

◆ Scissors or X-Acto blade

◆ Journaling pens (The ink of dye-based markers usually breaks down over time and they are not waterproof; use a pigment-ink pen or marker that is permanent, fade resistant, waterproof, and chemically stable.)

Widdershins

Use only acid-free material in your book. Acid is used in paper manufacturing to break apart the wood fibers and the lignin that holds them together. If acid remains in the materials used for a Grimoire or a Book of Shadows, the acid can react chemically with photographs and cut-outs and cause their deterioration. Acid-free products have a pH factor of 7.0 or above. It's imperative that all materials (glue, pens, paper, etc.) used in books be acid-free.

There's only one direction: Be creative! Scrapbooking is an adventure, so share it with friends. Besides enjoying the opportunity for a get-together, it's the perfect chance to share supplies.

Tools and Embellishments

Feel free to use stickers, decorative rulers, punches, pinking shears, beads, feathers, shells, material, buttons, or charms to add interest to the pages of your Book of Shadows. A Book of Shadows is not a work of art. It is a work of heart. You might not be a gourmet cook, but you make meals every day. You might not be a fashion designer, but you dress for success every day. You may not be an interior designer, but your home is a warm and welcoming place. The person you ultimately need to please is *yourself*. Have fun!

Widdershins

Never use another coven member's mundane name in your Book of Shadows! We have magick names for our protection and sense of security. Safeguard yourself and your friends by using only your magickal or coven names in your writings. Unfortunately, there is still prejudice out there and persecution does happen. Be safe!

Make Your Own Paper

For those of you who want more challenging projects, making your own Book of Shadows from scratch is amazing and satisfying. A rewarding group project that can add a special touch is to make your own paper. You will need a few special supplies and some practice, but the results are well worth the effort. Fresh or dried flowers and leaves, spices, fabric threads, and stamped-out paper shapes add great variety. Fragrant herbs, potpourri, lavender, or rose petals make extra special papers, although the scent will fade as the paper dries.

Make Your Own Mold and Deckle

The first thing you need is a mold and deckle. These are the two frames you will use to shape a piece of paper. The size of the mold and deckle will determine the size of the final sheet of paper. You can buy a mold and deckle inexpensively at most hobby shops. Or, with minimal effort, you can make your own.

Here's what you'll need:

- $1/2$-by-$1/2$-inch thick wood, four 10-inch pieces and four 8-inch pieces
- Wood glue
- Angle iron
- 16 small finishing nails
- Varnish
- Fine-mesh nylon netting
- Staple gun with thin U-shaped staples (Tell your friendly hardware dealer what you're using them for and ask for advice; staples that are too thick can split the frame.)

Arrange the wood pieces in a rectangle. You will be making two frames, but only one will have mesh netting. Glue them together, using an angle iron to get the corners square. When the glue is dry, hammer two small nails at each corner to hold the sides in place.

Paint the entire frame with varnish—two coats is best—and allow it to dry overnight. This seals the wood so it will not discolor the paper.

Cut the netting into a 10-by-12-inch rectangle. Wet the netting and staple it to the frame using a staple gun. Start by stapling the middle of one side, then the middle of the opposite side, pulling as tightly as you can. Then staple the other two sides. Now staple all around the frame, making sure the netting is taut. As it dries, it will become tighter. Cut away the extra netting.

Note: You can also use picture frames that are the same size, but they do need to be flat so they don't slip when you are making the sheets of paper.

Making the Paper Pulp

The heart of papermaking is the pulp you use. Pulp can be made with recycled paper or cotton linters, which are ready-made sheets used specifically for papermaking. If you choose to use recycled paper (*not* newspaper!) be sure to remove all traces of glue and remove any staples. Junk mail is great for this and can add some interesting colors to your final sheet. Here's what you'll need:

- Paper or cotton linters

- One or two plastic buckets

- A blender (It's best to use a blender reserved for this purpose—you don't want paper fibers in your next margarita!)

- Small flowers, herbs, leaves, or spices (optional, but their addition makes a very unique sheet of paper)

- One large tub such as a plastic dishpan (It must be bigger than your mold and deckle.)

- A mold and deckle

- Strainer or colander

- Palette or butter knife

- Several small kitchen towels or white felt squares to absorb water from the sheets

- Two boards for pressing the sheets of paper

- Bricks or other heavy weights

- Jars for storing excess pulp

Widdershins

Newspaper has lignin, the material that holds wood fibers together as a tree grows. If lignin remains in the final paper, it will become yellow and brittle over time. Therefore, newsprint should not be used in making paper.

Tear, do *not* cut, the paper into small pieces or rectangular strips 2 to 4 inches long and 2 to 4 inches wide. Tearing allows the water to better penetrate the paper. Put the torn paper into a bucket of clean cold water and let it soak overnight. If using cotton linters, soak for just a few minutes.

Pour off any excess soaking water and put small batches of the pulp into a blender, making sure there is plenty of water—about $1/3$ cup pulp to $2/3$ cup water. Blend well enough to break up the paper's fibers, about 15 to 30 seconds, stirring half-way through.

Flowers, leaves, spices, and other material can be stirred into the batch of liquidized pulp or pressed on to the still-wet sheet of paper once it's finished.

Fill a rectangular plastic tub with about 2 inches of water and pour in a blenderful of pulp. The amount of the pulp in the water will determine the thickness of the sheet of paper.

As sheets of paper are made, keep refilling the plastic tub with pulp and water if necessary.

Making a Sheet of Paper

Gently stir the pulp (and flowers or herbs) and wait for the water movement to stop, but don't allow the pulp to settle to the bottom. Hold the mold and deckle together at the sides with the mesh-covered frame, mesh upwards, underneath the empty frame. Holding the frames together tightly, slide them under the water starting at the far side of the tub and pulling them toward you.

Keeping the frames even and flat, lift them from the water. A layer of pulp should completely cover the mesh. If you aren't happy with the way the pulp is distributed, just dip the frames back into the tub and try it again. You may need to add more pulp. When you're satisfied, tilt the frames so that some of the water drains away.

Remove the empty frame. Press flower petals or herbs into the wet surface if you didn't stir them into the pulp. Use a palette or butter knife to help loosen the paper from the mesh.

Unmold the paper onto one half of a cotton kitchen cloth (not terrycloth) by "rock-ing" the mold from one edge to the other. You can also unmold it onto white squares of felt. The rocking process is easier if you place several layers of fabric beneath the top piece of fabric to form a "pillow." This allows the sheet of paper to roll over the blotting cloth while keeping in close contact with it. Fold the end of the towel to cover the paper or top it with another piece of felt. Continue adding sheets of paper and cloths in this way until you run out of pulp. Place the stack between two boards and weight the boards with bricks to squeeze out any extra water.

Leave the sheets of papers to dry overnight or up to several days. Carefully separate the papers from the blotting materials. Paper sheets can be ironed after flattening to make a smoother finish. Place them between sheets of clean paper or cotton fabric and press with a medium heat. If the paper is still slightly damp, the texture of the pressing paper or cloth will add an interesting imprint on the surface.

If you have any leftover pulp, store it in jars in your refrigerator so it won't mold before you use it again. Strain the pulp through the strainer or colander to eliminate excess water but leave it moist. You will have to add more water when you're ready to use the pulp again.

Congratulations! You've made your own paper for a special page or section in your Book of Shadows. Celebrate by decorating the paper with your growing skill and artisanship as a calligrapher!

> **CAUTION**
>
> **Widdershins**
>
> Do not empty the remaining tray of pulp down your sink. Liguana made this mistake once and is fairly certain that she paid her plumber's next mortgage payment to get it fixed!

A Small Book of Spells

Suppose you want to start small. Here are two projects for mini-books to commemorate special rituals or as Grimoires of spells by topic, or for any magickal purpose!

Say It All in Six Pages with One Sheet

This project makes a six-page book with a front and back cover out of one sheet of paper. A decorative $8^1/_2$–by-11-inch sheet of paper makes a cute little book; bigger paper makes a bigger book.

Here's what you'll need:

- A sheet of paper—the size depends on how big you want your finished book to be

- Scissors

- Black markers or pens

- Stamps (optional)

Fold the sheet of paper in half the long way. Open it flat and fold it again the short way.

Place the paper in front of you like a tent, short fold on the top, short edge facing you. Fold the edge of the paper facing you back to meet the fold. Turn the paper around and fold the other edge back to meet the fold. You should see a w when you look at the end with the long fold on the top.

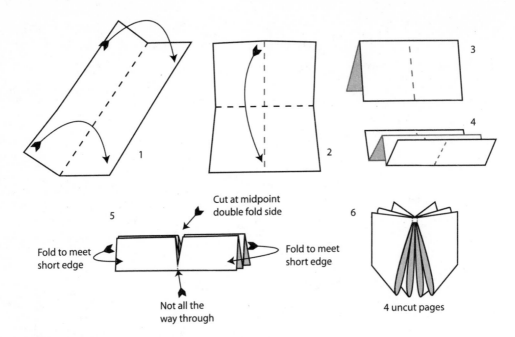

Folding the paper.

Use the scissors to cut down the center of the middle fold. You'll be cutting through two layers of paper, stopping at the long cross fold.

> **Summon and Stir**
>
> An experienced priestess or priest may share his or her Book of Shadows with a promising student or apprentice, allowing spells or rituals to be copied by hand.

Hold the two halves of the middle fold and bend them to the sides. You will have an open book with four sections.

Fold all four sections flat. There you go! You've made a book with six small pages and a cover and back. Using your black marker or pen, write in the spell, recipe, or memory you want to keep.

If you want to make several copies of your book to share a special spell or recipe, this is a perfect format. Make the book; write and illustrate it any way you choose with black marker or pen; unfold the sheet and lay it face down on a copier. Make as many copies as you want. Fold and cut each one according to the directions.

Little Lasting Book of Shadows

This little Book of Shadows is the perfect project for a group of friends who are looking for an easy, do-in-an-afternoon craft with stunning results. Depending on what kind of paper you use (witches can be on a budget, too), this little book can be made for as little as $1 to $5.

These books can be made to any size, including tiny books (1-inch square) you can wear as a pin or necklace. This piece of "jewelry" can be used on your altar as a symbol of yourself or worn only when you perform a ritual. (See the formal dedication ceremony in Chapter 2.)

The number of pieces of paper you use will depend on how many pages you want in your book. It's best not to make it too thick, but experiment with weight and color. You can use cardstock for all of the book's pages rather than just for the covers. This makes for a very stable book. If you do this, though, don't add too many pages or your book will be too thick to collapse easily.

Here's what you'll need:

- Three or more square pieces of text-weight paper (as in typing or drawing paper)

- Two square pieces of cardstock or decorative paper (index card is a good weight to try) for your covers

- Adhesive—white glue or rubber cement works well

- Stamps and inks of your choice

- Beads, charms, and trinkets (optional)

- Ribbon in a color that complements your cover

- Scissors and a ruler

These books are intended to be small, so start with a 4- or 5-inch square. Fold one of the text page squares in half from top to bottom. Open the square and fold it in half from side to side. Reopen the square again and *turn it over* (this is important!). Fold diagonally just once. Reopen and turn the square back over.

Place the square on the table with the diagonal fold facing up horizontally in front of you. Using your thumb and index fingers, pinch together the corners on either side of the diagonal fold. Press the center of the square down (if you're using card stock, it will pop inside out) while pushing the diagonal folds together. At this point, fold the other two points of the square together as it collapses into a little square. Make sure that the folds and creases are tight. Repeat with all of the squares, including the two pieces of cardstock that will form the covers.

Now you're ready to assemble your book. Start by laying your squares out on the table. You're going to be gluing one square, points up, to another square, points down. Repeat, alternating open points "up" and open points "down" until you have the desired number of squares.

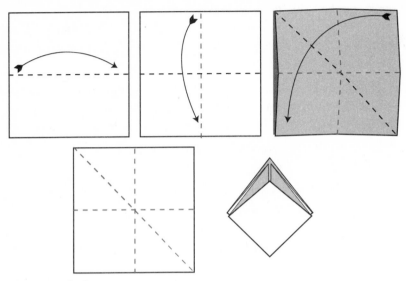

Folding the book.

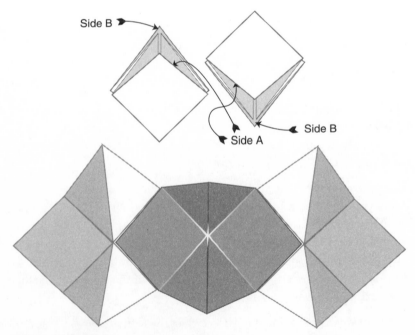

Gluing the folded pages together.

The front and back covers of the book are made with a square of cardstock (as in index-card weight) that is cut ¼ inch larger than the finished size of the folded squares that make up the pages.

Stamp and decorate your cover as desired. You can add beads, charms, and other trinkets as well. Add a ribbon to the inside of both of the covers to have your book tie on the sides. You may want to tape the ribbon to the cover before gluing in the pages to give the ribbon extra strength.

Next, glue the pages of the book inside the covers. The ribbon is tied on the sides (or front) to keep the book closed shut.

Your book is now ready for jotting down a special spell or a blessing and for decorating any way you'd like. You will generally treat each square or triangle of the book like a page. Or write only on the squares and use scraps of paper—origami paper works well—to decorate the triangular spaces.

Craftworking

Make a template of the triangle sections if you plan to cut out pictures to fit. That way you'll be sure your pictures will fit in the desired space and be centered appropriately before pasting them into place. Or you can treat the triangle areas that touch each other as one square, cutting through the photo where the fold will be to allow the book to fold back up.

Binding Your Own Book of Shadows

There are many ways to bind your own book, but the following instructions are easy. This method isn't suitable for too many pages, but it makes a lovely finished book.

Branching Out

This particular binding technique uses a tree stick, which seems particularly appropriate for a witch's book. If you cut a live branch from of a tree, be sure to ask the tree's permission first and thank it afterwards.

Here's what you'll need:

- Regular cardstock or heavy-weight specialty paper
- Text-weight paper for pages
- Scissors
- Two bulldog clips or binder clips (you can find these in office supply stores)
- A stick (any size will do)

- Hole punch or a pushpin
- Large needle
- Heavy thread or thin cord for binding
- Your favorite embellishments and stamps

Decide what size to make your Book of Shadows. For our purposes, these instructions will use card stock and text pages that are 8½ by 11 inches. Folded in half, the finished book will be 5½ inches wide by 8½ inches tall. Begin by folding the cardstock in half.

Next, trim about ¼ to ½ inches off both the length and the width of four pieces of text-weight paper. These will be the pages. Fold them in half and insert them into the fold of the cardstock.

When the pages are aligned inside the book cover, attach the bulldog or binder clips to the top and bottom of the book to hold the pages and cover in place.

Choose a stick that is at least the height of the book or just a bit shorter. The circumference of the stick isn't critical but it will give a slightly different look to the binding, depending on how thick it is.

This binding uses seven holes. Place the holes approximately 1 to 1½ inches from the spine edge of the book. Space the holes approximately 1¼ inches apart starting in the middle—4¼ inches from the top. Using a pushpin or an awl and a hammer, punch the holes through all the papers' thicknesses.

Craftworking

If you aren't a whiz with a ruler, take a narrow piece of paper the length of the book. Fold it in half and continue folding to the halfway marks until you have the right number of points. Now you have a template you can use to make your holes for the binding. Witches are nothing if not resourceful.

Measure your thread so that it's four to five times the height of the book. A fatter stick will require more; a skinny one less.

Thread your needle and starting at the top hole, insert the needle stitching from the front to the back. Draw the thread almost all the way through, leaving about 5¼ inches worth of tail. For the moment, secure this tail beneath the bulldog clip at the top of the book.

Place the stick against the line of holes and stitch around it as you work your way down the spine. Follow the diagram for stitching down the book.

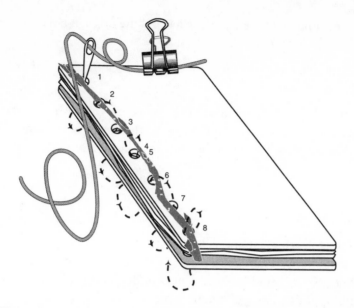

Threading the spine together.

Down in 1, up in 2, around the stick and down in 3, up in 4, around the stick and back down in the same hole for 5, up in 6, around the stick and down in 7, up in 8.

To stitch back up the spine, follow the diagram. Around the stick and down in the same hole for 9, up in 10, around the stick and down in 11, up in 12, around the stick and back down in the same hole for 13, up in 14, around the stick and down in 15, and up in 16.

Threading back up the spine.

The remaining tail should be on the left of the stick and the original tail on the right side. Tie the ends together over the stick.

When you finish, you should have an *X* over the stick between the 2nd and 3rd holes and between the 5th and 6th holes.

Now comes the fun part. Embellish and decorate the cover as you wish. Use stamping, collage, drawing; glue on beads, glitter, buttons, feathers, or whatever strikes your fancy. I know Wiccans who have used the mate to lost earrings as decorations. Be creative!

Just the Beginning

Obviously, entire books are written about techniques such as stamping, calligraphy, papermaking, and bookbinding. This chapter is a sampler of several different techniques you can consider as you begin keeping your own Book of Shadows. If any of these projects really appeals to you, go online or to your favorite bookstore for more ideas and information.

The Least You Should Know

- A Book of Shadows is a witch's diary that tracks her or his spiritual growth.

- Making a Book of Shadows should be a fun, spiritual activity, but does not have to be a showpiece for artistic talent (although talent is a wonderful gift). Don't be critical of your creative ability; just enjoy the process.

- There is no one right size for a Book of Shadows. Make one large book or keep spells in individual, decorative books that are small and easy to tuck away.

- However you choose to keep a Book of Shadows, make it your own and don't share it lightly with strangers.

Part 2

Celebrating the Craft: Esbats and Sabbats

Every religion has its holidays. For Wiccans, there are 8 major holidays called sabbats and at least 12 Full Moon esbats. What better time to decorate your house and your sacred space, plan a celebration or two, honor the change of seasons, and renew your life in service to the Lady and Lord. Here are projects for every sabbat, esbat, and Moon phase, including Drawing Down the Moon—for group rituals and solitaires, too.

Chapter 4

Make and Maximize Moon Magick

In This Chapter

- ◆ Coordinating your spells with the phases of the moon
- ◆ Easy directions for sewing and decorating a ritual robe
- ◆ Moon oils and other ritual tools for Drawing Down the Moon
- ◆ Using moon cords to harness the moon's energy
- ◆ A ritual or two for Drawing Down the Moon
- ◆ Creating sweet treats for the Goddess

I see the moon and the moon sees me,
Down through the leaves of the old oak tree,
Please let the light that shines on me,
Shine on the one I love.

For Wiccans, the moon is much more than a silver orb in the night sky who often appears as the main character in children's stories and rhymes. She is the embodiment of the Goddess—Maiden, Mother, and Crone. The Wheel of the Moon (one complete cycle) is approximately 28$\frac{1}{2}$ days long, waxing to Full Moon and waning to New Moon. The position and phase of the moon are considered one of the main deciding factors in determining when to celebrate or use magick. Practical witches time their spells and rituals so that they are performed at the right lunar phase for maximum results.

This chapter gives you some projects to help you make and maximize your own moon magick, from a ritual to Draw Down the Moon to some spiritual tools you can use to complete the ceremony.

Moon Phases and Tools to Use

Spells work best when you time them to coincide with the correct moon phase. A *New Moon* is one you can't see in the night sky. Magickal work which involves the start of something new or projects that favor growth are best performed under a New Moon. Starting a new job, having a baby, taking on a writing project, beginning a relationship—all of these are appropriate New Moon undertakings.

A *Waxing Moon* appears as a backwards *C* in the night sky. During this period, as the moon heads toward being full, spells that attract or bring about positive changes are best. Spells to draw something to you—love, luck, wealth, knowledge, health—are most powerful during this phase. Consider this a time of growth and development.

The *Full Moon* is a time of fruition and achieving goals. The Goddess's energy is at its most powerful at this time. It is best to do magickal work that involves power, strength, healing, and nurturing three days before, during, and three days after the Full Moon.

A *Waning Moon* appears as a capital *C* in the sky. Magickal work designed to end or otherwise release something unwanted is most potent during the Waning Moon as it heads back to the New Moon phase. Think of this as a period of banishment, release, and completion. End a relationship, let go of a grudge, lose some weight, quit a job. Whew!

The phases of the moon.

New Moon	Waxing Moon	Full Moon	Waning Moon
New starts	Building and growth	Heart's desire	Banishing

With spells in hand, you're ready to begin making moon magick. Let's think about a few projects you can do to deepen and enhance lunar energies.

I Haven't Got a Thing to Wear: Ritual Robes for Moon Magick

Although it is perfectly acceptable to perform rituals in your street clothes, wearing a robe is a symbol that you are moving from the mundane world into the spiritual. Just as you dress differently to go to work during the week than you do to run errands on the weekend, dressing for rituals indicates that outwardly you are embracing your religion as well as inwardly.

This robe is a basic, simple style that requires very little sewing and it fits any weight from 80 pounds to plus sizes. The front and back are the same—all you have to sew here are the sides and neck, which you can do by hand or with a sewing machine.

It's best to make your robe out of natural fabric such as cotton, linen, wool, or silk—although silk is a little pricey and can be difficult to clean. Keep in mind that soft fabrics drape better than stiff ones. Choose fabrics that breathe well and work well for your climate, especially if you conduct rituals outdoors. You don't want to be sweating during the summer and full of goose bumps all winter. Also, be sure to pick a washable fabric, as robes inevitably get wine, food, or candle wax on them. (Liguana says she loathes polyester. Use it if you have to but don't admit it to her—she refuses to be responsible.)

> **CAUTION**
>
> **Widdershins**
>
> Bedsheet material looks like bedsheet material no matter what kind of decorations you sew on. Investing in a length of dress fabric will give you much more pleasing results in the long run.

Black for the Full Moon, White for the New

In Chapter 11, we'll talk more about styles and colors for ritual robes, but for our Drawing Down the Moon robes we'll focus on a black robe for the Full Moon and a white robe for the New Moon.

If you can only make one robe, make it black and wear a white tabard for a New Moon ritual. A tabard is a short cape or scarf to drape over your shoulders.

Here's what you'll need to make your robe:

◆ A length of fabric 36 to 45 inches wide and as long as *twice* the distance from the top of your shoulder to your feet (for example, if you're 5 feet tall, you will need 10 feet of fabric)

◆ A few straight pins

◆ Dressmaker's chalk or a soft colored pencil

◆ A good pair of scissors

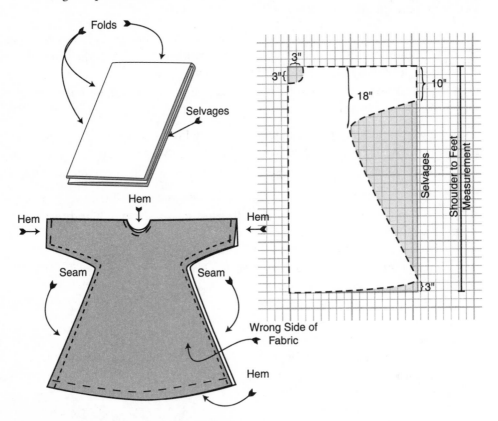

Use this pattern to create your own ritual robe.

Fold the fabric into quarters: once across (width—although most fabric comes already folded this way), and once the long way (lengthwise). Make sure that all four edges are even. Pin the edges together for added stability before you start cutting.

Important tip: If you have chosen a material with a pattern, there's an extra step you'll need to do. Cut across the width at midpoint, turn one half around and with the right sides facing, seam the 2 edges together. The seam will become the shoulder-and-sleeve seam of the finished robe, instead of the seamless top line made by folding. Be *sure* the upper ends of the design face *toward* this seam!

In the upper left-hand corner of the fabric you folded into quarters, measure 3 inches down both edges—horizontally and vertically. Make a quarter circle with the dress chalk on the fabric. Now cut it out, following the curved line you just made. This will become the scoop neck of your robe, which you'll see when you unfold it later.

Measure 10 inches down from the outside edge (selvage), and make a mark with your colored pencil. This is part of your sleeve.

Measure 18 inches up from the bottom along the outside (selvage) edge and make a mark with your colored pencil. This is your waist.

Measure 3 inches up from the bottom along the outside (selvage) edge and make a mark with your colored pencil. This is your hem.

Draw a line (essentially a sharp 45-degree angle) from the 3-inch hem mark up to the 18-inch waist mark. Stop. (Trust us on this, it's much easier this way!)

Now draw a wide gentle curve from the 18-inch waist mark out to the 10-inch sleeve mark. Remember, this is your sleeve, so the more generous you make this curve, the more roomy your sleeve will be. You need every inch you can allow to raise your arms above your head for rituals.

Now cut along the lines you just made. Unfold the robe. It should look just like the one in the previous illustration.

Now all you have to do is sew up the sides, hem the arms, the neck edge, and the bottom hem, and add trim if you want.

Decorating Your Robe

Decorate your black Full Moon robe with lots of silver. This can be with beads, embroidery threads, or textile paint. Use Goddess symbols such as shells, spirals, or circles. Sometimes less is more. Start simple and add designs and trim as you see fit.

New Moon robes should be decorated with repetitive patterns or designs to call in energy or magick power to the priestess or priest. Knot patterns or actual knots, dots, stars, or triangles all make powerful patterns— and gold is a good color to use.

Craftworking

However you chose to decorate your robe, make sure it's washable! In other words, gluing on glitter or sequins is a recipe for disaster.

Some Ritual Tools to Use in Drawing Down the Moon

Drawing Down the Moon is another way to invoke the Goddess. This ceremony can be simple or complex, solitary or group-oriented, and might (or might not) involve a variety of tools. Using oils, mirrors, bowls, or cords are all ways to help you tap into moon power. But just going out into the night, spreading your arms and talking to the moon works, too. The Goddess always listens.

Oils for Moon Magick

In some ceremonies for Drawing Down the Moon, Wiccans anoint themselves with a ritual oil depending on what phase the moon is in at the time. Here are two simple recipes to try.

Full Moon Oil

- A base oil such as sweet almond oil, avocado oil, or jojoba oil
- 3 drops sandalwood oil
- 2 drops lemon oil
- 1 drop rose oil

Mix all ingredients well pour into a decorative ¹/₂-ounce bottle. Store in a cool place.

Moon Oil When the Moon Is Other Than Full

Craftworking

You can use olive oil as a base oil, but it does have a slight odor that might alter the resulting fragrance.

- A base oil such as sweet almond oil, avocado oil, or jojoba oil
- 4 drops sandalwood oil
- 2 drops lavender oil
- 1 drop lemon oil

Mix all ingredients well and pour into a decorative ¹/₂-ounce bottle. Store in a cool place.

Moon Mirror

In a Drawing Down the Moon ritual, you will want to use a small mirror that you can carry easily and that you use only for Wiccan practices. Although any mirror will do, you can empower a mirror with your spirit by painting or refinishing the mirror's frame. Hobby shops carry mirrors with unpainted frames that you can decorate using Goddess or moon symbols. Or haunt antique shops, Goodwill stores, and yard sales. Find a mirror that appeals to you—oval or round shapes are especially appropriate for the Goddess, but any shape will do. Refinish the frame in any way you like—painting, varnishing, covering the frame with fabric. Just remember to keep the mirror small enough to carry into your circle.

Moon Bowl

If you want to try sculpting a bowl to use in your Drawing Down the Moon ritual, you can use the Sculpey modeling compound you used to create your Goddess and God statues in Chapter 2. Follow the directions on the Sculpey box once you're ready to bake and paint your finished bowl.

A moon bowl.

However, you may want to try a different technique if you don't feel like a talented potter. You can make something that looks like pottery using the papier-mâché technique, a craft in which layers of paper are pasted together to make a form. In this activity, we'll create a bowl and invent our own pictographs to use as surface decoration. By recycling newspapers and bags as art materials, we can help save natural resources and landfill space.

Here's what you'll need:

- ◆ Newspapers, including color comics section
- ◆ Wax paper
- ◆ Plastic wrap
- ◆ Small glass or ceramic bowl the same shape you want your papier-mâché bowl to be
- ◆ Masking tape
- ◆ Plastic container for paste
- ◆ Paint brushes and pan
- ◆ Wallpaper paste or white glue thinned with water

Summon and Stir

Wiccans pride themselves on protecting the environment. After all, Wicca is a nature-based religion. Papier-mâché is the perfect way to recycle at the same time you're creating sacred items. A bonus!

♦ Brown paper bag

♦ Acrylic paint

♦ Clear acrylic varnish

Cover the table with newspapers topped with a sheet of wax paper. Cover the outside and rim of the bowl with plastic wrap. Smooth it, pull the wrap tight, and tape it to the inside of the bowl. This makes it easier to remove the papier-mâché bowl from the mold. Place the bowl upside down on the wax paper.

Mix the wallpaper paste according to the manufacturer's directions or mix the white glue with enough water to make a thin paste.

The brown bag is the first layer of paper applied to the bowl. To help soften the bag, tightly roll the paper into a ball. Smooth it out, and tear it into small squares or rectangles. Dip a paper strip into the glue mixture, and remove the extra paste by running the strip between your fingers and thumb.

Starting at the rim, lay the strip onto the bowl and smooth it. Repeat with another strip, being careful to slightly overlap the first one. Continue pasting the paper in this way all around the rim of the bowl. When you've finished, cover the rest of the bowl with strips of brown paper.

Now apply a layer of black-and-white newsprint starting at the rim, as before. When working with papier-mâché, it's better to tear the strips of paper rather than cut them because torn strips lay better than cut ones. Also, the fibers in newspaper run in one direction, so tear the paper along the "grain" to obtain long strips.

Next, paste a layer of the colored comics to the bowl. Continue alternating between the newsprint and the comics until you've pasted at least four layers of each to the form. Using the two kinds of newspaper will help you keep track of the number of layers you've added. If you'd like to make a heavier bowl, just add 5 to 10 more layers of papier-mâché to the form.

Finish the papier-mâché by applying another layer of brown paper. Allow the bowl to dry for at least 12 hours. Remove the bowl from the papier-mâché form, and finish the rim by pasting brown paper all around the edge. When the bowl is completely dry, you're ready to paint it.

Summon and Stir

Challenge yourself to decorate your bowl without using modern art tools. The aborigines of Australia have been painting beautiful dot designs with sticks for thousands of years! You can try your hand at stick painting by using short lengths of dowel rods, cotton swabs, or similar materials. Dip the stick into paint, and apply it to the bowl. Repeat until an area is covered with a repetitive design.

You can invent your own pictographs to use in decorating your bowl. Make symbols or designs to represent important ideas or to record events in your life. Use pictographs to express who you are, where you live, and what you like to do. After you've created a few symbols, draw them on the outside and/or inside of the bowl. Use acrylic paint to fill in the outline. When you've finished painting the bowl, set it aside to dry. Finish the bowl by coating the inside with a coat of acrylic varnish. If you skip this final step, don't put water in your bowl or it'll turn to mush.

Moon Cords

The idea behind moon cords is to embrace and preserve specific attributes of moon power that are available during a specific moon phase. These attributes are directed into a length of cord and held there by knots; thus the attributes are available to a witch at any time.

For example, you may wish to perform some magick that is appropriate to the Waning Moon. Ideally, you would be wisest to wait until three days after the moon is full to utilize the most compatible energies for your work. But what if you have good reason not to wait, and what if it's the time of month when the moon is actually waxing? No problem! If you have prepared a Waning Moon cord, you can draw upon the Waning Moon power at any time of any month. You can prepare a cord during each phase of the moon, and have available to you the power of each phase. However, Liguana strongly suggests that you use the cords only when absolutely necessary and try to work with the phases of the moon in the sky whenever you can.

You'll need a length, or five lengths, of colored yarn or embroidery thread about 2 feet long. (You can use four different colors if you prefer and prepare four cords—one each for New, Waxing, Full, and Waning.)

To prepare a cord during the appropriate Moon phase, light a Goddess candle and sit at your altar or work table or go outside. Call on the power of the Goddess who rules all phases of the moon. This is called charging the cord—in other words, empowering the cord with spiritual energy.

It's a good idea to use your athame for this, because the process is related to Drawing Down the Moon. In a sense, you are drawing her down for each phase to enter your cord, so you may draw a pentagram over the face of the moon, or over the candle flame that represents her, and trace a line of power from the moon or flame into your cord. Use the following incantation or one of your own choosing:

> *Mother Goddess, I call upon you to charge this cord with your power. Bring the light of the moon into my spirit for the good of all, for the work of positive magick only. Aid me in my work in your time, according to your will, as these knots are tied.*

Then tie nine knots in the cord, placing them equidistant from one another and use the ninth knot to tie the cord into a circle. End by saying, "*So mote it be.*"

Place your circle of knots on the altar around your Goddess candle and leave it there while you meditate on the phase of the moon with which you have charged the cord. When you feel your work is complete, wind the cord into a compact little ball and enclose it in a tiny pouch or box on your altar.

When you work with a moon cord, either hold it in your hand or place it around your Goddess candle as you do specific magic for which you need its aid. When you are finished, put it back in its holder. You may take it out and hold it under the moon during its name phase, to recharge it, but this is not absolutely essential. Moon power doesn't drain away like a battery. It's there to stay.

Drawing Down the Moon Ritual

Drawing Down the Moon is a fancy way of charging yourself with divine energy. Just as you charge the tools of your craft, you charge yourself. There are as many different ways to do this as there are Wiccan practitioners. You can choose to do this ritual with sacred tools and trappings or without them, solitary or in a group.

Here is one of Liguana's famous 10-minute rituals for a solitary practitioner to Draw Down the Moon. Perform a self-blessing or take a ritual bath to prepare yourself to accept the Goddess's energy. Using your 27-foot rope or a bowl full of flour and barley (put the grain in your newly made moon bowl), go outside to a place where you have a good view of the moon in its fullness. Cast a magick circle using either your rope or by drawing a circle on the ground with your flour and barley mixture. Welcome the benevolent entities of each direction into your sacred space.

Recite out loud some version of "The Charge of the Goddess." Here is a copy of the traditional version translated by Charles Leland in the 1897 book, *Aradia, Gospel of the Witches:*

> *Whenever you have need of anything,*
> *one in the month and be it better when the moon is full,*
> *then shall you assemble in some secret place and adore*
> *the spirit of me, who am the Queen of all witches.*

> *When I have departed from this world,*
> *Whenever you have need of anything,*
> *Once a month, and when the moon is full,*
> *Ye shall assemble in some desert place*
> *or in a forest all together join*

To adore the potent spirit of your Queen
My mother, great Diana, She who fain
Would learn all sorcery yet has not won
Its deepest secrets, then my mother will
Teach her, in truth all things as yet unknown.

And ye shall all be freed from slavery,
And so ye shall be free in everything,
And as a sign that ye are truly free,
Ye shall be naked in your rites, both men
And women also: this shall last until
The last of your oppressors are dead.

There are several updated versions you can find online if you want something a little more modern. Or see *The Complete Idiot's Guide to Spells and Spellcraft* (Alpha Books, 2004) for several ideas. You can also write your own version, which is always powerful magick.

Focus on what "The Charge" means to you. Then, when you feel *centered* and *grounded*, take a mirror that you use only for your Wicca practice. Hold the mirror so you can see the moon reflected in it. Allow yourself to be filled with the Lady's light as you chant the following:

You are the Mother of the moon.
You are the Goddess strong and bright.
I am a sister (or brother) of the moon.
Let me be filled with Goddess light.

When you feel the energy build in you and you feel touched by the Lady, the ritual is done. Perform whatever other magick you wish; blessing a tool or casting a healing spell is especially good at this time. When you're finished, thank the benevolent entities and especially the Goddess. Open your circle, taking with you as you leave the blessing and extra boost of the Drawing Down the Moon ritual.

Magickal Properties

When preparing for a ritual it necessary for you to clear out any doubts or wandering thoughts. This is called **centering** and **grounding**. Center yourself by slowly bringing your awareness inward. Ground yourself by connecting to the Earth through your feet. For moon magick, visualize a cord of energy from your body that reaches down into the Earth, and a similar cord that reaches up to you from the Earth, with the two cords weaving together as they climb through you from Earth to Moon.

A Group Moon Ritual

If you are looking for a fancier ritual where your friends and coven family can participate, here is a nice one. Decide where you will go for sacred space, preferably where the moon can be clearly seen. (Liguana says candlelight can be used to represent the moon if the night is cloudy or rainy. Just hold the candle high so you gaze up at it. *Don't* hold it right above your head. The last thing you want is hot wax dripping down in your face. Trust her. She knows!) Cast your magick circle and call the quarters as usual. Everyone stands in a circle within the boundaries of the magick circle and, one at a time, participants enter the center of the circle where you have placed some reflective surface: a magick mirror, a silver plate, or a dark bowl with water in it. All will work. (Liguana prefers the mirror.) For more about casting magick circles and magick circle projects you can do, see Chapter 8.

The center person raises the mirror slowly to the sky until her arms are fully extended upward. The other people also sweep their arms slowly upward, as if pulling Earth energy into the center of the circle. While they do this it is good to tone or hum or chant together to raise energy. Now the center person lowers the mirror enough to see clearly the reflected moon and lets the divine energy wash over her while everyone else maintains a steady drone of humming, toning, or chanting. When the time feels right, the center person sets down the mirror and steps back into the circle of coveners. The next person steps forth and the process is repeated until all are charged and blessed by the moon and the coven. Now you can conduct whatever other rites you had in mind for the night, and thank the elementals of the four quarters and the Goddess, of course. Open your magick circle and celebrate with your friends. You have invited the Goddess to fill you with her energy to help you be the best priestess or priest you can be. That's no small thing, and it's worth celebrating!

Sweet-Tooth Treats for the Moon Goddess

Of course, traditional cutout moon-shaped sugar cookies would be perfect for a Drawing Down the Moon celebration. If you have children, involving them in decorating the cookies with icing and edible decorations is a great way to include them in precelebration preparations. But if you're looking for a different kind of cookie, here are two delicious treats to share with friends after a Drawing Down the Moon ritual.

Sweet Crescents

This buttery-rich cookie is easy to make and provides a melt-in-your-mouth treat that adds a lovely touch to a Drawing Down the Moon table. This recipe makes approximately two dozen cookies.

- ◆ $1/2$ cup powdered sugar

- ◆ 1 cup (2 sticks) softened butter (real butter makes them melt in your mouth and you can't beat the taste)

- ◆ 1 tsp. vanilla

- ◆ $2^1/4$ cups flour

- ◆ $1/4$ tsp. salt

- ◆ $3/4$ cup very finely chopped nuts (Black walnuts add a wonderful flavor, but pecans, almonds, English walnuts, or hazelnuts work equally well.)

Tip: The finer you chop the nuts, the better. These are rich, delicate cookies and large nut chunks tend to make them break.

Preheat your oven to 400°F. Cream together the powdered sugar and the softened butter until well blended. Stir in the vanilla. Work in the flour, salt, and nuts until the dough comes away from the sides of the bowl and holds together.

Pinch off pieces of the dough to form approximately 1- to $1^1/2$-inch balls. Next roll the balls into long ropes $1/4$ to $1/2$ inch thick and bend them into crescent moon shapes. Place on an ungreased baking sheet and bake 10 to 12 minutes or until set but not brown. While still warm, dip each cookie into powdered sugar gently, although you get to eat any you break! The sugar will melt a little and form a sort of shiny glaze (appropriate for moon cookies, don't you think?). Once they are completely cool, dip them again into powdered sugar.

Dark of the Moon Pies

These cookies require a little more effort, but they are so worth the time. This is a good cookie to make with a friend—one of you can be in charge of the cookies, one in charge of the filling, and both of you in charge of "sand-witching." This recipe makes approximately 18 cookies but can be doubled for a crowd.

For the filling:

- ◆ 2 TB. flour
- ◆ $1/8$ tsp. salt
- ◆ 1 cup whole milk

- ◆ $3/4$ cup shortening
- ◆ $1^1/2$ cups powdered sugar
- ◆ 2 tsp. vanilla

For the cookie:

- $1/2$ cup unsweetened cocoa powder
- $1/2$ cup boiling water
- $1/2$ cup shortening
- $1 1/2$ cups white sugar
- 2 eggs
- 1 tsp. vanilla

- $2 2/3$ cups flour
- 1 tsp. baking powder
- 1 tsp. baking soda
- $1/4$ tsp. salt
- $1/2$ cup buttermilk

To make the filling, begin by stirring together the flour and salt in a small saucepan. Whisk in the milk and cook over medium heat, stirring constantly until thickened, 5 to 7 minutes. Cover and refrigerate.

While the filling is cooling in the fridge, stir together the cocoa and boiling water for the cookie mix. Set aside. Meanwhile, cream together the shortening and sugar until smooth. Beat in the eggs one at a time. Add the vanilla. Combine the flour, baking powder, baking soda, and salt. Stir the dry ingredients into the sugar mixture alternating with the buttermilk. Finally, stir in the cooled cocoa.

Preheat the oven to 350°F. Drop the cookie dough by rounded tablespoons about 2 inches apart onto greased cookie sheets. Bake for 10 to 12 minutes.

While the cookies are baking, finish the filling. Cream together the shortening and powdered sugar and beat until light and fluffy. Add the vanilla and the milk mixture, continuing beating until well blended. Once the cookies have cooled, sandwich the filling between two cookies.

The Least You Need to Know

- For maximum magickal results, conduct your spells with the right moon phase for your intention.
- Drawing Down the Moon is a way to empower yourself with the Goddess's energy.
- Putting on a ritual robe is an outward symbol of your internal commitment to the Craft.
- Recycling material to create sacred items serves a dual purpose.
- Eliminating negative thoughts is the first step in casting a spell, and it begins with grounding and centering.

Holiday Projects: Celebrating the Wheel of the Year

In This Chapter

- Celebrate the circle in all its forms
- Holiday sabbat projects year 'round
- Honoring nature-based Wicca traditions
- Start with Samhain, Wicca's New Year

If you spend enough time around witches, you'll notice how much they love circles. Magick circles, the moon, the sun, the earth, a pregnant tummy, a ring, the rim of a chalice or bell, a shell—so many of the things that surround our lives are circular.

Circles are eternal with no beginning or end, and all points on a circle are equal. Witches look at a year as a circle or a wheel. In every year we travel through the seasons of reproduction, growth, fruitfulness, decline, death, and rebirth. There are eight sabbats, or holidays, on a witch's calendar, although many witches celebrate all of the standard holidays, too. The difference is that the sabbats won't find you obsessing about shopping for gifts, sending out greeting cards, or putting up with obnoxious television commercials.

There are, of course, activities for every Wiccan holiday, some of them symbolic and some that are just plain fun. Wiccan holiday projects could fill a book by themselves. This chapter offers you a few activities just to get you started. Gather up the coven, the family, and the kids and celebrate, celebrate!

Wicca's holiday Wheel of the Year.

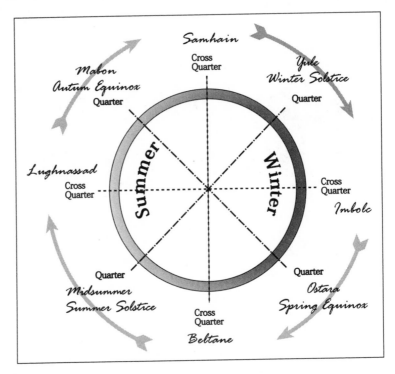

Samhain: October 31

Samhain is considered the most important of the eight sabbats, for it is the beginning of the Wiccan New Year. Like any new year, Samhain (pronounced *SOW-en*) is a time for reviewing the past and looking toward the future. The Lady is in her crone aspect, older and more sedate. Wiccans believe October 31 is the night when the veil between this world and the spirit world is at its thinnest because the Lord is in the otherworld and his crossing causes the veil to become thin for a while. This is the perfect night to receive messages and make contact with our ancestors and friends who have already passed. During this holiday, witches reflect upon and honor departed friends and loved ones. Samhain also celebrates the end of the Goddess-ruled summer and the beginning of the God-ruled winter. The meaning of Samhain is "Summer's End."

Summon and Stir

Liguana celebrates three days of Samhain on October 29, 30, and 31. The first day is a thanksgiving to the plants. She sets up a shrine on black cloth and puts out symbols of the plant blessings her family has received. They eat vegetarian meals and thank all the spirits of the plant world that have given themselves up for their comfort. The second day is thanksgiving for the animal spirits that have blessed them. October 31 is the feast of the ancestors and of all those who have gone before them. She makes a simple shortbread to put on the shrine, and then shares them as soul cakes to honor their ancestors at cakes-and-ale time.

Hazelnut Good-Luck Charm

This is an easy craft to add to your pre-Samhain celebrations, and an activity to involve the youngest Wiccans, too. This good-luck charm will protect you and your loved ones all year long. If you want, make several, and after consecrating them, give them to other pagan family and friends as gifts, or hang one in every room in your own home if you wish.

If you make them every year, the old ones can burned in the traditional Samhain bonfire. Then, consecrate the new ones.

Here's what you'll need:

- ◆ Nut pick and small hammer
- ◆ Nine whole hazelnuts
- ◆ Black- or red-colored twine or yarn
- ◆ Needle with a large eye (a creweling needle works well)

Using the nut pick and hammer, bore small holes through the middle of the nuts. (This is the adult's job.) Use whole nuts, and don't shell them! Thread the needle with the twine or yarn. String the nuts onto the twine, making it long enough to hold the nine nuts with a little bit of extra space, then tie it off in a circle. On the night of Samhain, consecrate it in the bonfire (or in a candle flame), passing it back and forth three times, and chanting:

 **Craftworking**

Nine is the sacred number of the hazelnut in the Celtic Tree Calendar. To attune yourself with the cycle of birth and death, save some of the nuts to bury during the Spring Equinox.

Hazelnuts all nine in a ring
By the smoke of the fire bring
To those within our lives and home
From the Goddess a protective cone

Guard for a year, I charge of thee
And as I will, so mote it be.

Hang these hazelnut charms over the doorjambs in your front and back doors (don't forget patio doors) and in windows to keep your good luck safely inside your house and bad luck out.

Make a Samhain Luminary

Because Wicca is a nature-based religion, witches like to take care of the earth by recycling. Empty metal food containers are perfect for creating pierced lanterns, small luminaries which hold votive candles. Make this a family or coven project and you'll have plenty to decorate the patio or line the sidewalks for Samhain.

Here's what you'll need:

- Metal cans (any size will do, but 5-pound coffee cans allow plenty of room to light a candle without burning your fingertips)

- Plain white paper wide enough to wrap around the can

- Rubber bands

- Pencil

- 10-penny nails, or the size of your choice

- Hammer

- An old throw rug or pillow

The luminary is made by tapping holes into the sides of the can with a hammer and nail. If you wish, you can plan a design using paper and pencil first, and follow it as you make the lantern. It's also possible to create the luminary as you go by just piercing the can along the edges and making simple patterns.

To start this project, rinse the empty food can and remove the paper label. If there are any sharp edges on the inside, hammer them flat.

Fill the cans with cold water, leaving at least $1\frac{1}{2}$ to 2 inches of space at the top. Place them in the freezer. Allowing room at the top is necessary because the water will expand as it freezes. This can cause the bottoms to bulge, making them unstable and unusable as luminaries. Leave the cans in the freezer until they're solid. The ice prevents the cans from becoming misshapen as you pound in the luminary holes.

If you've made a pattern on paper, use rubber bands to hold the pattern in place or tape your drawing to the container.

Place it on some form of cushioning such as an old throw rug or pillow.

Use the hammer and nail to tap holes through the can and ice. Simply follow the lines on your pattern, leaving spaces between the holes.

When finished, allow the ice to melt and empty the can. Place a votive candle in the bottom and line your sidewalk with your luminaries.

> **CAUTION**
>
> **Widdershins**
>
> According to an old legend, it's bad luck to bake bread or to travel after sunset on Samhain. However, lighting an orange candle at midnight and letting it burn until sunrise will

Winter Solstice or Yule: December 20–23

Yule is the longest, darkest night of the year, but it also marks the beginning of the time when days grow longer and nights grow shorter. It is a festival which honors the sun's rebirth symbolized by the Horned God who rules the dark half of the year. It is during this time that the Mother gives birth to her son and future consort. Pagan customs include decorating a tree, hanging mistletoe and holly, and burning a Yule log. Sound familiar? Christmas is actually the Christianized version of the Pagan Yuletide feast. On this sabbat, witches also concentrate on spells and rituals that focus on love, peace, prosperity, and family togetherness.

Witch Orbs

Hanging witch orbs (also called "witch balls," but Liguana hates that name) in your windows is not only festive, it provides added magick and protection to your Yuletide house. Buy good-sized orbs for this project. Small ornaments that come 24 to a box will work, but the end result won't be as satisfying.

> **Summon and Stir**
>
> A traditional Yule beverage is mulled wine, which dates back to medieval times. "Mulled" means to heat a beverage and add spices. Adding cinnamon, nutmeg, cloves, and lemons and oranges to red wine that has been slowly heated (*not* to the boiling point, which destroys the flavor) makes a soothing beverage. For a non-alcoholic version, substitute apple cider for the wine.

Here's what you'll need:

- White or silver glass ornaments
- Paint and brushes (nail polish works well, too)
- A variety of herbs and oils (see below)

This is as simple as filling the orbs with a variety of herbs and oils and hanging them in your window.

First, paint your orbs with whatever magickal designs you choose. Let them dry thoroughly. Then carefully fill them with the herbs and oil you've chosen. Liguana prefers putting a few drops of oil on a cotton ball rather than mixing it in directly with the herbs.

Following are some suggestions, but feel free to experiment.

Herbs:

- Dragon's blood resin for potency, love, and purification (it makes all your magick stronger)
- Sagebrush or white sage for purification and to drive away evil
- Mugwort for healing and dreaming
- Vervain for love and peace
- Myrrh for purification and protection
- Frankincense for blessing and protection
- Rosemary for cleansing, healing, and protection

Oils:

- Primrose for protection and love
- Sandalwood for purification and healing
- Heliotrope for dreaming, healing, and wealth

Avoid using hard resin or stones in the witch orbs; they are fragile and apt to break.

Cinnamon Cutouts

For another fragrant decoration, try these cinnamon cutouts to hang on your Yule tree. This is another good activity to share with children. You mix; they cut out. This recipe makes approximately eight cutouts, depending on the size of your cookie cutters. Even though the cutouts smell delicious, they are not edible and are for decoration only!

Here's what you'll need:

- 1 cup cinnamon (Yes! 1 cup)
- 1$^1/_2$ tsp. ground cloves
- 1$^1/_2$ tsp. allspice
- 1$^1/_2$ tsp. ginger
- $^1/_2$ to $^3/_4$ cup applesauce
- Decorative cord
- $^1/_3$-inch wide ribbon in assorted colors

In a small bowl, combine the cinnamon, cloves, allspice, and ginger with $^1/_2$ cup of the applesauce, mashing with a fork or a pastry blender until well blended.

Gather the dough into a ball, kneading with your hands until it's smooth and elastic. Add more applesauce, 1 teaspoon at a time, if the mixture is too crumbly.

Sprinkle a flat surface with cinnamon. Dust a rolling pin with cinnamon and roll out the dough to a $^1/_4$-inch thickness.

Using a medium cookie cutter, cut out shapes from the dough—for example, stars, moons, pine trees, or bells. Carefully center a smaller cookie cutter on some of the shapes; cut out centers, as desired. (Hors d'oeuvre cutters work well for this.)

Preheat the oven to its lowest setting (120–140°F) and using a toothpick, make a small hole at the top of each cutout, if desired; gently transfer cutouts to an ungreased baking sheet.

Continue cutting out shapes with remaining dough, adding more applesauce to moisten, if necessary.

Craftworking

These cutouts will keep their aroma for years. Small cutouts of this dough can be added to potpourri for additional scents and texture. Store them in an airtight container in a cool, dry place between seasons. To rejuvenate the scent, sprinkle them with warm water. (Mice love these, so if you don't make the container rodent-proof you'll end up with nibbled cutouts!)

Bake cutouts for 1 hour and 30 minutes; turn off oven but don't open the oven door to peek! Leave the cutouts in the oven overnight to dry completely.

Tie loops of cord through the toothpick holes for hanging, if desired. Make a bow with a length of ribbon; tie to the top of the cord to decorate.

Candlemas: February 2

Candlemas is a fire festival which celebrates the coming of spring. The Lady recovers her youth after giving birth and becomes a maiden again. The Lord is in his infancy. This is a time for sweeping out the old; streams start to flow again and, in some places, snowdrops and crocuses peek through the last crust of snow. Witches consider this the first of the three sabbats of the growing light and sometimes celebrate with rituals to invoke wisdom and prophecy.

A Wiccan Wakeup Wand

Children love the sound of this magickal wand as they walk about pointing and shaking it at plants, bushes, and trees, encouraging them to wake up from winter's long sleep to celebrate the union of the Lady and the Lord of the Forest.

Here's what you'll need:

- Small tree branch
- Thin brown or gold string or thread
- An acorn
- Craft glue
- Yellow, green, and gold $\frac{1}{4}$-inch ribbon
- Small gold and silver jingle bells

Select a small branch about $\frac{1}{2}$ to $\frac{3}{4}$ inch in diameter. Cut the top end flat. Approximately $\frac{1}{2}$ inch below the top, score a notch all the way around the branch with a sharp knife (have an adult do this!). Take a piece of string 1 foot long and tie it into the groove, keeping the ends even. Take another 1-foot long piece of thread and tie it into the groove also, knotting it on the opposite side of the branch. This should give you four strings, each approximately the same length.

Place the top of the acorn at the top of the branch and adhere with some glue. Now pull the string up over the cap and wind once around the acorn. Repeat

> **Summon and Stir**
>
> Candlemas is also called Imbolc, which means "in the belly," and refers to all of the animals just beginning to start the cycle of life over again. Most specifically, sheep are usually carrying young at this time.

with the other three ends of string. Pull the strings back down to the groove in the branch and tie off. This will hold the acorn in place.

Decorate the branch by wrapping it with the ribbons, leaving enough length at the top for streamers. Tie gold and silver jingle bells to the ends of the ribbons. Tell the children about how the acorn-wand is a symbol of the Lord of the Forest, and how this magickal wand helps the sleeping plants and animals wake up and prepare for spring.

Bread-Braid Crowns

A lovely ritual for Candlemas is to have the young ladies and lords in the group wear bread crowns with lit candles and dance joyously to welcome the upcoming spring.

Use any pretzel dough recipe (you'll find one in Chapter 9), but make sure you use enough flour to make a thick dough, not mushy.

Have folks roll out three dough snakes each. If children are helping at this point, you can talk about the symbolism of the snakes coming up out of the Earth to greet warmer weather. Measure the children's head circumferences with string; their snakes should be a few inches longer than that. It may take just a bit of experimenting to get the right length. Luckily, the dough is a bit stretchy, and if it's still not right, you can squish it together and start again. Just remember that making these hats isn't an exact science. Generally, if you measure the widest circumference of your head with the string and stick to that measurement, the rising of the dough will make the bread braid sit more like a crown. If you make them bigger than the widest circumference of the head, you stand the chance of having bread braid necklaces instead of crowns.

Pinch the three snakes together at one end and braid them, connecting both ends of your braid by pinching them together and reshaping nicely. Wrap little foil squares around a finger and press into the braid where candles will go. Birthday candles or Chanukah candles are a good size—any larger and they will fall out easily. Bake the braids with the foil in. (It should be enough foil that it sticks out a bit for easy removal later.)

When the bread begins to brown, remove the foil bits, brush with beaten egg to make it shiny, and sprinkle on coarse salt for a sparkle factor. When they are done, remove from the oven and let them cool before putting the candles in.

The joyful dancing should ideally happen around a bonfire. Tie back long hair so it doesn't accidentally float into a candle flame. Have a bucket of water and a hose nearby. We *don't* want to set our friends or children on fire, so make sure the candles are firmly embedded before the dancing begins.

Spring Equinox or Ostara: March 20–23

Ostara is a fertility celebration heralding the birth of spring and the Earth's awakening to new life. On this day, light and dark are equal in length. It is a time of balance, and many witches' thoughts turn to things within themselves that they wish to balance—the practical and the frivolous, stubbornness and submission, logic and intuition, acceptance of the status quo and motivation to change. It is a time to celebrate growing things and to ask for blessings for the projects we start after a winter of planning. The Lady is a youth again (in her maiden aspect), as is the Lord.

Celebration Eggs

Dyeing hard-boiled eggs is an Easter tradition, but the custom has its roots in the pagan Ostara holiday. Rather than following the usual egg-dyeing routine, try this variation.

Here's what you'll need:

- Fresh eggs

- Large darning or embroidery needle

- Clear tape

- Herbs, confetti, glitter, birdseed, or other lightweight items for filling

- Colored pens, paint, or tissue paper and glue to decorate the eggs

Empty the eggshells by making a small hole in the larger end and a slightly larger hole in the small end with the needle (be sure to puncture the yolk but be careful not to crack the rest of the egg). Then, gently blow on the larger end of the egg to gently push out the egg's innards. (Save these for scrambled eggs or omelets.)

Rinse out the eggs with cool water (gently!) and let them dry overnight.

Craftworking

If the weather is nice, you might want to be outdoors for this celebration in case cleanup is an issue. Filling the eggs with birdseed is an added bonus for the birds!

Close the smaller hole with a tiny piece of tape or a bit of glue.

Carefully fill the shells with a mixture of herbs, confetti, or other lightweight filling. You might need to enlarge the hole a bit; just be careful not to crack the egg. When full, seal the top hole with tape or glue.

Carefully decorate the outside of the egg using the paint, pens, or tissue paper.

On Ostara morning, take turns breaking a filled egg over the heads of your family and friends. As the filling sprinkles down, everyone is blessed with love, luck, and new life for the season.

Pashka

This is a lovely, light dessert to celebrate spring made with nuts, fruits, and cottage cheese. Make it a part of your Ostara brunch. Serve it right after the omelets you make from the egg "innards" you saved when you blew out the eggs to make the decorative eggs.

- 1¼ cups sugar
- 2 sticks butter, melted
- ¼ tsp. salt
- 2 cups evaporated milk or cream
- 2 eggs
- ¾ cup chopped almonds or pecans
- ¾ cup chopped peaches
- ½ cup maraschino cherries
- 1¼ tsp. vanilla
- 2½ lbs. small-curd cottage cheese

Whisk together the sugar, melted butter, salt, evaporated milk or cream, and eggs in a large pan over low heat. Stir constantly until it thickens to the consistency of pudding.

Remove from heat, stir in the nuts, peaches, cherries, and vanilla and allow the mixture to cool completely.

Mix in the cottage cheese and beat well for about 4 minutes.

Place the mixture in a decorative mold and chill overnight.

Unmold the pashka onto a plate. Decorate with jelly beans, flowers, chocolates, candied flowers, or other spring delicacies. Surround with fresh seasonal fruit if you like. Keep refrigerated until it's time to serve.

Beltane: May 1

Beltane is the last of the spring fertility festivals. The Lord and Lady are in young adulthood and their union inspires all things to grow and flourish. Flowers and trees are in all stages of blooming, being pollinated, and preparing to bear fruit. Most Wiccans turn their thoughts to love magick at this time—pulling love in, expanding their capacity to love, and learning to love themselves. It is a time of union, both physical and spiritual.

Beltane traditionally begins with a bonfire at moonrise on May Day eve to light summer's way. Coven members might dance clockwise around a decorated maypole, a phallic fertility symbol.

Tabletop Maypole Centerpiece

If you don't have access to a full-sized maypole, you can make a small one to use as a centerpiece for a Beltane luncheon. Serve fresh fruits and vegetables and bake fresh muffins or scones to accompany them.

Here's what you'll need:

- Empty paper towel roll
- Paint and small paintbrush
- Small piece of flat cardboard
- Wrapping paper
- Tape
- Ribbons or streamers

Paint the paper towel roll a bright spring color. Set it aside to dry. Cover a small square of cardboard with wrapping paper to use as a base. When the paint is dry, tape one end of your painted paper towel roll onto the cardboard so it stands upright. Wrap a ribbon around your maypole leaving some of the painted towel roll showing and secure it with tape. Cut lengths of ribbon to hang on the outside of your maypole. Tape these on the inside of the top edge of the paper towel roll. If you like, you can scatter flowers around your maypole centerpiece.

Tiny May Day Basket

An old tradition on May Day is to leave baskets of flowers and sweets on your friends' doorsteps. Anyone who gets caught leaving the treats must forfeit a kiss!

Here's what you'll need:

- ◆ Empty toilet-tissue roll
- ◆ Tape
- ◆ Construction paper or wallpaper scraps
- ◆ Markers or paint
- ◆ Pipe cleaners

Cut the toilet-tissue roll in half so you have two small pieces. Cover one opening with construction paper as a base and tape securely it in place. Cut a strip of construction paper or wallpaper to cover the outside of the toilet tissue roll. Using a hole punch, make two holes opposite of each other near the open end of the tissue roll. Thread the pipe cleaner through the holes to make the handle. Fill your minibasket with real or homemade flowers (violets and clover are a perfect size) and try to hang it on your neighbor's doorknob without getting caught!

Summer Solstice or Midsummer: June 20–23

Midsummer marks the longest day of the year and symbolizes the power of the sun; it is a great turning point in the Wheel of the Year. After today, the days grow visibly shorter. The God is at his most powerful now; he makes the fields grow green and produces food for the coming harvest. The Goddess is in her aspect of Mother, guiding the world into bountiful fullness. Witches typically begin harvesting the herbs they will use later in potions and spells. This is a good time for healing rituals and divinations. All forms of magick, especially love magick, are potent on Midsummer's Eve; and, it is believed that whatever is dreamt on this night will come true.

> **Summon and Stir**
>
> European farmers of old kept the tradition of marching their livestock between two bonfires to cleanse them of negative energies on Midsummer's Eve.

Dream Pillow

Because a Midsummer night's dream (apologies to Shakespeare) is an especially important one if it's destined to come true, an herb-stuffed pillow will ensure sweet dreams and a pleasant future. For those who are sitting up all night on the Solstice, this is a special dream pillow you can make for prophetic dreams when you go to sleep the next night or throughout the year.

Here's what you'll need:

- 1–4 oz. of each of the following dried herbs and flowers (or substitute your favorites):

    Chamomile

    Mugwort

    Peppermint

    Catnip

    Rosemary

    Rose petals

    Lavender

- One or two whole oranges and lemons
- One cinnamon stick, broken into small pieces
- Scraps of lightweight cloth 4 by 7 inches (two for each pillow), optional bits of ribbon, embroidery floss, scraps of lace, or a few small beads

Mix the dried herbs in whatever proportions you desire. More lavender will lead to more prophetic dreaming; more rosemary will lead to a deeper sleep; more catnip may encourage pillow sharing with a cat.

As the night passes, eat the oranges and use the lemons (minus their peels) in teas, punches, or hot drinks. As you use them, try to remove the peels in large chunks or in easy to work with sections. Using a spoon, carefully scrape out as much of the white inner rind as you can without damaging the zesty outer peel. Scatter the remaining outer peels on a cookie sheet and dry them on low heat in the oven (200°F or less). Watch them to make sure they are drying but not scorching. This will take an hour or two. Remove them from the oven, and let them cool.

Crumble the dried peels up into smaller bits and add them to the spices. Mix well.

If you want to use the ribbons and floss to embroider protective or other magical symbols or representative designs, it will be easier to do before you stitch the sides together. Next, sew the scraps of material into small pillows, 3 by 6 inches. Leave one side open. As you sew your pillow, think of the season and what it means to you. If these are intended as gifts, think kindly and lovingly of the folks you will be giving these to.

Fill each of the bags with the herb/spice mixture, but not so full that it is hard: people will want to smell them, but they need to be soft enough to sleep with. Fold the last side inward, and stitch closed. When you go to bed, slip one or more of these into your pillowcase, and inhale deeply as you relax into sleep. Watch for special dreams as you sleep.

Make a Witch's Ladder

This is a great family activity and the end product is a whimsical but powerful amulet. Gather up feathers on a nature walk, or purchase them at your local hobby shop.

Here's what you'll need:

 ◆ Three different colored yarns about 5 feet long (Red, black, and white are traditional, but use any three colors that appeal to you.)

 ◆ Nine feathers (see the color suggestions that follow)

Tie the yarns together on one end and braid them together. The braid should be 3 feet long. Tie a knot so the braid won't unravel. Weave the quill end of the feathers into the braid. Use all one color for a specific charm or various colors for diverse charms. Following are some color suggestions:

 ◆ Red feathers for vitality

 ◆ Green for prosperity

 ◆ Blue for peace and protection

 ◆ Yellow for joy and awareness

 ◆ Brown for stability

 ◆ Black for wisdom and courage

 ◆ Black and white for balance

 ◆ Patterned for clairvoyance and insight

Hang your ladder on a sheltered porch or patio or on a tree branch. If you make one every year, you can burn the old one in a Midsummer bonfire.

Lammas: August 1

Lammas is the first festival of the harvest. Food is plentiful now, signaling the weakening of the God. In some traditions, Lammas is a wake for the Lord, who prepares to take our negative habits and thoughts with him to the otherworld and leave them there so we may start living newly reborn. This is a time to pay off debts, thank those to whom we owe thanks, and repair any damage we may have thoughtlessly done to relationships. Although the days are still warm and long, now is the time to start canning and preserving fruits and vegetables for the winter.

Corn Necklace

Corn necklaces make fun party favors, or place one on your altar to honor the God who will be leaving us soon.

Start with an ear of fresh corn. Choose one with large tough kernels—in fact, the larger and tougher, the better.

Remove the husk and break the ear in half, then begin popping off the kernels, beginning at the broken end of each half and going around the cob. Try not to break the kernels in half, but leave the white points on them.

Then, with about 2 or 3 feet of heavy thread on a large needle, begin stringing the kernels by putting the needle through the very center of each one. When the strand is long enough to make a necklace (one ear is usually more than enough) tie the ends of the thread together and hang the necklace in a warm, dry place for a few weeks.

The kernels will shrink as they dry, so it may be necessary to tighten the knot.

You can also use Indian corn that has been field dried because it has beautiful colors, but if it's too dry you might have trouble pushing the needle through the kernels.

If you want to be able to use this necklace year after year, you'll want to spray it with polyurethane or varnish it to protect it from moths and mice.

Pumpkin Apple Butter

With apples especially plentiful this time of year, putting up apple butter is a great way to use up the surplus. This is a great butter for your toast, muffins, bagels, or crackers. If you bake a pork loin, apple butter is a lovely accompaniment. This recipe makes approximately one pint.

- ◆ 1 cup apple juice or cider
- ◆ 1 cup (about 1 medium) peeled, cored, and grated apple
- ◆ $1/2$ cup packed brown sugar
- ◆ 1 tsp. pumpkin pie spice
- ◆ $1^3/4$ cups canned or fresh pumpkin

Combine all ingredients in medium-sized, heavy saucepan and bring to a slow boil.

Reduce heat to low; simmer uncovered for $1^{1}/_{2}$ hours, stirring occasionally. (Low temperatures are important because this mixture scorches easily.)

Pour into a small container, cover, and chill. Pumpkin apple butter can be stored in the refrigerator for up to two months.

Fall Equinox or Mabon: September 20–23

Mabon is the second harvest festival and a time of thanksgiving for Earth's bounty. The Lord walks between the worlds, sometimes with us and sometimes crossing the veil between life and death. The Lady anticipates his leaving and mourns the time she will be without him. This is the time when witches rededicate themselves to the Craft and welcome new witches into the Craft. As the smoke from autumn bonfires rise, we celebrate with gratitude the bounty of the harvest and look forward to winter—a time of darkness, rest, and anticipation of the future.

Fall Leaf "Stained Glass"

This is the perfect time of year to bring some of autumn's splendor inside. This project is simple and inexpensive and starts with a nature walk. What could be better? You can involve children in gathering up the leaves and in arranging them into a pattern, but adults only in charge of the ironing, please.

Here's what you'll need:

- Fall leaves
- Wax paper
- An old towel (towels made of flour sack or some other thin cloth work best)
- An iron
- Tape
- A picture frame (any size will work, but 8 by 10 inches or 9 by 12 inches will give you a nice surface area to work on)

Begin by going for a walk and collecting as many different fall leaves as possible. Try to find different shapes, sizes, and colors.

Cut two pieces of wax paper slightly larger than your picture frame.

Lay one piece of the wax paper on the towel and arrange the leaves in a pleasing design. Don't hesitate to overlap some of the leaves or to place some of them upside down.

When you have the pattern you want, lay the other piece of wax paper over the leaves and press the two together using a hot iron. Start by "tacking" the wax paper into place with the tip of the iron so it won't shift. Then, press firmly but quickly from the center out.

Tape the "stained glass" to the picture frame and cut off the excess. Hang in a sunny window for best results.

Pinecone Bird Feeder

Migrating birds begin gathering to fly south for the winter at this time, but there are plenty of birds who hang out all winter hoping to find food. Now is the time to begin feeding birds so they fatten up for the upcoming winter. Making a pinecone feeder is fun, inexpensive, and easy.

Here's what you'll need:

- Several pinecones (if you purchase pinecones rather than picking them up off the ground, be sure they haven't been sprayed with chemicals)
- Some red ribbon
- Peanut butter (a generic brand works just fine, either creamy or chunky)
- Birdseed (any kind will do, but adding sunflower seeds and cracked corn will attract cardinals if they're in your area)
- Small butter knife or cheese spreader
- Shallow pan or pie plate

Tie a length of ribbon around the top of the pinecone. You will use this ribbon to tie your bird feeder to a tree branch or to a metal flowerpot hanger, so make it long enough for your needs.

"Paint" the pinecone with peanut butter—spread it to a medium thickness all over the pinecone. Pour the birdseed into a shallow pan and roll the pinecone in the seed until it's well covered.

Hang the feeder in a tree near a window so you can watch your bird friends enjoy the treat.

Celebrate the Seasons

Wiccan holidays celebrate the seasonal changes as the Lady turns from Crone to Maiden to Mother and alternately mourns the death of the Lord, celebrates his birth, and rejoices in him mating with the Lady, which starts the cycle all over. Whether you chose a solitary celebration, a family get-together, or a coven gathering, the sabbats are a time of joy and reflection.

The Least You Need to Know

- ◆ The sabbats celebrate the turning of the seasons, whether you choose to be a solitaire or share the celebrations with friends and family.

- ◆ The Wheel of the Year symbolizes the Goddess in her aspects of Maiden, Mother, Crone, and the God who is born, mates with the Goddess, and dies, only to be reborn again.

- ◆ Wiccans should choose holiday traditions that make the sabbat celebrations their own.

- ◆ Every sabbat offers us a time to reflect on how we exist in the world and provides an opportunity for joy.

Chapter 6

Homage to the Lord and Lady

In This Chapter

- Why honor the God and Goddess?
- Making candied flowers
- Invite the blessings of the Goddess with a Brigid's Cross
- Honor the God by making a stag staff
- Planting a tree to honor a deity
- How to make blessing bundles

So who are the Lord and Lady and how do Wiccans honor them? This is a tricky question to answer. First let's look at some generally accepted Wiccan cosmology.

Most Wiccans recognize a divine force or energy, variously referred to as the All, the Cosmos, Spirit, or All That Is. Some Wiccan traditions call this the Mother and use no other deity in their practices. However, many Wiccan traditions recognize two distinct aspects of the All—the Goddess and the God. The natural cycles of their existence correlate to the cycles of life here on good old planet Earth. As we pointed out in Chapter 5, we honor Goddess and God by celebrating the seasonal changes and the turning of the Wheel of the Year.

The projects in this chapter can help you connect more deeply to the Divine in all of its many forms. Though we might name specific deities whose personality types seem to correspond to an activity, there are probably hundreds more we could name. A common Wiccan practice is to use the divine pantheons from other cultures and religions to connect with various traits and abilities of Gods and Goddesses worshipped in times gone by or in distant lands. Most Wiccans research and update their knowledge of mythology and world religions regularly. We highly recommend this.

Honoring the Goddess

In the Wiccan religion, the Goddess is the universal mother. She is the source of all creation and is viewed in three aspects:

- Maiden: the young woman, not yet come into her full womanhood
- Mother: the woman of childbearing age, the nurturer
- Crone: the Matriarch, the giver of justice, swift and sure

Some symbols honoring the Goddess are the cauldron, the cup, five-petaled flowers, a pentacle, the mirror, a necklace, seashells, pearls, silver, emeralds, and moons. Some of her most favored animals are the rabbit, bear, owl, cat, dolphin, lion, horse, scorpion, spider, bee, and turtle.

Candied Flowers

Here is a fun group project, perfect for spring and summer holidays. It honors the Lady in several of her aspects.

Here's what you'll need:

- 1 extra-large egg white, at room temperature
- A few drops of water
- About 1 cup superfine sugar
- Edible flower blossoms, separated from the stem, rinsed well and dried (suggestions: hollyhocks, borage flowers, lilac florets, roses, geraniums, violets, cornflowers, marigolds, impatiens)

- ◆ Small paintbrush
- ◆ Baking rack covered with waxed paper

This job takes a little patience so it's a good group activity. Chatting with friends makes the chore less tedious and the results are well worth it. This recipe will coat quite a few flowers depending on which types of flowers you use.

In a small bowl, combine the egg white with the water and beat lightly with a fork or small whisk until the white just shows a few bubbles. Pour the sugar into a shallow dish.

Holding a flower or petal in one hand, dip the paintbrush into the egg white mixture with the other and gently paint the flower or petal completely on both sides with a thin coat.

Holding the flower or petal over the sugar dish, gently sprinkle sugar evenly all over on both sides. Shake off any excess and place the flower or petal on the waxed paper to dry. Let the flowers dry completely in a cool place out of direct sunlight. This could take a day or two.

Store the dried, candied flowers in airtight containers until ready to use. They will keep up to one year. These leaves and flowers may be used on cakes and cookies or may be handed out as candies during feast times.

Craftworking

Many flowers correspond to a specific Goddess or God. For example, use rose petals for the Goddess Aphrodite, mint leaves for the Goddess Mentha, calendula or marigold blossoms for the Goddesses Lakshmi, Brigid, and Aphrodite, and borage flowers for the Goddess Athena and also for the God Mars.

Brigid's Cross

One of Ireland's most beloved saints, Brigid, spent her childhood serving the family of a Druid priest, performing the burdensome tasks associated with running a household and a farm. Early in her life she became a Christian. Brigid's feast day is February 1, long held sacred as Imbolc, the Celtic festival of spring.

Brigid is a goddess of the Tuatha De Danann. She was one of three daughters of the Dagda. We don't know which one, as they were all named Brigid! She is often viewed as a triple-aspected goddess instead of just one of three sisters. The Christian Saint Brigid may represent the church's attempt to sway pagan people into the fold by incorporating one of the old gods into the new religion and calling her a saint. She may also have been a real historical figure. We don't know for sure.

At Imbolc, the Maiden aspect of the Goddess might be represented in a great variety of ways. One popular way is to braid straws or wheat into an intricate design called a Brigid's Cross. Although the original design may well have been made from rushes, wheat versions have been recreated for centuries. Make a cross for each room in the house to invite the blessings of the Goddess into them.

You'll need 28 long, large diameter wheat straws without heads (or any long, flexible reeds or grasses).

Soak straws in a tub of cool water for half an hour before starting, then wrap in a towel for another 15 minutes.

Make the core first by positioning two straws to make a plus sign, placing the horizontal straw on top. Pull the upper section of the vertical straw down on top of its other half.

The first step in making the cross.

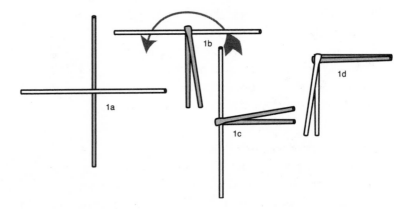

Turn the weave 90 degrees counterclockwise. Repeat to fold down the straw that is now vertical.

The second step.

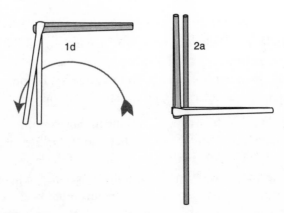

Turn the straws 90 degrees counterclockwise again. Add the next straw by placing it to the right of the vertical folded straw and under the horizontal folded straw.

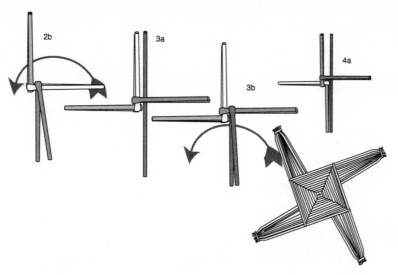

The third step.

Fold the added straw, turn the straws once again, and add the fourth and final straw to this round in the same fashion.

Continue to add folded straws. Avoid letting them bunch up or lie on top of those in a previous round. Instead, build the weave outward, resting the straws side by side. At first, you might find it difficult to hold the arms together and at right angles, but as the cross gains substance, this will become easier. Just remember to watch for gaps and fill them by adjusting and tightening the straws as necessary.

When all 28 straws have been woven in, tie each arm off about 4 inches from the center of the design. Trim the ends of the straws and threads.

To perform a simple ceremony using your Brigid's Cross, place a red, pillar-sized candle at your front door. With a Brigid's Cross in your hand, light the candle, open the door, and say:

> *Welcome, Goddess, into my house, we seek the turning of the Wheel away from winter and into spring. Enter and relax.*

If you have made a cross for other rooms of your house, take the candle with you and as you enter each room say:

> *Great Lady, enter with the sun and watch over this room.*

Leave a cross in each room and proceed throughout the house. Save the kitchen for last. There you say:

> *Mother of the Earth,*
> *Keep us safe and warm in your embrace,*
> *As over our home you extend your blessing.*

Summon and Stir

Wiccans are very accepting of other spiritual paths and religions. We see other gods and goddesses as aspects of the Lady and the Lord. We want to connect with their traits and abilities. Creating things that represent the Gods and Goddesses is another example of the microcosm reflecting the macrocosm. Like calls to like. We call the divine.

Honoring the God

The God is the universal father. He is viewed in two aspects:

- Horned God of the Hunt: the hunter, the protector
- Father: consort to the Mother Goddess

Some symbols honoring the God are the sword, horns, a spear, gold, brass, diamonds, arrows, magickal wands, and knives. His favored creatures include the bull, dog, snake, fish, stag, dragon, wolf, boar, eagle, falcon, shark, and lizard.

Stag Staff

This project is easy and honors the Horned One in his aspects as Herne, Cernunnos, and Pan.

The quest for a forked branch is part of the project. Search nearby woods or the seashore. (A driftwood staff may also honor Poseidon.) When you have found your staff, remove any loose bark so that your hands can slide up and down without wood flaking off or giving you splinters.

Using almond, lemon, or olive oil, condition the wood by rubbing it in thoroughly, especially the ends. (This is best done on a waning moon.) Leave it alone in a safe place for three days to drink in the oil. Now you are ready to decorate it to suit you and your chosen God.

Some Wiccans like to use animal hide and glue it in strips around the staff. Or you may fasten a leather band around the staff where your handhold will be. Feathers and fur and rawhide are common materials used to decorate staves. If you do use animal bits, please take a moment to honor the spirit of the animal and all its descendants and ancestors. Never use hide that you cannot identify. You may carve or burn runes or other symbols into your staff. You may also use shells and beads as ornamentation. However, don't use any metal on your staff. Metal ornamentation seems to arrest the energy flow. Your staff is like your wand in that you want to draw energy up through it and send energy out of it.

Once you have crafted your staff the way you like it, it can accompany you to any ritual and help you connect with the essence of the Horned One.

> **Summon and Stir**
>
> Poseidon is a God of many names. He is most famous as the God of the sea. The division of the universe involved him and his brothers, Zeus and Hades. Poseidon became ruler of the sea, Zeus ruled the sky, and Hades got the underworld. The other divinities attributed to Poseidon involve the God of earthquakes and the God of horses.

Plant a Tree

Planting a tree to honor a deity and call his or her energy is a life-affirming ritual that adds a touch of beauty to the world at the same time. Although lists exist that suggest which tree is associated with which deity, as in all magick, plant whatever type of tree you are drawn to. (And whatever type of tree suits your climate. You can't grow an orange tree in Minnesota!)

Newly planted trees do best when exposed to moderate temperatures and rainfall. They need ample time to root and before being exposed to the intense heat and dryness of summer or the freezing temperatures of winter. Therefore, spring (on or just before Beltane) and early fall (on or just after Lammas) are generally the best planting seasons (depending on your location), with spring preferred over fall in more northerly latitudes. In the southern United States, however, where winters are usually mild, planting can take place during the winter months and can make a festive Yule celebration.

Although planting different types of trees differs in the details, all trees eventually end up in a hole. But not any old hole will do. The most common mistake when planting a tree is digging a hole both too deep or too narrow—too deep and the roots don't have access to sufficient oxygen to ensure proper growth, too narrow and the root structure can't expand sufficiently to nourish and properly anchor the tree.

As a general rule, trees should be transplanted no deeper than the soil in which they were originally grown. The width of the hole should be at least three times the diameter of the root ball or container or the spread of the roots in the case of bare root trees. This will provide the tree with enough worked earth for its root structure to establish itself.

The shape and depth of the hole you create to ground your tree will help it anchor strongly in Earth energy. The way you plant its roots will help it draw water's nurturing energy to your magickal purpose in honoring the Lord and Lady.

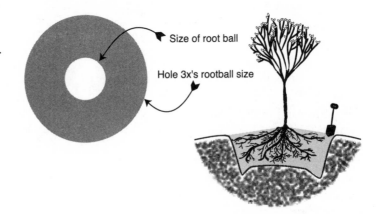

Size of root ball

Hole 3x's rootball size

Once you have a proper hole size and before you place the tree into it, blessings and wishes written on small bits of paper can be placed into ground where the tree will grow. Participants should recite the following as they lay their paper into the freshly dug hole:

> *Hear my wish now, Honored Spirit,*
> *Help this tree grow tall and strong,*
> *Grant guidance to those living near it,*
> *And may your blessings last as long.*

Balled and burlapped trees should always be lifted by the ball, never by the trunk. The burlap surrounding the ball of earth and roots should either be cut away completely (mandatory, in the case of synthetic or plastic burlap) or at least pulled back from the top third of the ball (in the case of natural burlap). Any string or twine should also be removed. Backfill soil (combinations of peat moss, composted manure, topsoil, etc.) is then placed in the hole surrounding the tree just to the height of the ball or slightly lower to allow for some settling. Be careful not to compress the backfill soil, as this may prevent water from reaching the roots and the roots from expanding beyond the ball.

The procedure for planting trees in a container is similar to that for burlapped trees. In the case of metal or plastic containers, remove the container completely. In the case of fiber containers, tear the sides away.

Once carefully removed from the container, check the roots. If they are tightly compressed or "potbound," use your fingers or a blunt instrument (to minimize root tearing) to carefully tease the fine roots away from the tight mass and then spread the roots prior to planting. In the case of extremely woody compacted roots, it may be necessary to use a spade to open up the bottom half of the root system. The root system is then pulled apart or "butterflied" prior to planting.

Once the tree is seated in the hole, the original soil is then backfilled into the hole to the soil level of the container. Again, remember not to overly compress the backfilled soil, especially by tamping it down with your feet. Compress gently using your hands instead.

> **CAUTION**
>
> **Widdershins** _____
>
> Loosening the root structure before you plant a tree that has been in a container is extremely important. Failure to do so may result in the roots being tightly bound and killing the tree. At the very least, the roots will have difficulty expanding beyond the shape of the original container.

Newly planted trees should be watered at the time of planting. Say something like the following as you offer your tree its first drink in its new home:

> *We call upon the guardians of the North and West,*
> *Elements of Earth and Water,*
> *Watch over this living energy; strengthen and nourish it,*
> *Even as its presence enriches our lives.*

In addition, during the first growing season, they should be watered at least once a week in the absence of rain, more often during the height of the summer. However, care should be taken not to over-water, as this may result in depriving it of enough oxygen.

If you are uncertain as to whether a tree needs watering, dig down 6 to 8 inches at the edge of the planting hole. If the soil at that depth feels powdery or crumbly, the tree needs water. Adequately moistened soil should form a ball when squeezed.

Regular deep soakings are better than frequent light wettings. Moisture should reach a depth of 12 to 18 inches below the soil surface to encourage ideal root growth.

Decorate your tree's branches with holiday trinkets or place a birdhouse in its limbs to attract feathered friends. A tree can also provide a shady space to place an outdoor altar.

Blessing Bundles

Blessing bundles are simply bundles of herbs, leaves, flowers, beads, shells, or twigs gathered together, laid on plain muslin or cotton fabric, and tied into a bundle with twine or embroidery thread (or just tied together by the plants' stems). Hang them over doorways or on trees surrounding a sacred space or in a child's room. Their specific purpose dictates what plants are used. It is good to have several kinds of plants in each bundle. The search for these plants is part of the project.

Use the larger leaves and branches first. Lay the smaller plants on top with stem over stem. Tie each bundle with string colored to your purpose.

You'll want to research which plants to use in your bundle to enhance your spell. Here are some examples of blessing bundles for specific intentions:

- For a good sea voyage, cruise, or beach vacation, with pleasant mild weather, include pine (sacred to Poseidon), chamomile, and marigold. Use a green string to tie the bundle together.

- To assist with studies and exams, tie together grape leaves, lily-of-the-valley, rosemary, and spearmint. Use a white or yellow string or twist the two together.

- To increase your psychic abilities, use a purple string to bundle yarrow, mugwort, peppermint, and cinnamon sticks.

- To bring healing energies to a sick room, braid white, green, and magenta strings and use them to bundle rosemary, thyme, willow, and carnation.

Putting It All Together

As we've emphasized, there is no one way to honor the Lord and Lady, and there are no "rules" for calling the divine. Although lots of sources link specific elements with certain gods and goddesses, if a particular plant or rock "speaks" to you, by all means use it in any ritual or spell you perform. Likewise, writing your own spell can invoke powerful magick because it comes from inside you. We encourage you to research different *cosmologies* and the gods and goddesses from a variety of *pantheons* to find the ones with whom you most closely identify. Listen to your inner voice, write from your heart, and come into the Craft with good intentions—these are the real elements of magick.

You'll learn more about how to make the ritual tools of the Goddess and the God in Chapter 12.

Magickal Properties

Cosmology is the study of the order of the universe. In a religious context, it means the hierarchy of Gods and Goddesses in a given religious system. A **pantheon** is a group of deities worshipped by a certain people. For example, the Hindu Pantheon includes Shiva, Vishnu, Ganesh, and many others. Hindu people may worship all or some of the deities in this pantheon.

The Least You Need to Know

♦ Wiccans use the divine pantheons from other cultures and religions to connect with Gods and Goddesses worshipped in times gone by or in distant lands.

♦ Tedious projects are more fun in a group. For example, gather your coven or a group of friends to make candied flowers or Brigid's crosses; then, everyone gets to take some home.

♦ You can do research and discover the many trees, plants, and herbs that are associated with specific Gods and Goddesses, but use your own "plant sense" when planting trees or making bundles.

♦ Practicing Wiccans should research and update their knowledge of mythology and world religions on a regular basis.

Part 3

For Every Magickal Purpose

From pocket altars you can carry with you to a permanent indoor or outdoor altar you can build, we'll give you projects for creating the perfect sacred space for your magickal purpose. We'll also show you how to lay out the boundaries for your magick circle, do spiral casting, plant a magick circle, and form a scarf circle. You'll also enjoy projects to make and use the pentagram and pentacle, the witches' symbol.

Chapter **7**

Altars: Portable, At-Home Solitaire, and for Group Ritual

In This Chapter

- ◆ Setting up a temporary altar in a small space
- ◆ Portable altars for Wiccans on the go
- ◆ Establishing a permanent altar
- ◆ How to set up your altar
- ◆ Instructions for building your own altar
- ◆ Altars for group ceremonies

Most Wiccan rituals have an altar at their centerpiece. An altar may be a permanent fixture in your home, a space or corner that you set up and take down as needed, or even a portable altar you carry with you. The most important thing to remember when planning your altar is to make it your own—a place of comfort, peacefulness, and spirituality.

In this chapter, you'll find practical altar suggestions no matter what your living situation is. We'll suggest ways to place your tools and symbols on your altar as well as ways to refurbish a "found" altar or, for the carpenter witches, a blueprint for building your own from scratch. Altars are not meant to be static or sterile, but vibrant working spaces. In other words, you will want to tend your altar, adding or removing tools and symbols depending on the season or the ritual you are performing. Only a lazy witch lets an altar gather dust.

Temporary Altars for Small Spaces

The simplest and easiest way to "build" an altar is to find a place in your living space that will allow you to set up an altar when you need it and to take it down when you're finished performing the ritual or spell. An alternative is to use a box or boxes that not only double as your altar but can also be used as storage for your ritual tools and sacred items.

Use What You Already Have

Perhaps you live in a small house or apartment, where there is limited space. Or maybe you live with people who might misunderstand your religious preference. You will want an altar you can set up and take down easily. Almost any flat surface can be used to set up an altar: a kitchen table, a coffee or end table, the top of a dresser, a TV tray, a shelf in a bookcase, a trunk, or even a board that you lay on the floor. Look around your living space and see what's available to you.

An easy way to transform your space into something sacred is to drape a piece of cloth over it. This also helps define the altar's boundaries. There is no standard size, but make sure the cloth is large enough to encompass all of your altar tools and symbols. The color of the cloth can be your personal preference or it can be attuned to a particular element or Goddess or God.

Directional altar cloth colors are traditionally white or yellow for the east, red or orange for the south, blue or sometimes green for the west, and brown, green, or black for north. Seasonal altar cloth colors depend on how eclectic your coven is. Here are some standard sabbat altar cloth colors.

Sabbat Altar Cloth Colors

Sabbat	Colors
Samhain	Black or brown
Yule	Red, green, or white
Imbolc (Candlemas)	Yellow, white, or silver
Ostara	White, yellow, sea green, or purple
Beltane	Pink, red, or green

Sabbat	Colors
Midsummer	Red, orange, or gold
Lammas	Brown, orange, or gold
Mabon	Brown, yellow, or gold

Use a material that doesn't crease or wrinkle too much and that will lay flat when it is spread out. A material that is too stiff to lay smooth once it's unfolded can cause items on your altar to tip over. This is especially bad when candles are involved! Silk works well, as does soft cotton or linen. (Keep in mind that altar cloths may occasionally need washing or cleaning. If your cloth isn't washable, you might incur some dry cleaning costs.) Your altar cloth can be used to wrap up your sacred tools before you put them away.

Making an Altar Box

You will want to have a small box or container to hold your tools when your altar is not in use. Sometimes you can find interesting containers at flea markets or second-hand stores. Or you can make your own altar box just the size you want it to be. A bonus is that the box can be draped with the altar cloth for an instant, portable altar.

Craftworking

If you would rather not spend the time it takes to build your own box and are looking for an easier solution, you can buy sturdy cardboard storage boxes at most office supply stores. Then just follow the instructions for covering them with decorative paper.

Here's what you'll need:

- Card stock to make the boxes (it should be strong enough not to sag, but thin enough to cut easily with a craft knife or scissors; mat board, Bristol board, mechanical or illustration board, or Pasteline board are all good choices

- Pencil and eraser

- Ruler and straight edge (preferably metal) to cut against

- Cutting mat or thick magazines to protect your work surface as you cut

- T-square or set square (an L-shaped tool to make 90-degree angles)

- Craft knife and sharp scissors

- Clear craft glue for the box

- Masking tape or gummed brown tape to reinforce folds

◆ Paper to cover the box (Wallpaper works best because it will lay smoothly, won't tear easily, and is wide enough to cover the box and lid without any seams; wrapping paper is an alternative, but it is more subject to gouges, wrinkles, and tears.)

◆ Spray adhesive for the wallpaper, or white glue thinned with water and a thick brush

◆ An awl or hole punch and decorative cord (optional, for handles)

Decide what size box you want, and with a ruler and a square, draw the base rectangle. Cut out your base using the craft knife and pressing onto the protected work surface. (If you're unsure of what size to make your box, try putting your tools into some cardboard boxes you have around your house and enlarge or shrink your altar box accordingly. We can already warn you, shoe boxes are much too small.)

Mark out and cut the two box sides the same length as the base and as tall as you want them to be.

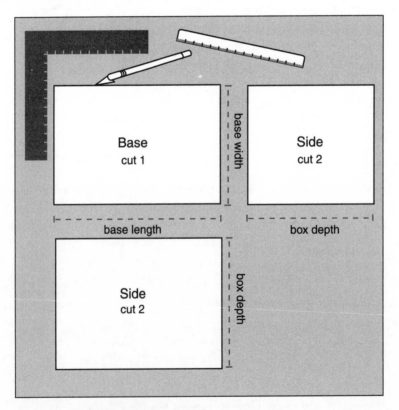

Use this pattern to make the box.

Run a strip of clear craft glue along one edge of the base and butt one side piece against this at right angles. Hold the side to stick it in place and anchor it with small pieces of masking tape. Repeat with the other side section.

Measure the outside width at the base of the box, including the thickness of the sides you've already glued on. Cut out two end pieces the same height as the sides. Run the glue along the side and base edges of one end and press an end piece into place. Secure with tape and repeat at the other end.

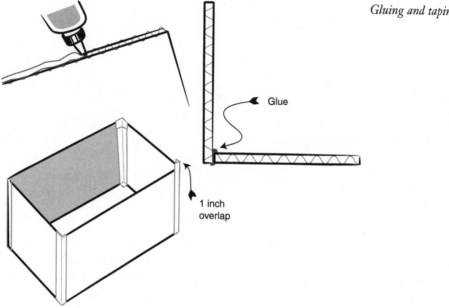

Gluing and taping the box.

Glue

1 inch overlap

When the glue is dry, stick masking tape along the edges on the outside of the box to reinforce it. Extend the tape by 1 inch at the top and turn this to the inside. Stick tape along the inside edges, too.

To make the lid, measure across the outside width and depth of the box and write down the measurements, adding ³/₈ inch to each measurement. Draw a rectangle this size on a sheet of the cardstock. Extend the lines and mark out the depth of the lid, between 1¹/₂ and 2¹/₂ inches.

Cut out around the lid, and then gently score along the lid outline (the inside rectangle

Widdershins _____

You might be tempted to use self-adhesive contact paper for this project, but it's difficult to use and unforgiving of mistakes. It adheres permanently on contact and can quickly become more frustrating than fun. In addition, contact paper isn't as wide as wallpaper, so for a fairly large box you will have to piece together seams. Only try contact paper if you're up to a challenge!

without the extensions). Bend the edges into a lid shape. Run a strip of glue along the edges and press them together to stick. Hold each corner in place with a piece of tape. When the glue is dry, secure with longer strips.

Use this pattern to make the lid.

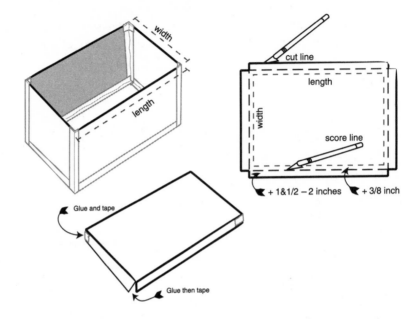

To cover the box, unroll the wallpaper and lay the box on its side on the wrong side of the paper, at right angles to the edge. Wrap the paper around the box and cut. Leave enough paper to make a 1½-inch overlap. Trim the depth of the paper so that there is an overlap at the top of between 3 and 5 inches, and an overlap at the base between 2 and 3 inches.

Spread the white glue thinned with water over one long side of the box, or spray with adhesive. Lay the paper on the glued side of the box. Run a strip of adhesive down the back of the overlap and press it into place.

Work around the box, gluing each side in turn and pressing the paper flat. When the overlap is reached, glue along the back edge of the paper and press it over the overlap so that the cut paper edge is level with the corner of the box. Trim the edge if necessary.

Lay the box on its side and made a straight cut at each corner, up to the box's base. Fold the flaps over to the base. Draw a straight line diagonally from corner to corner, across the folded flaps and trim the paper along these lines. Glue the overlaps flat.

Cover the base with a rectangle of paper cut ½ inch smaller than the base. Glue in place.

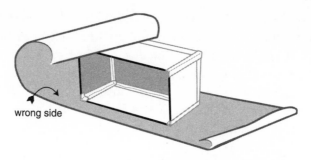

Covering your box with wallpaper.

wrong side

Sit the box upright and slit the overlap paper at each corner down to the edge of the box. Spread adhesive on the wrong side of each overlap flap and smooth them down onto the inside of the box.

To cover the lid, lay it upside down on the wrong side of the paper and draw around the outline. Remove the lid and extend the lines on all four sides the same depth as the lid sides. Mark these lines. Draw a second extension the same depth to fold inside the lid top. Then, mark ³/₈ inch for side overlaps on each end of the longest lid sides.

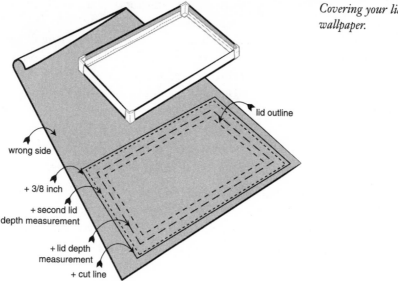

Covering your lid with wallpaper.

lid outline

wrong side

+ 3/8 inch

+ second lid depth measurement

+ lid depth measurement

+ cut line

Cover the top of the lid with glue and lay it onto the paper. Spread glue on the backs of the longest side pieces and overlaps and press into position.

If you plan to carry your altar box from place to place, adding handles can make that easier. Start by marking where you want the handles to be on each end. Use a thick cord—curtain cords with tassels, for example—or braid several thinner cords together for added strength.

Pierce one hole where you've marked your handle position and a second hole about 2 inches below that one. Repeat with two holes for the other side of the handle. (The resulting four holes look a little like the four on a pair of dice, only a little further apart. The holes should be just large enough to thread the cords through.) Push one end of the handle through the bottom hole, thread up and back through the top hole, then back through the bottom hole. Repeat on other side of the handle. Adjust for correct handle size and knot firmly. Repeat on other end.

Portable Altars

If you're a traveling witch, or if you share a living space that requires that your altar be even smaller than a couple of storage boxes, then a portable altar is for you. The biggest trick to putting together a portable altar is to think small.

> ### Craftworking
> Turn your whole house or apartment into an altar by placing tools or symbols on your windowsills—a candle in a south window, a bowl of salt in a north window, a seashell in a west window, and a feather in an east window. Or use whatever symbols of the elements appeal to you.

Start with a container. A small cosmetic travel bag or shaving kit with several pockets is perfect. Choose a square of cloth to use as your altar cloth. Wrap your most fragile altar tools in the cloth before you tuck them into a pocket. Keep your tools to a minimum: a votive candle for Fire (South), a small rock for Earth (North), a 1-ounce bottle of water for, well, Water (West), and a feather for Air (East). Add a shell to represent the Goddess, a forked twig to represent the God, and a pin or a ring to represent yourself, and presto! You have an altar. Keep a supply of small candles and matches in your bag and add whatever other small items seem right to you.

Lay your altar out on any flat surface available to you. Don't forget, floors are flat places! Cast your magick circle, invite in the four corners and the Goddess and God and perform whatever spell or ritual you have in mind. As you put away your altar, thank the Lady and Lord for joining you in your efforts. Don't let your portable altar become a hodgepodge of stuff crammed into a too-small bag. Treat it with as much reverence as you would a permanent altar.

Permanent Altars

If you're lucky enough to have a space in your house or apartment where your altar can live permanently, there are several choices you can make. Pick a piece of furniture or a space in your house where the altar won't be disturbed. Call the Goddess to bless the area and set out your altar tools and symbols. Visit your altar regularly. Add seasonal touches—pine boughs, fresh flowers, ripe fruit, gathered nuts—if you feel the urge.

Don't overlook unused corners in your house, or spaces under windows. Hang Goddess or God symbols on the wall above your altar; place a special rug under the altar to help define the space. Remember that a permanent altar can still be small, tucked away out of the normal day's traffic. Or it can be the focal point in a room set aside for meditations and rituals.

Decoupaging Your Altar

Of course, a traditional way to refurbish an old table is to paint it or to strip off old varnish and put on a new coat. But if you want to make your altar an especially exquisite piece of furniture, the art of *decoupage* might be for you. An added bonus is that decoupage can cover a multitude of imperfections on the surface of an old piece of furniture.

To begin, you will need to pick a theme for your altar. Cut out pictures and symbols that fit your theme. You might use goddess and god figures, flowers and herbs, trees, buildings, bodies of water, seashells—let your imagination soar. The paper shapes should be approximately the same thickness and must be able to withstand the effects of paste and varnish. Magazine pages may be too thin to be suitable. Avoid using thin paper with printing on both sides, as the "wrong" side can bleed through. Experiment with types of paper, for example, greeting cards, posters, Tarot or playing cards, brochures, wallpaper, empty flower seed packets, record jackets, canceled stamps, family photographs, and catalogs.

Magickal Properties

Decoupage is a French word which means "cutting up." The technique first became popular in Europe during the seventeenth and eighteenth centuries, inspired by the elaborately decorated lacquered furniture imported from China and Japan.

Here's what you'll need:

- A table, box, board, or other piece of furniture to be used as your altar

- Medium-grade sandpaper, a fine-grade sandpaper, and very fine steel wool

- Paint (if some of your altar top will be left exposed, you might want to paint it using a water-based vinyl primer or sealer and oil-based paint for wood)

- Paper cutouts, enough to cover your altar's top (have more than you think you'll need)

- Small scissors (manicure scissors work well) or an X-Acto knife for cutting out shapes

- Wallpaper paste or craft glue that dries transparent

- Brayer or wallpaper-seam roller

- 3½-inch brushes for applying paint, glue, and varnish

- Clear satin-finish interior varnish, enough for 10 to 20 coats (you can choose a tinted varnish, but use a light color or your images will be obscured)

Craftworking

Antique shops often carry old greeting cards, which can provide interesting images to use on your altar. Cruise second-hand stores for books, posters, and old photographs as well. One word of caution: If you are uncertain whether a purchased photograph depicts a "happy" or pleasant occasion, don't use it. You don't want to accidentally introduce negative energy onto your altar.

Make sure the altar's surface is smooth and oil-free. It should be thoroughly stripped of flaking paint or old varnish. Sand the altar with the medium-grade sandpaper, paying attention to the rough corners and edges. If it is unfinished, seal it first using a coat of primer and varnish. If you want to paint the table, now is the time, then finish it with varnish. Let it dry thoroughly before continuing.

Begin by laying out the largest images first. Spread glue evenly across the backs of each cutout and press them gently into place. Use a piece of plain white paper to protect the cutouts while you press them in place with a brayer or wallpaper-seam roller, or with gentle hand pressure. Overlapping the images provides an attractive three-dimensional illusion.

Continue adding paper shapes in this way, leaving edges of overlapping shapes unstuck so that new images can be slipped underneath if desired. Consider arranging the cutouts so they can be folded over the edges of the altar and glued into place. This helps prevent the paper from lifting after it has been varnished.

When you have the altar covered as you want it, let it dry for 24 hours.

Apply a coat of varnish sparingly, brushing in one direction only. When the varnish has dried, rub it gently with fine-grade sandpaper and wipe away the dust.

Repeat the varnishing and sanding process until there are 10 to 20 layers of varnish. Alternate the direction of the brush strokes between each layer.

Ultimately, the edges of the paper cutouts should be undetectable to the touch. Finally, run the surface over very gently with fine steel wool and polish the surface with clear-paste furniture wax using a soft cloth.

Setting Up Your Altar

There are as many "rules" for setting up an altar as there are Wiccans. Most traditions suggest putting your altar up against a north wall. Other traditions put the altar against an eastern wall to aid in starting new projects or creating new spells, symbolized by whatever is placed on the altar. And, hey—sometimes you just put the altar in the space you have available that isn't occupied by muddy boots or the television. In other words, the only rules are what work best for you. Most importantly, put your altar somewhere you can get to it easily, where you can reach everything you need and where no one will trip over it.

The right side of the altar is usually dedicated to the God. Place your God symbols there— for example, an athame, a *boline*, a staff, or a bowl of salt.

The left half of the altar is dedicated to the Goddess. Place a Goddess symbol there—for example, a cup, a bell, a cauldron, a broom, or a crystal.

A pentagram or pentacle, an object used as a symbol for yourself, and a variety of candles, as well as symbols for the four directions or elements, can be added as desired.

> **Magickal Properties**
>
> A **boline** is traditionally a white-handled knife used for cutting in the physical world, as opposed to your athame, which cuts on the spiritual plane. Use it to cut wands; chop herbs or vegetables; inscribe symbols onto candles, wood, clay, or wax; and in cutting string or cords used in magick.

Building Your Own Altar

For those of you who like a challenge, building your own altar from scratch can be satisfying and result in a truly magickal space. You can use almost any materials— bricks, a tree stump with a board nailed to it, adobe, or mud—whatever materials seem to appeal to you.

If you want a simple design, start with this one. You'll need a 4-by-4 board 3 feet long (just ask the lumber people for a 4 by 4 cut to 3 feet long; they'll know what you mean), a piece of ¼-inch plywood 2 by 2 feet square and another piece of ¼-inch plywood 3 by 3 feet square. Center the smaller piece of plywood on the end of the 4 by 4 and hammer into place with at least two nails (so it won't spin around). Then flip it over and do the same thing with the larger piece of plywood. With the smaller bit on the bottom for a base, you have a little platform table. Pretty it up with an altar cloth, decoupage, or linoleum-like tile. This is not the strongest design, especially at the edges, but it's easy for noncarpenters.

If you're looking for a little more challenging altar-building project, you can always find blueprints online or in home stores for a small table or bench. The following project is slightly more challenging than the previous one, but it still doesn't require super carpentry skills.

Here's what you'll need:

◆ Two 1-by-4-by-³/₄-inch boards cut 2 feet long (or as wide as you want your altar to be)

◆ Two 1-by-4-by-³/₄-inch boards cut 4 feet long (or as long as you want your altar to be)

◆ Four 2-by-2 boards 3 feet high

◆ A 2-by-4-foot piece of ¹/₄-inch plywood

◆ Hammer and nails

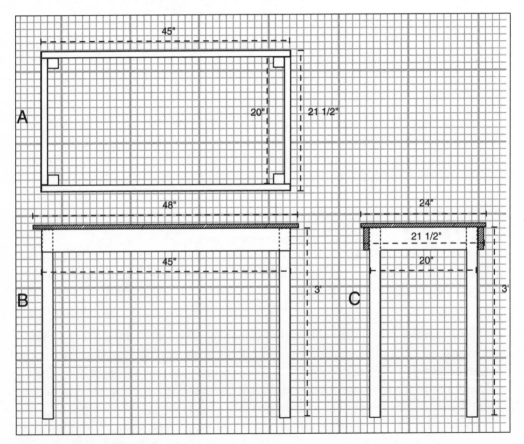

Altar blueprints.

Build a frame out of the 1 by 4s, making sure that the corners are at 90-degree angles.

Nail (or screw) the 2-by-2 boards inside the frame at each corner for the altar's legs.

Finally, nail the plywood top to the frame and stain, paint, or decorate your altar according to your taste.

Group Altars

You can use those same plans to make a much sturdier altar that can double as an outdoor bench for group ceremonies. Use 4 by 4s for the legs, 1–by-6-by-1-inch boards for the frame, and $1/2$- to 1-inch plywood for the top. This will create a bench sturdy enough to sit on when it isn't in use as an altar. In addition, it will be heavy enough to live outdoors without being in danger of being blown away. You will want to seal the altar with a waterproofing sealant. Thompson Co. has a wide range of products available online.

A group altar is a lot like a potluck supper. Most often it is temporary, set up for sharing and community-building based on a single theme. For example, the intent of a ritual may be to honor the ancestors.

The altar cloth is chosen by group consensus. Each person invited to the ceremony brings a symbol best suited to him or her to help invoke the image of those who have gone before. It might be a picture, a favorite pocket knife, an old corsage, or a special piece of jewelry. A three-dimensional collage is created as each person adds a symbol to create the focal point of the ritual.

A group altar is most often in the center of a magickal circle. Cast a large circle using flour and barley or use an athame. Invite each participant to come forward, place the symbol on the altar, and say a few words about the ancestor or ancestors being honored. When everyone has had a chance to participate, recite the following together:

> *To all those who have gone before,*
> *Within this sacred circle soar,*
> *We honor your memories and your grace,*
> *And welcome you to this sacred space.*

Spend a few moments meditating on your ancestors, thank the spirits for joining you, and then open the circle.

The Least You Need to Know

◆ However you choose to create an altar, make sure the space reflects your own personal spirituality.

◆ The size of your altar or whether the altar is permanent or temporary doesn't reflect on your commitment to the Craft.

◆ Visit your altar regularly and keep it dust-free and well tended.

◆ Change the tools and symbols on your altar depending on the ritual you're planning or on what season you're celebrating.

Chapter 8

Magick Circles to Put Up and Take Down

In This Chapter

- ◆ Casting a magick circle
- ◆ Planting a magickal flower or herb circle
- ◆ From the physical to the spiritual: the magick circle as sacred space
- ◆ Creating a scarf circle

A magick circle is used by Wiccan folk to establish sacred space, making it separate from the mundane. It is a way to create a temporary temple both in the physical world and in the etheric or astral realm. Remember the microcosm reflecting the macrocosm? Here is another example. The space created by casting a magick circle and calling the four elements reflects the sphere of the Earth and all that makes her powerful. A magick circle, whether drawn in the air with an athame or visualized within a stone circle, grants protection for those within. A common saying upon casting a circle is:

Only love may enter.

You might cast a circle to contain energy or to keep unwanted energy out. Some witches cast circles as a way to get into a certain frame of mind for what they plan on doing. A circle can be cast in many ways as well. You can use great pomp and circumstance, really hauling out the ceremonial magick, or simply acknowledge the elements and directions and create a circle within your mind. Some Wiccans only cast circles when working with groups and never when they are working solitaire. What you choose to do is up to you, as each of these ways is perfectly valid.

Casting a Circle

Circle dimensions vary according to need, magickal tradition, and the whim of the practitioner. Common tradition says the circle should in some way be a product of the numbers 3 or 9. For instance, the circle caster may walk three paces from the center and walk the pattern of a circle deosil (clockwise), walk three paces out again and walk another circle, walk three more paces out and walk yet another circle. With each circuit, a circle is traced in the air with an athame, a wand, or two fingers, and conjuring words are said:

> *Three times round the circle's cast,*
> *Great ones, Spirits from the past,*
> *Grant us, Goddess, strength times three,*
> *All spells we spin, so mote it be.*

Craftworking _____

Some common circle etiquette: Try to always keep the flow deosil—clockwise or sunwise—unless banishing work is being done (in which case you flow widder-shins, or counterclockwise). Do not move freely back and forth across the circle perimeter. If you must leave while the circle is in place, quietly speak to the person who cast the circle and wait for a "doorway" to be cut for you. On returning, wait outside the circle until the doorway is recut.

If you have your own place with floor space (not carpet), here are a few fun ways to work with sacred space: You will need brightly colored masking tape and symbolic objects you probably have displayed in your home or on your altar.

Before the formal ritual, use masking tape to mark a large circle on the floor. Within the circle, mark out a five-pointed star, thus making a large pentagram. (This is a good project for the least mathematically and dimensionally impaired coveners!) Place symbols of the four elements at four of the points. Put a symbol of Spirit (the Divine, the All, the Cosmos) at the fifth point. You can also mark the points with symbols of Lord,

Lady, Mother, Maiden, and Crone. Cast your circle as usual and make part of your ritual a walking meditation as you walk the star and contemplate all the possible meanings of each point.

There are many ways to invite the elements into your circle. Here is one example, but writing your own can be empowering:

I call upon the guardians of the watchtowers of the East, elements of Air and breath—enter this circle, and be witness to and aid in my purpose.

I call upon the guardians of the watchtowers of the South, elements of Fire and passion—enter this circle, and add warmth with your wisdom and desire.

I call upon the guardians of the watchtowers of the West, elements of Water and intuition—enter this circle with your powers of rebirth and change.

I call upon the guardians of the watchtowers of the North, elements of Earth and body—enter this circle, and bless this ground from which all things come.

I invite the Spirit, the Divine, to bring to this time and place the power of the universe. May everything I do here be for the good of all, so mote it be.

Spiral Casting

A similar project is to lay down the masking tape in a spiral design. Make it wide enough so people can walk a spiral inward and outward again without crashing into each other! You can also take turns spiraling in and out, one person walking the spiral, the others singing, chanting, drumming, or toning to further energize each person's journey. The spiral is a symbol of death and rebirth, with the center being the womb of the Mother. Going in represents reunion with the Divine. Coming out represents renewal and transformation.

Widdershins

What you say in a consecrated circle has a lot more impact than it might ordinarily. Be very aware of the words you use. Also, metaphors and colorful slang may meet with literal interpretation in the etheric realms. You would never want to say, for instance, "Holy cats, Moonwoman! That's a huge mole on your arm. Thought about having it tested for skin cancer?" This could become a "huge" concern for Moonwoman, forcing her consciousness to the negative, not the positive. As a bonus, you could end up with a yard full of stray cats looking for their next meal. Don't scoff—Liguana has seen it happen.

Planting a Magick Circle

If you have a big enough space in your yard, planting a magickal flower or herb circle is a lovely way to honor the Goddess. And it gives you a semipermanent space to use for rituals all through the spring and summer, and even into the fall. If you're planting flowers, choose plants that bloom at different times to keep your magickal circle vibrant all season long. Before you begin planting, make a diagram: tall flowers in the back, shorter flowers in the front. Making a plan may seem compulsive; however, designing the flower bed before ever looking at a flower or entering a garden center ensures that the flowers will fit the design, instead of the other way around.

The first thing to do is to measure the size of the circle. Then, use graph paper and draw the beds to scale. Typically, make one square on the paper equal 1 square foot. Make the drawings as accurate as possible to the actual shape of the bed; and then make several copies.

Next, use colored pencils or crayons to start the design. Draw in borders and group plantings, indicating desired colors and mixes. Play around and have fun with the design. Do not think about what type of flowers you're going to buy, just use the colors and pretend any color is available. If you don't like the design, you can always grab another copy and start again.

You don't have to be an artist to design a beautiful flower bed. Warm colors such as red, yellow, and orange bring a sunny feeling to a cool shady area. Cooler colors such as blue, green, and violet bring a soothing coolness to a hot patio or walkway.

Complementary colors, which are opposite each other on the color wheel, provide eye-catching, dramatic plantings. These might include planting blues with oranges, purples with yellows, or reds with greens. Spiritually, this kind of natural pairing helps provide inner balance—balancing passion with cool-headedness, acceptance with irritation, optimism with pessimism. Spending some moments meditating in your complementary-colored garden can help you eliminate the extremes in your life.

Harmonious colors are next to each other on the color wheel. Examples would be combinations of red with purple or orange, blue with purple or green, yellow with green or orange, or orange with yellow or red. These plantings are not as vivid but have a more softening effect. Meditating in a harmonious

> **Summon and Stir**
>
> If you want a low-maintenance garden, choose perennials. These are plants that come up every year, either through their original roots or by self-seeding, and spread easily. It will require a little work to keep your circle in shape, but you won't have to replant every year. If you like gardening and want to change your choice of plants every year, choose annuals.

garden can bring you peace, contentment, and self-love. These gardens are meant to be soothing, so adding the background splash of a fountain is a nice touch.

Monochromatic plantings can also be quite attractive. These color schemes use different flowers in a single color throughout a flower bed. For example, an all-yellow garden might use tulips, daffodils, foxglove, yellow daisies, and marigolds. The different hues and forms add interest and appeal. A mono-chromatic garden is planted in order to focus on one goal—for example, reds to incite passion, yellows to invoke optimism, greens and blues to attract prosperity, and white to purify your intentions.

After determining the colors needed to fill the design, calculate the amount of flowers by counting the number of squares on the graph paper in any color. Most annuals are planted on about 1-foot centers.

Begin planting by marking off a circle and spading up the earth in a clockwise position. Plants should be put into the ground clockwise as well, following the planting directions for each type of plant. As you plant, meditate on what the season means to you. You can also tuck wishes and blessings on small pieces of papers into the soil.

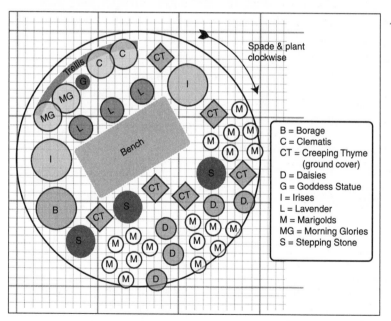

A magick circle plan.

For added privacy, place trellises in strategic places and plant climbing flowers that will form a natural curtain around your circle. Morning glories, which signify hope and optimism, or clematis, which invoke inner strength and determination, make lovely additions. As a final touch, a stone or wooden bench in the center of your circle can double as an altar.

Herbs to Grow from Seed

If you're planting herbs to create your magick circle, here are some suggestions. A bonus is that the herbs can be dried to use in magickal recipes (in and out of the kitchen!) all year long.

- **Basil:** Plant the seed where it is to grow directly in the garden in mid-May. Grows to 18 inches; space 12 inches between plants. Dark Opal has beautiful deep-red foliage and lovely pink flowers and is excellent to use along a walk or as a solid bed for decoration in the garden. Basil is very good to use to flavor tomato juice and tomato pastes and in spells for love, wealth, and protection.

- **Borage:** This plant has pinkish blossoms which turn blue. It is an annual and should be planted directly in the garden in early May in the northern United States. Growing to 2 feet, it should be spaced 10 inches apart. It is excellent in tossed salad to add a most elusive flavor and for use in spells requiring courage or psychic powers.

- **Chives:** This is a perennial plant whose tiny little plants look like fragile spears of grass. When transplanted they wilt slightly but even during a drought they grow very well. Mature plants grow to 12 inches; space 6 inches apart. They are very hardy even in cold locations. Flowers are pretty enough so that chives can be grown as a border or in a rock garden. They add an excellent flavor to salads, egg dishes, and sauces of all kinds. Potted up, chives will grow on a sunny windowsill all winter. Spiritually, they drive away illness and evil intentions.

Craftworking

Although herbs, flowers, and trees are associated with specific rituals and deities, don't let anyone dictate how or which ones to use. Let your own spirit make the choices.

- **Dill:** This is an easily grown annual with feathery foliage. Blossoms are tiny and pale yellow. It grows to $2^1/_2$ feet and may be spaced as close as 4 inches apart. Dill is excellent for use in pickling and to flavor fish or in spells for protection, money, or luck.

- **Marjoram:** This is a perennial in frost-free sections of the south but is grown as a hardy annual in the north. Sow seed indoors; grows to 12 inches; space 6 inches apart. Plants may be potted up and grown in a sunny window over the winter. This herb adds a delicate flavor to lamb, fish, salads, and soups; and can be used in spells for love, happiness, health, and money.

- **Mint:** Mint is very easy to grow. It is a hardy perennial, grows to 2 feet, and is rather sprawling. Space 12 inches apart; it's at its best in good, rich soil. Mint is fine to use for mint jelly and in mint juleps, lemonade, and other fruit drinks; or in spells for protection, travel, love, healing, and money.

♦ **Rosemary:** Rosemary is a perennial that grows best in warm, dry climates. In cooler climates in the north, plants should be wintered indoors but in warmer climates they can be left in the garden. Plant the rosemary 2 feet apart in rich soil. It is excellent to flavor beef, chicken, sausage, and wild game; or in spells for protection, love, mental powers, healing, sleep, or youth.

♦ **Sage:** This is a hardy perennial and is often grown in gardens for its pretty foliage and spikes of bluish flowers. Seed sown indoors germinates in 14 days. It grows to 2 feet and should be spaced 12 inches apart. It can be sown outdoors in May with germination in 21 to 30 days. This is a fine herb for dressings for chicken, turkey, pork, and for flavoring sausages. In spells, sage is used for wisdom and learning, psychic awareness, long life, and protection.

♦ **Thyme:** This is a hardy perennial, being of somewhat shrubby growth. Leaves are cut for drying before the blossoms are open. It is easily grown from seed sown indoors but it grows slowly when young. Space the plants 8 inches apart and plant in rich soil. Thyme is used for flavoring soups and poultry dressing; or in spells for courage, health, sleep, or love.

Drying Herbs

To dry herbs for winter, cut off the tops of the leafy varieties in midsummer and wash them off with cold water. Hang them up just long enough for the drops of water to evaporate, then tie the stems together and place in a paper bag with stem ends at the opening and close the bag with a rubber band. Use a paper clip as a hook through the band and place the other hooked end over your line where you are going to hang the herbs to dry, indoors. After two or three weeks remove from the paper bags, crumble the leaves, place on a shallow pan, and dry out in the oven with the setting at warm or at least not over 100°F.

Using dried herbs in spellcasting is every bit as effective as using fresh ones. Even gathering and drying herbs can be a spiritual experience. As you harvest your herbs, meditate on the magickal properties of each one. After they're dried, say something like the following as you store them for future use:

> *I invoke the power of the Lord and Lady*
> *that their blessings blend with these herbs*
> *to be used only for good, magickal intentions.*

To dry seed heads, allow them to grow until the seeds are mature and ready to drop from the plant. Cut seed heads on a very dry day and spread on clean paper (not newspaper). It is better to keep them in the sun the first day as little insects, which may have been hidden inside the heads, will leave as the seeds dry out. Store herbs in glass jars or other airtight containers in a cool, dry place.

Using the Garden Circle

Cast a spiritual circle inside the physical circle of flowers or herbs using your athame, wand, or staff. Invoke the Gods or Goddesses you are inviting into your circle and invite in the four corners. Breathe in the garden scents and ground yourself in the moment. Perform any spells or rituals you have in mind. Release the circle, thanking the deities who were walking in the garden with you.

From the Physical to the Spiritual

Although the mundane world can be used to create circles anyone can see, magickal circles are, of course, invisible, although many Wiccans can "see" the energy rising like a blue or white light in their mind's eyes. For those of us more rooted in the physical world, circles can start with the mundane, like your garden circle, and then be consecrated as sacred spaces.

You'll need to collect a few things—at least four or five candles in holders (votives in glass are fine). You can use all one color, or have a special color for each direction or element. To get a bit more fancy, you can have an object that represents the element at each corner as well. Set up the candles in each appropriate corner, and if you're going to have an altar, or some place of focus, place a fifth candle here. Now you are going to invoke the direction and element—you can do this vocally or mentally. Some people like to also invoke a deity that is associated with that direction or element as well, so how you go about it depends on what feels right to you.

Trace the spiritual circle with your athame or wand. Or use stones, shells, flower petals, grain, or reeds to create a physical circle first. The size of the circle depends on the number of people involved in the ceremony or ritual.

Scarf Circle

This is a fun group activity—first decorating your scarves, and then forming the circle. Each participant brings a scarf or piece of cloth 3 by 3 feet, hemmed on all sides. (Make sure the material is soft enough to be flexible.)

You'll also need the following:

- ◆ A good selection of fabric markers, textile paints, beads, embroidery thread, and embroidery needles

- ◆ A large plate to use as a template to trace a circle in the center of the scarf

Mark a large circle in the center of each scarf. Within this circle, each person can decorate his or her scarf with symbols representing the Self, the Gods and Goddesses, and the elements. Use the textile paints, beads, and embroidery thread as the spirit moves you. Be sure to leave the corners and very edges of the scarves unadorned.

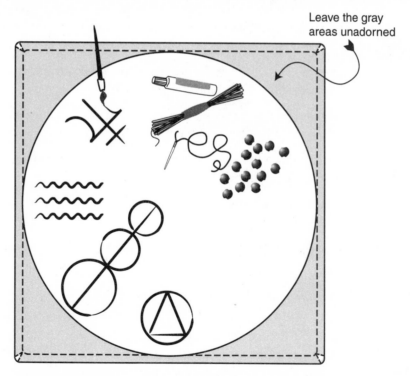

Making a scarf circle.

When everyone has decorated their scarves, they can be sown together at the edges and hung on the wall of your meeting place. They may also be used in a coven binding or community ritual, in which everyone brings his or her own decorated witch scarf to the event. A circle is cast; the elements and the Lord and Lady are called. The covener standing in the east begins by holding up the scarf, flapping it gently a few times and extending one corner to the person to the left. This person flaps his or her scarf and then extends a corner of the scarf and the two work together to tie the corners tightly. Then, the third person in the circle flaps his or her scarf a few times and the second scarf is connected to the third scarf the same way. Continue until all of the scarves are tied together in a colorful circle. This circle may become part of a group dance where people together raise and lower it while moving clockwise around the circle. It may also be used to physically mark the circle perimeters while coveners sit inside. There are hundreds of uses for witch scarves. Proceed as inspiration and imagination guide you.

The Least You Need to Know

- A magick circle is a way Wiccans create a sacred space to perform ceremonies and rituals.

- Circles should be cast deosil (clockwise) unless the spell or ritual involves eliminating or banishing something from your life.

- Releasing negative energy or taking down a magick circle is done by walking or casting in a widdershins motion (counterclockwise).

- A physical circle made out of the mundane becomes a spiritual place when the God and Goddess and the elements are invited in.

- Planting a magick circle allows you to incorporate the plants' energies as well as creating a sacred space.

- Scarf circles are a festive and colorful way to create a group circle for spell-casting.

Pentagrams for All Occasions

In This Chapter

- ◆ The difference between pentagrams and pentacles
- ◆ Pentagrams and the five elements
- ◆ Creating pentacles for all occasions
- ◆ Tasty pentagrams from the kitchen

The pentagram, a five-pointed star, is a powerful Wiccan symbol. A pentacle is the five-pointed star within a circle. These are symbols that are thousands of years old, even though what we now call Wicca is not nearly that old.

A pentacle crafted from silver represents Moon energy and psychic forces. The same symbol made in gold represents the Sun's energies of power and strength. Many pentacles include embedded stones which can represent birth months or a particular energy that the wearer wants to attract.

During magickal rituals, the pentagram can be drawn in the air using an athame or sword. Used on the altar, it becomes a focal point to draw in and send out the intentions of spellwork.

Pentagram Magick

Traditionally, each of the five points on a pentagram is related to an element:

- Earth (lower left-hand corner) represents stability and physical endurance

- Fire (lower right-hand corner) represents courage and daring

- Water (upper right-hand corner) represents emotions and intuition

- Air (upper left-hand corner) represents intelligence and the arts

- Spirit (at the topmost point) represents the All and the Divine

The circle around the star in a pentacle represents the God or Goddess; it brings to the wearer intelligence, universal wisdom, and protection.

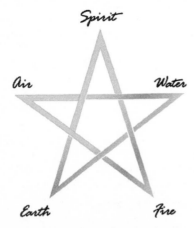

The witches' symbol, the pentagram.

The circle around the star yields the pentacle of protection.

Making a Wire Pentagram

An easy way to make a pentagram is to form one out of thin wire. Depending on the size you make them, they can be turned into earrings, necklaces, altar tools, or a frame for pictures or pillar candles. Each kind of wire has its own magickal associations:

- Copper is sacred to Venus and associated with Earth energies. It brings stability and balance to any pentagram work.

- Silver is sacred to the moon and the feminine aspects of all things. It is good for working on internal issues and creating harmony and spiritual comfort.

- Gold is sacred to the sun. It is a masculine metal and often used for calling in good fortune and health.

Here's what you'll need:

- 16-, 18-, or 20-gauge wire (¹/₂ hard wire will work best if available)

- 24- or 26-gauge wire

- Wire cutters

- Round-nose pliers

- ¹/₂-inch plywood—the length and width depends on the size of your pentagram

- Five finishing nails (it's important to have no head on the nail so the wire will slip off easily)

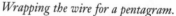

Summon and Stir

Liguana was taught that you are blessed if you wear the pentacle, twice blessed if you wear it concealed. In plain talk this means being a practicing Wiccan is a blessing, and it is especially a blessing if you don't feel you have to go around blowing your own horn in public about it. This is also important if you're around people who might have misconceptions about your religion.

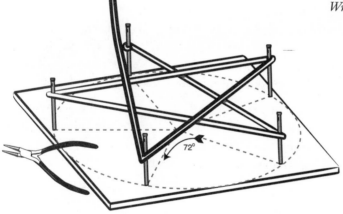

Wrapping the wire for a pentagram.

There are two techniques that are involved in making these pentagrams. The first is to make the basic wire component by wrapping 16-, 18-, or 20-gauge wire around the nails on the board. The second technique is to use very fine wire (24- or 26-gauge) to wrap around the larger wire, setting the shape in place.

1. Cut and straighten a piece of 16-, 18-, or 20-gauge wire. The length depends on the size of your pentacle.

2. Make a loop in one end of the wire.

3. Place the loop over nail 1 and wrap the wire around all five nails in turn, returning to nail 1.

4. Make a final loop around nail 1 with the end of the wire.

Craftworking _____

Most people wear a pentacle necklace over the heart center. This confers courage and faithfulness to Wiccan ideals. If you don't mind letting people see the symbol, wearing it as a ring assists in the flow of magickal energies. Worn as earrings, pentacles assist in the reception of psychic flows. Pentacle tattoos anywhere on the body confer protection against negative energies.

5. Before removing the wire from the board, gently squeeze the wire together on either side of the nails using your fingers. This is done to make the points of the star sharper and less rounded. This step may not be necessary with ½ hard wire.

6. Remove the star from the board and cut the excess wire tail off. Close the ending loop where you just cut the excess wire with a round-nose pliers.

7. Cut and straighten 12 inches of 24- or 26-gauge wire.

8. Insert ½ inch of this fine wire through the two loops around nail 1. Wrap this wire around the top of the two loops, threading it back through the loops to fully encircle the two loops. Pull tight. This should begin to hold the two loops together. Do this again at least three times. Cut the excess wire at both ends (beginning and ending). Use your pliers to squeeze the wire ends flat.

9. Now wrap the fine-gauge wire around all the places where the heavy wire crosses itself. There are five total places. Make at least three full loops around the wire. Pull tight, then cut any excess wire from both ends. Using your pliers, squeeze the loose wire ends flat. Now step back and admire the finished piece.

Wrapping the wire to stabilize the star.

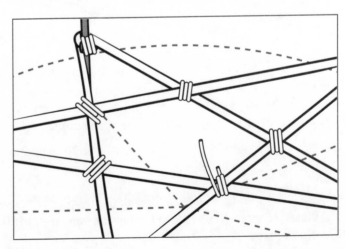

"Carving" Pentagrams

Use your imagination when it comes to carving pentagrams. Take your boline and carve one into a candle. (See Chapter 14 for suggested candle colors for your spell or intention.) Or use a lump of wax or paraffin. Flatten it into a disk, carve your five-pointed star, and place it on your altar.

This also works well with modeling clay or the Sculpey we used in Chapter 2. Use a glass cutter to etch one into a piece of glass or a small mirror. Embroider one onto a witch scarf or on the collar of a shirt. The possibilities are unlimited.

Summon and Stir
In more dangerous times, the pentacle was crafted from disposable materials such as wax, clay, or dough. To be caught in possession of a pentacle in those days could very well endanger your life.

Use this template as a starting point.

The template we've provided can be enlarged with a copy machine. Or trace a cookie cutter to get a "perfect" star. Better yet, draw your own pentagram freehand and love the imperfections.

Pentacles for All Occasions

Adding a circle around your pentagram turns it into a pentacle—presto! Use the pentagram inside the circle with the "top" point, of course, in upright position.

Dream Catcher Pentacle

A pentacle dream catcher is not difficult to make. And dream catchers really do work. Hang one over a child's bed to help him or her attract and remember pleasant dreams, or over your own bed to help harness the power of dreamwork for your spellcraft.

Here's what you'll need:

- ◆ A ring, such as a large curtain ring (or make a ring out of a clothes hanger)
- ◆ Thread, string, or heavy crocheting thread to weave the design upon the ring
- ◆ Tiny beads, small shells, or little feathers

To begin, tie one end of the thread to the ring. Stretch the string across the ring to the opposite side and wind the thread tightly around the ring three times. This will form the straight horizontal line at the top of the star. Now stretch the string at a slight angle down and to the left. Wind the string around the ring, three times each time.

Keep stretching and winding the string into a star shape—up to the top, down to the right, and back up to the original knot.

If you carefully check the angle of the thread each time you prepare to wind it at another point on the ring, you can adjust the design. Make a small loop for hanging at the top of the pentacle.

> **Summon and Stir**
>
> In a deck of Tarot cards, pentacles is the suit of money, abundance, and earthly wealth.

If you want to string beads on the thread, slide the beads on each section before you wind the thread around the ring. You can finish off your dream catcher by tying three or four lengths of string each approximately 5 inches long to the bottom and tying feathers or shells to the ends. You might have to make a small hole in the shell with a finishing nail to thread the string through. Be careful not to shatter the shell.

An Altar Pentacle

Pentacles have an important role to play on an altar. The simplest spells of this kind are those involving candle magick. A candle of the appropriate color is charged and placed on the pentacle. And, as we said earlier, a pentagram can help you draw in and send out energy. The pentacle's circle can act with a magick circle's powers of protection and healing.

Here's what you'll need:

♦ A small unfinished wood board or plaque; check hobby shops for plaques with decorative borders (Liguana says bread boards work, too.)

♦ A soft pencil and a compass

♦ Sandpaper

♦ A wood-burning tool

♦ Paint—red for Fire or South; blue for Water or West; yellow for Air or East; either green or brown for Earth or North; and purple to represent the Deities

♦ Varnish (optional)

♦ Clear shellac

Smooth out any rough spots on your board with your sandpaper. Lightly sketch out your pentacle using the pencil and compass. Don't worry if it isn't totally symmetrical. Variations make it your own.

Once you have the pentacle sketched out, burn the figure into the wood board using the wood-burning tool.

Decorate the pentagram star with the paint as desired, matching corresponding colors with the elements the pentagram's points represent. Choose the color most appropriate to raise the magickal energy you desire for the pentacle circle's healing protection.

Stain the wood with varnish if desired and seal it with a thin coat of clear shellac. Place the finished pentacle on your altar and use it to draw in positive energy.

"Stained Glass" Pentacles

This project produces decorations that look like stained glass that can be hung on any wall or window. This project is fairly easy to do for children ages about seven and older. It involves permanent markers and requires a bit of patience.

Here's what you'll need:

- Permanent magic markers with pointed tips, in an assortment of colors as well as black

- Plain white paper

- Transparency sheets (available at office supply stores)

- Tape

- Paper plates (about 8 inches in diameter)

- Aluminum foil

- Plastic wrap

- Ribbon or yarn for hanging (optional)

- Construction paper to cover the back (optional)

For this project you'll be drawing the stained glass designs onto the transparency, and then putting them onto foil-covered plates. This creates a beautiful sparkling decoration whenever light shines on it.

Draw a pentagram about 5 or 5½ inches across on the white paper. Draw a circle around it using a compass or a small plate or lid.

Tape the white paper pentacle pattern to your work table at the four corners.

Then take a piece of transparency that is large enough to easily cover the plates—at least 11 inches square—a bit bigger is better than too small.

Tape the transparency to the table over the pattern. Tape all four corners and the centers of all the sides—eight pieces of tape. This keeps the transparency from sliding as you color in the pentacle.

Craftworking

Younger children will probably want help with outlining the pentagram in black. Let them color the star and have an adult trace the outline.

Let each person color his or her pentagram onto his or her transparency. Be careful, these are permanent markers! The markers will smudge if you color one color into another, so it is easier to color all the *colored* areas first, and then draw the black outlines later. Otherwise, you'll likely touch the black lines with the tip of the marker, and the black will smear into your color and dirty up the marker. When tracing the black outlines, take your time—that is the most important part of the project.

Next, cover the paper plate with the aluminum foil. Crumple the foil a bit, then smooth it out, and cover the bottom of the plate with the foil, shiny side showing. Wrap the extra foil around to the top of the plate.

Carefully remove the tape that's holding the transparency to the table. Cut the transparency into a circle the same size as your paper plate. Turn your artwork over so that the markered side of the transparency is down. Place it on the foil-covered side of the plate. Center it and then wrap the entire plate with plastic wrap to hold it on. Wrap it around to the other side and tape it.

If you want to hang your ornament with a ribbon, take a 10-inch piece of ribbon or yarn, and tape it in a loop to the back of the plate.

Take an uncovered paper plate and trace around it onto a piece of construction paper. Cut out a circle a bit smaller than the one you drew, so that it will only be on the back. Make some double-sticky rolls of tape to attach it to the back, or glue it down with a good craft glue, one that will stick to the plastic wrap.

Pentagrams from the Kitchen

If you aren't wearing pentagrams or using them on your altar, you could be eating them. Decorating a cake or twisting dough into star shapes can add a festive touch to a sabbat table. Or carve a pentagram into pats of butter; decorate sugar cookies; lay out hors d'oeuvres in a star shape. Kitchen witches will have more ideas.

Vasilopita (New Year's Cake)

This cake is of Greek origin and is traditionally served on New Year's Day. Because Samhain is considered the Wiccan New Year, witches get a chance to serve it twice!

- $^1/_2$ tsp. baking soda
- $^1/_2$ cup milk
- $^3/_4$ cup orange juice
- $4^1/_2$ cups all-purpose flour
- 1 tsp. baking powder
- 1 tsp. salt
- $^1/_2$ cup (1 stick) unsalted butter, softened
- 5 eggs, separated

- Zest of 3 to 4 oranges

- 1 clean silver coin

- Confectioner's sugar

Preheat the oven to 350°F. Grease and flour an 11-inch springform pan. Mix the baking soda with the milk and orange juice. Set aside. Sift the flour, baking powder, and salt together. Set aside. Using an electric blender, cream the butter until it's light and fluffy. Add egg yolks one at a time. Beat the yolks and butter together.

Widdershins

Be sure your guests or family know there is a hidden surprise in the cake, whether it's a coin or a wire pentagram, *before* anyone starts eating. It isn't lucky to break a tooth … and you wouldn't want any children (or adults) present to swallow the prize!

Alternate adding the flour and liquid mixtures to the butter mixture, starting with flour and ending with flour.

Whip the egg whites to medium peaks. Using a rubber spatula, fold in whites with batter, then fold in the orange zest. Pour the batter into the springform pan, spreading the batter evenly.

Drop a clean silver coin into the batter. Bake 40 to 50 minutes in a 350°F oven. Sprinkle with confectioner's sugar, stenciling a pentagram on top. The person who gets the coin in his or her slice will have good luck for the year!

Instead of a silver coin, you could make a small, silver wire pentagram. Boil it in hot water before adding it to the batter.

Pretzel Pentagrams

Shaping dough into pentagrams is fun and yummy at the same time. These are a little labor intensive but well worth the effort. This recipe makes about two dozen pretzels.

- $\frac{1}{8}$ cup hot water

- 1 package yeast (active dry yeast)

- $1\frac{1}{3}$ cups warm water

- $\frac{1}{3}$ cup brown sugar

- 5 cups flour

- Extra flour, kosher salt, baking soda, water

Preheat the oven to 475°F. In a large bowl, mix the hot water and yeast until it dissolves. Stir in the warm water and brown sugar. Slowly add the 5 cups flour, stirring constantly. Continue stirring until the mixture is smooth and does not stick to the sides of bowl. Put dough on a lightly floured counter. Flour your hands and knead the dough until stretchy and smooth.

Grease two cookie sheets very well (this is the key—go heavy on the grease). Sprinkle each with kosher salt (go heavy on the salt, then brush off after baking—this will keep the pretzels from sticking.) Pinch off a piece of pretzel dough about the size of a golf ball. Roll the dough into a rope and then shape into a star. Fill a pan with water. For each cup of water add 1 tablespoon of baking soda. Bring to a gentle boil. Lower the pretzel into the water with a spatula. Leave the pretzel in the water for 1 minute; lift the pretzel onto the greased cookie sheet after water is dripped off.

Repeat until all the dough is used. Bake for 10-15 minutes or until golden brown. Eat while warm.

The key to making nice-looking pentagrams is to pinch where the pretzel overlaps, otherwise they will come undone in the water. This however is only cosmetic, because even the ugly ones taste great.

The Least You Need to Know

- ◆ A pentacle is a pentagram enclosed in a circle.

- ◆ Pentagrams can be worn, placed on an altar, hung on a wall or in a window, or even eaten.

- ◆ Don't worry if your star isn't perfect—the magick lies in your intentions, not in your artistic ability.

- ◆ Use these ideas as a starting-off point but incorporate pentacles in your life wherever they seem appropriate.

Part 4

Make Your Own Ritual Tools and Talismans

In the spirit of *"As above, so below,"* every tool or prop that exists in the mundane world represents something sacred in the etheric world. Here are ritual tools to make, to find, and to refurbish. Gather up your tools, put on your beautiful newly hand-sewn and decorated ritual robe, pick up your wand, cast your circle, and make magick. We'll also give you projects to make magick with your natural allies, from familiars to faeries and more.

Amulets, Talismans, and Jewelry

In This Chapter

♦ What amulets and talismans are used for

♦ Amulets to infuse with magickal meaning

♦ Talismans hold natural magickal power

♦ Pouches and boxes to hold your amulets and talismans

Many Wiccans use the words "amulet" and "talisman" interchangeably. For our purposes, we're going to make a distinction. An amulet is some small object used for protection and for keeping negative energy at bay. It may be carried or worn as a piece of jewelry. It is often a nature-based object like a rock or crystal, a pressed four-leaf clover, or even a small bottle of water or sand from your favorite ocean, but it doesn't have to be. You might already have a "lucky" charm that you carry—an old penny, perhaps, a bent nail, or a medal you won. What's important is that it means something to you.

A talisman is an object created and infused with magickal intent to create a specific effect. In other words, these are objects which possess magickal or supernatural powers of their own which are transmitted to their possessor. They are physical manifestations created especially to put your intent out into the world in an ongoing way. Usually, the solitary function of a talisman is to make powerful transformations possible. A talisman, like an amulet, may also be worn or displayed.

Amulets to Carry Along

Almost anything can serve as an amulet—a red string braided around your wrist, a bird's feather carried in your pocket, or a horseshoe nailed above your bed or front door. These objects from the mundane world are infused with meaning when you consecrate them to a God or Goddess.

An amulet may be used to protect its wearer from a specific negative energy or to call in positive energy, either specific or general.

Treasure Hunting for Amulets

All of us have boxes of "stuff" from our pasts—memorabilia packed away somewhere. It might be in an attic, a garage, or still stored in your parents' basement. Now is the time to go back through your past and explore. Maybe there is an old piece of jewelry you forgot you had, or a figurine or statue that holds special memories. If anything touches your spirit, it might be turned into an amulet.

Before you begin, carve an appropriate symbol into a candle with your boline. It can be a runic symbol, a Tarot symbol, an astrological symbol, or even a mundane symbol like a dollar sign or a question mark. Cast a magick circle and call down the elements. Invite the Lord and Lady into the circle. Pass the amulet through the smoke of the candle you are using to represent the positive energy you're calling in. It might represent love, wealth, health, a wish for an exotic trip, or luck in general. If you're dispelling negative energy, name it. You might want to give up jealousy or envy, cowardice, physical illness, or depression. As you pass the amulet through the smoke, chant something similar to the following:

> *Lady, come to me today*
> *Protect me as I go my way*
> *Grant me luck in love and life*
> *Take away and ease old strife.*

Thank the Goddess and place the amulet in a prominent place or wear it as a good-luck charm.

Sealing Wax to Help a Friend

Perhaps you have a friend who needs some well-wishing. Write him or her an encouraging letter of support and seal it with sealing wax stamped with a design pertinent to the friend's situation. For example, if your friend is suffering over an affair of the heart, stamp the wax with a rose or a cupid. If the problem involves the workplace, stamp the wax with a coin or a symbol of his or her profession. There are no right or wrong symbols to use. Name your intention and send the letter with your blessings. The sealing wax becomes an amulet of sorts.

Can't find a store that sells sealing wax in your town? You can order a wide variety of wax online. One good source is www.nostalgicimpressions.com. But just type "sealing wax" into any search engine to find a source that appeals to you. Keep in mind that a sealing-wax amulet should only be used with good intentions. Sending bad energy someone's way will just bring it back to you threefold.

There are many "generic" good luck symbols you can use: four-leaf clovers, rabbit's feet, horseshoes, wishbones. An interesting one to use is a frog. The frog figure is linked to the moon. This is because as it grows the frog actually changes shape during the phases of the moon. Frogs are also linked to creativity, immortality, and wealth. They are believed to protect against all evil influences.

The color of the sealing wax you use can also be a powerful influence. Try using yellow or gold for happiness; green for money; pink or red for love and passion; blue for peace; and brown for stability.

Craftworking

As an added good-luck touch, write your note on homemade paper suffused with the appropriate herbs or flower petals. See Chapter 3 for directions on making homemade paper.

Widdershins

Sealing wax has a very high dye content and stains easily—be careful not to drip it where you don't want it. Also, less is better. If you use too much sealing wax it tends not to adhere to the envelope and falls off, especially if it gets cold.

A Braided Bracelet Amulet

You don't have to be a silversmith to make attractive jewelry. Here is a simple braided bracelet that takes almost no time to make.

Here's what you'll need:

- ◆ Red cotton cording or twine (leather cords or shoelaces work, too, and are very durable if you want to wear your amulet all the time)

- ◆ Two small rubber bands or two twist ties (like the ones that come on a loaf of bread)

- ◆ A few small, well-chosen beads that "speak" to you

Lay three cords out together in front of you, each long enough to fit your wrist (8 to 10 inches). Secure one end with a rubber band or twist tie.

Braid them together about 2 inches. Thread a bead onto the middle cord naming your intention as you do—luck, wealth, health, love.

Continue to braid another inch, and add a bead. Braid another inch and another bead, and do it one more time.

Finish braiding and put a rubber band around the other end.

Knot the ends, remove the rubber bands, trim off any extra cord, and then tie the bracelet around your wrist.

Designing an Amulet Out of Nothing at All

There are as many ways to make amulets as there are practicing Wiccans. This is a project to really expand your imagination. Pick your talent and try any of the following suggestions:

- ◆ Use modeling clay to sculpt a small figurine, perhaps a Buddha or an animal totem.

- ◆ Take a small piece of tin or other metal and tool a design onto it.

- ◆ Make a small quilted square about 3½ by 3½ inches and embroider a symbol on it. Tuck it into a coat pocket.

- ◆ Take a small square of aluminum foil, pour some appropriate herbs (see Chapter 20) into the middle and fold it into an envelope shape. Carry it in a purse or wallet.

- ◆ Find a bead or crystal that appeals to you; sew a small silk square to carry it in.

- ◆ String a coin-shaped stone with a central hole onto a cord and wear it as a necklace. (These can be purchased at any New Age–type store, but if you find one on your own, it is exceptionally lucky.)

- Cross-stitch or crewel a pentagram or your astrological sign on a small square of cloth.

- Make a small envelope out of decorative paper with a design that appeals to you. Put your child's baby tooth in it, a cat's whisker or toenail, your pet's fur, or a bird's feather.

- Melt paraffin and pour it into a small lid to form a flat disk. Carve a symbol into the wax.

- Paint a symbol or design on a small stone.

> **Summon and Stir**
>
> Catherine de Medici, queen consort of Henry II of France, had a talisman which she constantly carried. It was a medal allegedly made from metals that were melted together along with goat's blood during favorable astrological signs. She believed the talisman conferred upon her clairvoyance and sovereign power.

Talismans to Keep in Your Home

A talisman is most often created within a magick circle for a specific intention. Making them during the appropriate phase of the moon or under an auspicious astrological sign makes their magick even more powerful. Talismans can be made for many endeavors such as winning the lottery, coming into unexpected money, falling in love, preventing illness, protecting your household, or even closing a successful business deal.

If you're making a talisman for someone else, be sure it's for an endeavor that person wants to take on. Don't impose your desires onto someone else. And, as always, keep your intentions toward your friends positive.

An Onion or Garlic Braid

If your goal is to draw positive energy into your home or to absorb negative energy, placing talismans strategically in different rooms of your house is a good place to start.

Start with something simple to hang in your kitchen—an onion or garlic braid. Onions, garlic, shallots, and leeks are very protective, help cleanse a space of negative energy, and attract money as well. (Liguana points out that in addition to no bad vibes, if you use garlic you won't have vampires, either.)

> **Craftworking**
>
> Knots and crosses and braids are symbolic holding places for magickal energy. In any craft you do, the more knots and crosses you include, the better the magick.

Here's what you'll need:

- Enough onions or garlic bulbs to create the size braid you want to form (You'll want freshly harvested plants that still have the long green tops.)

- Black and green string or cord (black for positive energy, green to attract money), two or three times the length of your greenery

- Dried flowers or herb sprigs (optional)

1. Choose three plants and tie them together just above the bulbs with your twine or cord.

2. Braid the green tops and twine together just like you would schoolgirl braids.

3. After a few crosses over and under, lay another bulb on your braid and include its greenery into your braiding. Proceed upwards adding a new bulb every few crossovers.

4. When you've used up all your plants or your braid is around 2 feet long, use your twine to tie off the top and act as a loop for hanging.

Hang your braid in a dry place for two or three weeks. After the braid is dry, you can weave in dried flowers or other shorter stemmed herbs. Rosemary sprigs are good for this. (Rosemary and garlic … what's not to love here?!)

Make a Mobile Talisman

You can increase the vibrational intensity in your household with crystals, shiny stones, or sea glass. Making a mobile is an easy project. The spiral invokes connection with the Goddess and also acts as a negativity trap. Light through the crystal increases positive energy flows and splashes pretty rainbows around to improve everyone's mood.

Craftworking

Liguana likes to keep colored sea glass in a pretty bottle on a windowsill. The sunlight through the glass draws in positive energy and banishes bad moods. You can create the same effect with crystals.

Here's what you'll need:

- Heavy-gauge copper wire

- Fishing line or clear thread

- A crystal with a hole in the top

- Black cord for hanging

Twist the copper wire into a spiral 6 to 7 inches in diameter at the widest point and make it however long you want it to be, depending on where you plan to hang it.

Thread the fishing line through the crystal and suspend it through the middle of the spiral.

Tie a black cord around the top to hang the mobile and place it in a sunny spot.

Talismans to Wear and Carry

Talismans have existed throughout all historical periods. The Egyptians and Babylonians used them when attempting to alter the forces of nature. In the Middle Ages, holy relics and other objects assumed talisman status in attempts to cure illnesses.

Talismans are also common in literature. Excalibur the sword was King Arthur's talisman, imbuing him with strength and power. In the book *The Clan of the Cave Bear* by Jean M. Auel, every child of the clan was given an amulet on naming day which made him or her a part of the collective spirit. Other objects were added when special things happened that were meaningful to the individual. The first piece placed in the amulet, which was a pouch made of leather and worn around the neck, was a piece of red ochre, symbolizing the blood of the mother from which all clan members came. When a boy became a man and made his first kill, he got a special rock or a fang or claw from the animal to put into the bag, symbolizing the event.

These next three projects are created in that same spirit.

Talisman Bags

A talisman bag can be worn as a necklace or carried in a purse or pocket. The idea is not to stuff the bag with things, but to choose objects carefully and to add them to the bag with reverence and ceremony, or at least with some thoughtfulness.

Here's what you'll need:

- ♦ A small bag, or enough cloth or leather to make one (natural fibers such as silk, cotton, linen, or wool are best)

- ♦ A length of thin ribbon or cord (red or black is good, but choose a color that complements your material, and make it long enough to slip over your head when it's folded in half if you intend to wear it as a necklace)

- ♦ One small object that represents luck to you or that represents yourself

If you're making your bag—which we highly recommend—cut a piece of cloth approximately 2 by 6 inches. Adjust the measurements depending on what size you want your finished bag to be.

Fold the cloth in half, right sides together, and stitch up the two sides, leaving the top open. Make a hem approximately ½ inch in the top, leaving a space open to thread the ribbon or cord through.

Thread a cord through the hem as a drawstring.

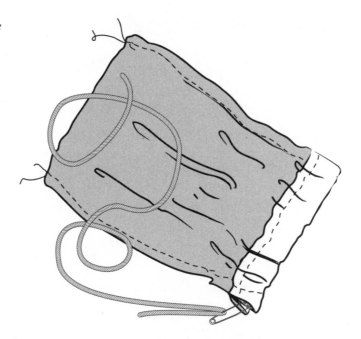

Widdershins _____

Talismans should never be used to try to manipulate another person. In other words, you can make a charm to bring true love into your life, but not to make a particular person fall in love with you. Always remember the Wiccan Rede: *An it harm none, do what you will!*

Put a small safety pin through one end of the ribbon or cord to help you thread it through the hem you've made. Remove the pin and tie the ends of the ribbon together to make a drawstring. Turn the bag right side out. Decorate the bag with fabric paint if you desire. Paint on a special symbol or decoration. Or write a spell on your bag with a toothpick dipped in fabric paint to add an extra touch of magick.

Then, cast a magick circle and consecrate the object you are going to place in your bag, naming your intention. Add other objects to your bag as they seem appropriate.

A Variation on the Theme

Another way to make a simple amulet pouch is to use wide ribbon (3 or 4 inches wide), the kind purchased where quilting supplies are sold. Ribbon amulets can be made in many colors and embellished with beads, charms, buttons, and other materials.

Measure out 10 inches of ribbon and put ¼-inch hem in both ends using a zigzag stitch on a sewing machine or hemming it by hand.

Fold one end into an envelope shape and stitch it in place. This will become the flap that closes the bag. Fold the other end of the ribbon up just a little farther than half way, wrong sides together, and stitch up the sides.

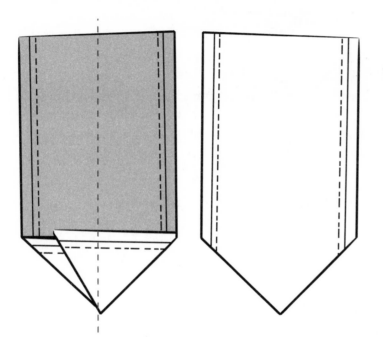

Fold one end into a point like an envelope.

Fold the envelope end down toward the other end; the fold should be right where the purse opening starts. The envelope end should reach almost to the bottom of the folded end.

Now you are ready to add the clasp. Stitch a button or a bead on the very edge of the envelope bottom in the middle. Next take the cord, and measure enough cord to go around the clasp. Stitch the knotted cord end to the bottom of the folded purse edge. Now you should be able to put the cord around the button and close the purse.

A simple clasp.

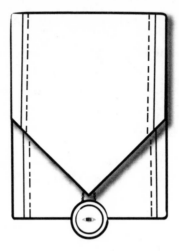

Matchbox Talismans

These little boxes can be transformed into decorative boxes in several different ways and in a variety of sizes. These directions use a small matchbox that can be worn as a necklace. Follow the same directions to turn a larger matchbox into an altar decoration.

Here's what you'll need:

- Small matchbox (save the matches for lighting altar candles!)
- Small paintbrush
- White craft glue
- Modeling clay (such as Sculpey)
- Rolling pin
- Craft knife
- Ruler
- Rubber stamp (optional)
- Craft chalks plus small applicators (optional)
- Two bamboo skewers or chopsticks
- Paint
- Cord or twine
- A small bead (optional)

Using the small paintbrush, coat all four outside surfaces of the matchbox with a thin coat of white craft glue. Set it aside to dry.

Roll out a sheet of clay to approximately $1/16$-inch thick. Using a craft knife and a ruler, trim the sheet to $4^1/_4$ by $2^1/_4$ inches.

If you plan to decorate the box using a decorative stamp, ink the stamp well and press the stamp firmly but gently onto the sheet of prepared clay. Add color carefully if desired using the craft chalks and small applicators.

Carefully wrap the sheet of clay around the matchbox. Make sure the clay is pressed smoothly onto the box. Trim the edges if necessary. You'll want the seam to be on the bottom.

Next, roll a piece of clay into a long snake and wind it loosely around a bamboo skewer. Press it firmly onto the side of the matchbox. Repeat on the other side. Bake at 275°F for 30 minutes. Gently slide the skewers out. Cool completely.

Paint the drawer. The drawer can also be lined with attractive paper. Glue a small bead on one end to serve as the drawer pull. Once the drawer is dry, insert it back into the box. Thread a cord through the spirals on the side and tie a knot in both ends.

Thread the cord through the spirals.

Add little trinkets to the box to finish your talisman.

Matchboxes can also be covered with wallpaper or wrapping paper to make decorative boxes. Take the drawer out first and smooth the paper over the edges of the box. Fasten the paper down with craft glue or tape. Paint the drawer and slide it in once it's dry.

The Least You Need to Know

- An amulet protects its wearer from negative energy and provides protection.

- Talismans are created for specific magickal intentions.

- Almost any object can be turned into an amulet; choose something that has special meaning to you.

- Talismans and amulets can be worn, carried, or placed around your home.

11

Ritual Robes and Other Clothing

In This Chapter

- ◆ Making a magickal robe
- ◆ A sleeveless tunic to wear underneath your robe
- ◆ A hooded cloak to chase away a chill
- ◆ Adding some accessories

"Witch wear" can be simple or elaborate, plain or embellished, hand-sewn or store bought. The most important thing is that you should feel great when you put it on. For genuine sewing witches, there are a number of commercial sewing patterns you can buy to make a cloak or robe.

Sewing an outfit for one of your nonsewing friends is a lovely gift. See if you can trade talents. If you're a seamstress, offer to make a robe for a friend if she or he cooks a gourmet meal for your next dinner party.

Make a Magick Robe

Although any ritual can be performed in ordinary street clothes, having a robe that you only wear when you cast spells or attend a ceremony can help put you in the proper mood. You can individualize your robe by adding symbols or decorative trim.

Selecting an Appropriate Fabric

It's best to choose a 100 percent natural fiber: cotton, cotton fleece, cotton knit, wool, or silk, for example. Natural fabrics breathe and tend to be more comfortable. In many cases, you will be using fire to light candles or incense for spellwork. Or at some times during group rituals you will be beside open fires. Most robes are loose-fitting and flowing, and it can be very easy to catch a sleeve or some part of your robe on fire. Synthetic fabrics tend to melt and stick to your skin should they catch flame. This may sound extreme, but better safe than sorry.

> **CAUTION**
> **Widdershins**
>
> Liguana strongly recommends staying away from flashy prints or heavily textured fabrics. Stripes and plaids are definitely patterns to stay away from unless you would like to use plaid for clan colors (and you're an experienced sewer).

As for color, you can be very creative unless your coven has specific color requirements. Choose a color that makes you look and feel good about yourself. If you can't decide on a color, choose one that represents a direction or element you particularly identify with.

The fabric you buy must be 45 to 60 inches wide. (Although silk makes a lovely flowing robe, be careful when purchasing silk fabrics. Most of them are only 36 inches wide.) We strongly suggest you watch fabric stores for sales because you will need a lot of material for this project.

Preparing the Fabric

To determine how much fabric you will need, measure in inches from your shoulder to the floor, then add 2 inches. Divide that number by 36 inches to determine how many yards of cloth you will need. It will most likely not end up with an even number, and it's best to buy a little extra. Ask your friend at the fabric store for an opinion about how much extra to buy. And make sure you know how to care for your fabric.

If the fabric is washable, prewash it. This will take out the chemicals used to treat the fabric and preshrink it so that it doesn't shrink after you have sewn the robe. If the fabric isn't washable, it will have to be dry-cleaned. You will want to think carefully about this, as it can become an expensive robe to use if you can't wash it at home.

Summon and Stir

In her early days as a witch, Liguana became pregnant with her first child. It wasn't long before her clothes were too tight and none of her jackets fit. One of her witch friends gifted her with a beautiful gray cloak to celebrate the pregnancy. It was a lovely thing but the wind blew right through it. Secretly, so as not to offend the first friend, another witch friend gifted her by lining the cloak. Unfortunately, the cloak had been prewashed but the lining had not. Liguana found this out after the first potluck spillage. The lining shrunk and the rest didn't, of course. For many years thereafter, she conducted ritual in the guise of a big gray boulder.

Here are the measurements you will need to take:

1. Shoulder to floor + 2 inches = _____ divided by 36 = _____.

2. The distance from shoulder to shoulder = _____.

3. The circumference of your head (to get the measurement for the neck opening) = _____.

4. The measurement of the fullest part of your upper arm = _____ + 4 inches (so that the sleeve won't be too tight) = _____.

5. The length of your arm from your shoulder to your wrist = _____ + 1 inch = _____.

Here's what you'll need:

◆ Scissors

◆ Measuring tape

◆ Chalk for use on dark fabrics

◆ Pencil for use on light fabrics

◆ Ruler

◆ Pins

◆ Hook and eye for closing the robe's center front

1. Fold the fabric in half widthwise, matching the cut edges. Cut the fabric in half at the folded edge. Lay aside one half of the fabric to use for the sleeves.

Folding the material.

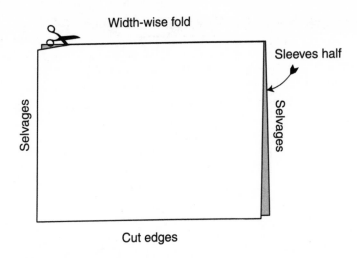

2. Take the other half of the fabric and fold it in half again so that the cut edges match. Then fold it again lengthwise so that the finished edges are together and there are four layers.

3. Take your chalk or pencil and from the single fold along the double-folded edge, mark one half of your shoulder-to-shoulder measurement plus ⅝ of an inch. From that point measure down half of your upper arm plus 4 inches measurement.

Pattern diagram.

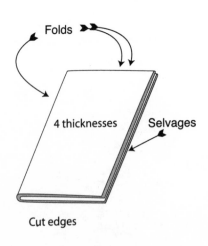

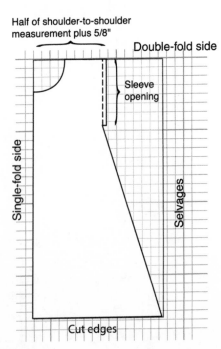

4. Measure from the double fold of the fabric to ½ inch of the upper-arm measurement along the single-fold edge. Make a small mark.

5. Measure from the small mark on the single-fold half of the shoulder measurement plus ⅝ of an inch. Make another mark meeting the mark at the mark made from the measurement from the upper arm. Draw a line between the two marks.

6. At the bottom of the line, draw a short horizontal line ⅝ inch long toward the single fold.

7. Draw a line down from the end of the ⅝-inch line with a ruler diagonally toward the corner where the finished edge and cut edges meet.

8. For the neck opening, start with the circumference of your head. Using the measuring tape like a drafting compass, start at the corner where the double-folded edges and the single-folded edges meet and make a quarter of a circle. This will be the neck opening of your cloak.

9. Make a mark on the single-folded edge along the fold from where you made the mark for the neck opening down the fold to the cut edge of the fabric.

Cutting the Fabric

Now you're ready to cut out the fabric. Be sure to use sharp scissors to make the task easier. Electric scissors work well, too.

1. Cut out along marked line through all four layers of fabric except for the line from the neck edge to the cut edge.

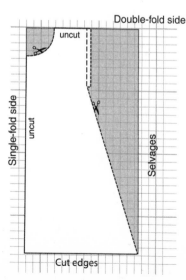

2. Unfold the fabric into two layers, leaving the cloak still folded lengthwise (at the shoulder line). Then make a small ¹/₈-inch clip in the fold, clipping from the sleeve opening toward the neck edge.

3. Cut away excess fabric as shown so that cut edges slightly curve up at the sides.

Front view of robe.

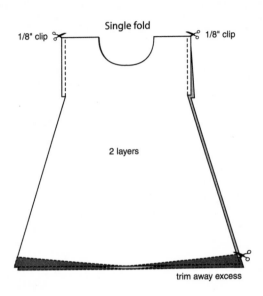

4. Unfold the fabric so that you only have one layer of fabric. From neck edge to cut edge on the marked line, cut a straight line from the center of the neck edge down the front of the cloak to the center of the cut edge. This will make the center opening of your cloak.

Cutting front opening.

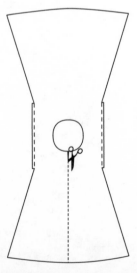

5. To make the sleeves, take the other half of your fabric. Fold it in half widthwise so that the cut ends meet. Fold it again widthwise so that the folded edge meets the cut edges.

6. From the finished edge on the right, using the measurement for arm length, measure from the right on the single fold the length of your arm plus ⅝ inch. Make a mark. Measure down from the single fold half of the upper-arm measurement. Make a mark. At this point, at the end of the line opposite the single-fold line draw a short ⅝-inch line horizontally toward the right finished edges. From the right end of the ⅝-inch line, draw a line diagonally from the end of the line to the right-bottom corner, where the finished edges and the folded and cut edges meet.

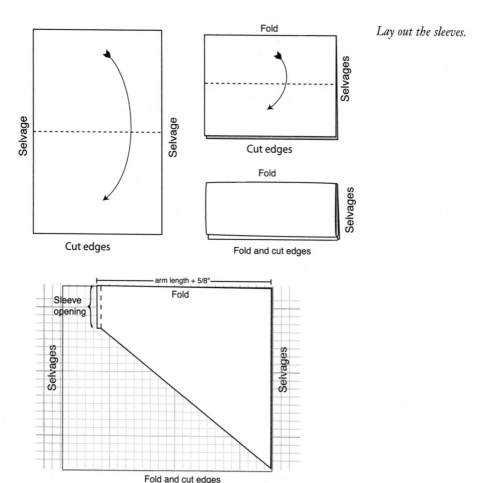

Lay out the sleeves.

7. Cut away the marked area as shown in the next illustration.

Attach front and back at the shoulders.

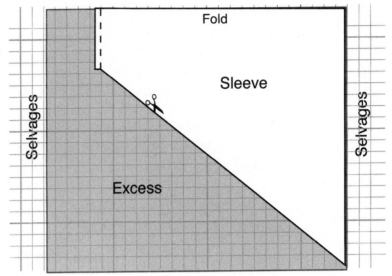

8. Make a small clip in your sleeve on the fold from the shoulder seam toward the bottom of the sleeve about $1/8$-inch deep to mark the center point of your shoulder seam.

9. Unfold the fabric. You will have two pieces of fabric shaped like a triangle with the top cut off. These are the sleeves.

10. To sew the sleeves to the cloak, lay out all three pieces. Take a sleeve and with the cloak place the right sides of the fabric together. Match the clip marks on the sleeve and the shoulder seam. Sew the sleeve to the cloak using a $5/8$-inch seam. Repeat with the other sleeve.

Sew the side seams.

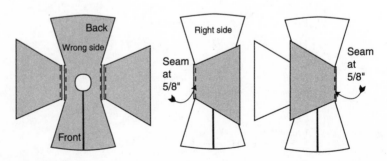

11. Fold the cloak in half. Matching sleeve seams at the bottom of the sleeve to the shoulder seam, pin the edges together. Pin together the side seams from the shoulder seams to the hem. Stitch from the bottom of the sleeve to the side seam and down to the hem using a $5/8$-inch seam.

12. To finish the neck edge, cut a strip of fabric the length of the neck opening plus $1^1/4$ inches and $2^1/2$ inches wide. Fold this strip in half lengthwise, wrong sides together. Pin it to the cut edges of the neckline and the cut edge of the fabric strip. Sew the strip to the cloak. Turn under $1/4$ inch of fabric on the center from the wrong side from the neckline to the hem of the cloak. Press, then turn again another $1/4$ inch to the wrong side. This will finish the center front opening.

13. At the neck edge fold the fabric over $1/4$ inch on the casing for the neck edge at the center-front seam and press. Stitch down.

14. Trim the seam on the neck edge through the casing and neck of cloak to $1/4$ inch. Press the facing out. Press a $1/4$-inch seam toward the casing. Turn the folded side of the casing to inside. Press, then stitch the casing to the garment.

15. To form a narrow hem on the sleeves and bottom of the cloak, tuck under the raw edge $1/4$ inch and press. Fold hem again a $1/2$ inch. Press, then sew.

16. Add the hook and eye at the center front to fasten the cloak shut.

Add a Sleeveless Tunic

Many times during the warmer months of the year, it isn't practical to wear a heavy cloak or robe. Or you may decide that you might like to wear different colored tunics under your cloak or robe when celebrating different sabbats or magickal workings. Making your tunic out of a lighter-weight fabric can keep you comfortable in summer months and make it easier to move about freely.

You will be using basically the same measurements and instructions you used for the robe pattern. The only measurement you don't need to make is the sleeve length. Remember to prewash the fabric as you did for the robe.

Sleeveless tunic.

Follow steps 2 through 8 as you did for the robe. For step 9, make a mark from the neck opening line down the single fold of fabric that is 6 inches long.

Follow steps 1 through 4 under "Cutting the Fabric," leaving out making the ¹/₈-inch clip in the fabric to mark the sleeve placement.

Next, measure from just above your knee to the floor. Use this measurement to mark a ¹/₈-inch clip on both side seams of the tunic. Hem up these side slits by turning them under ¹/₄ inch.

With right sides together, pin and sew the side seams from the arm opening to the top of the side slit.

On the 6-inch cut down the center front of the tunic, fold under ¹/₄ inch, press, and stitch in place.

Using the full measurement for the neck opening plus 24 inches, cut a strip of fabric 2¹/₂ inches wide. Fold the fabric in half lengthwise, wrong sides together, and press. Measure in 12 inches on either end of the fabric and make a mark. Pin the fabric onto the neck edge, matching the two marks to the front opening and the center clip marks together. Stitch the casing to the neck edge. The two 12-inch strips will be used for a tie to close the neck edge when finished.

To finish the ties, press the cut edges under and stitch all the way to the ends. Tie a small knot in the ends.

To finish the side seams of the tunic, press the seam open all the way from the hem to the arm opening. Then, make a running stitch all the way down both sides of the seam allowance, close to the cut edge. This will keep the fabric from raveling when washed.

Finish by hemming the sleeves and bottom of the tunic.

A Hooded Cloak Might Be Just the Thing

This project is a bit more difficult, but the results are well worth the effort. You might want to use the same types of fabrics mentioned in the instructions for the robe— natural fibers. If you want your cloak to be fancier, try using wool crepe or velvet. This will be considerably more expensive than the heavier cottons, but if you watch for sales after the winter holidays you can often find some good bargains.

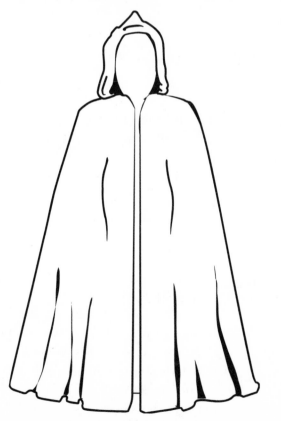

A finished hooded cloak.

You will want to line your cloak, so you will also need to buy some lining material. It's very difficult to find lining fabrics made of natural fiber. Rayon or silk are both good choices. Linings are fun because you can be more creative with them, using elaborate and colorful prints. Avoid fabrics that are too lightweight and slippery. They also have a tendency to pucker and gather when you stitch them.

Here's what you'll need:

- String

- Cloak fabric four times the measurement from neck edge to floor plus 1 yard (see instructions for determining yardage for a robe)

- Measuring tape

- Scissors

- Paper bag

- Lining fabric (use the same amount of yardage as for the cloak)

- Pins

- Matching thread

- One package of $^1/_2$-inch matching seam binding

- One heavy hook and eye

In addition to the measurement from shoulder to the floor and from shoulder to shoulder, you will want to measure for the hood. Put one end of the string at the center of the top of your head and let it drape down the side of your head. Then, bring the string up to the side of your neck as shown in the next illustration and cut. Lay the string flat, measure the length and then add 2 inches. This is for the cloak hood.

Widdershins

If you use velvet, you will have to use a velvet board and a cotton press cloth to iron the seams. Do not touch the velvet directly with the iron or you will leave permanent marks on your material.

Measure the circumference of your head, divide it by two, and then add $1^1/_4$ inches. This is for the depth of the hood.

Measure the circumference of the neck where your neck meets your shoulders. This measurement will be split into four parts—first in half and then in three equal parts, as shown in the next illustration. Use the first two thirds for the front neck edge of the cloak and the last third for the back neck edge of the cloak. Make a paper pattern for this out of a paper bag.

Measure for the hood with a piece of string.

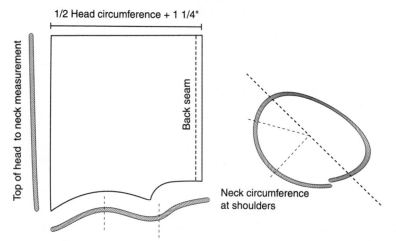

1/2 Head circumference + 1 1/4"

Top of head to neck measurement

Back seam

Neck circumference at shoulders

Pattern for neck edge.

For the front opening measurement, start where your collar bones meet at the base of your neck and measure all the way to the floor. For the center back measurement, measure from the base of your neck all the way to the floor.

Once you have all of your measurements, fold your fabric widthwise so that the cut edges meet and pin the edges together. Working from left to right from the cut edge of the fabric, mark the measurement for the center front.

Using the pattern piece made from measuring the neck, place the center front of the neck edge against the finished edge of the fabric, starting with the curved edge butted up to the center front mark you have previously made. Trace the neck edge.

Next, make a mark up from the finished edge using the line from the neck pattern. Measure up half off the shoulder measurement. Make a mark. From this mark measure left 1½ inches and make another mark.

From this mark, measure to the opposite side of the fabric. Draw a diagonal line using your measurement from the shoulder to the floor. Draw a line between the corner of the neck edge to mark 1½ inches down from the shoulder measurement and erase the old shoulder-measurement line. Then where the shoulder line and the line used to measure the length from the shoulder to the floor intersect, gradually round off the edge.

Laying out the cloak pattern.

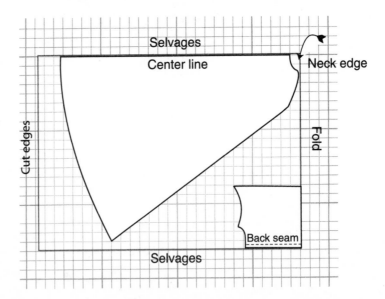

Follow the same steps to measure the back of the cloak on the opposite side of the finished edge. Remember to use the pattern piece for the back of the neck.

For the hood, on the folded edge, measure half of the circumference of your head. Then, take the measurement of the string plus 1 inch along the front of the line for the head measurement. Measure the circumference line of the head measurement on the fold two thirds of the way and make a straight line down using the string measurement. Then, at the end of this line, draw another line down the length of the string measurement minus ½ inch. Connect all three lines using a slightly curved line.

At the hemline of the back, draw a line from the center back to the side seam, gradually rounding the line as you go to connect the center back seam. Repeat the same procedure for the front hemline.

If you plan to line your cloak, use the pieces you've cut out as a pattern to cut the lining. Be careful not to cut into the pieces of the cloak!

After cutting out the pieces, take the back of the cloak and pin the right sides together. Stitch the back seam and press open. Do the same with the lining.

With the right sides together, pin the front panels to the back at the side seams. Repeat for lining.

Stitch all of the way around the neck edge. This is called stay-stitching and helps keep the material from stretching. Repeat for lining. With the right sides together, pin the lining to the cloak. Stitch from the neck edge, down the center front, around the hem, and back up the other side of the center front. Turn the cloak right side out and press.

Sew the center back seam of the hood from the fold to the cut edge. Repeat with lining. With the right sides together, pin and stitch the lining to the hood. Trim the seam to $1/4$ inch, turn right-side out, and press.

Using a larger stitch length, stitch along the neckline of the hood through all layers of fabric. Pull on one end of the thread to gather the hood so that it fits into the neckline of the cloak, right sides together. Pin the edges together and stitch around the neck edge. Be careful not to let the gathering on the hood bunch up all in one place. Once the seam is stitched, make several small clips, being careful not to cut through the stitching. This will help the seam be more flexible and easier to work with. After you clip the seam, trim it to $1/4$ inch.

Bind the seam at the neck edge using the $1/2$-inch seam binding. Unfold the binding and pin it to the cut edge of the neckline. Sew along the creased fold of the binding. Place a hook and eye at the center-front neck edge.

If you like, you can add different trims to the edge of the sleeves of your robe or around the hem. Think about embellishing them with embroidery or fabric paints or dyes.

Clip the neck seam.

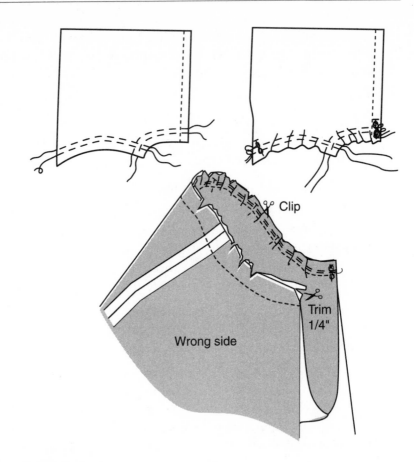

Clip

Trim 1/4"

Wrong side

A Few Additional Pieces

Once you're a well-dressed witch, you might want to add a few extra touches to complete your outfit. Adding a headband or a piece of jewelry is a nice touch.

Priestess Headband

Priestess headbands can be made very easily. Obtain a piece of black suede 9 inches long and 1 inch wide. With an awl or leather punch (or hammer and nail, if you're rustically supplied), punch a hole ³/₄ inches in from each end. Obtain two 12-inch strips of leather lacing or sturdy ribbon (shoelaces work, too, in a pinch). Fold each lace in half and, pushing the loops up through the holes, make a slip knot on either side. With silver textile paint, decorate the band in the middle with the crescent moon or the triple moon design. You might also use your coven's *sigil*, if you have one.

This design can also be used for a high priestess's garter. Measure the thigh where the garter is to be worn and take off 1 inch. That's how long the suede band should be. Use 7-inch laces for the ties.

Either of these designs can use wide ribbon instead of suede. If you use ribbon for the band, you'll want to hem the ends to avoid fraying. Be sure to give yourself a little extra length to do this.

Magickal Properties

A **sigil** is a magickal sign or symbol. Many covens adopt one as their own and use it to decorate robes, headbands, and witch scarves, as well as using it on an altar during group rituals.

Safety Pin Bracelet

This easy project can be made in just an hour. It's also a nice project for a junior high–age girl's party. Choose beads that complement the color of your robe or cloak. Silver pins generate moon magick; gold pins attract sun energy. Jewelry designed to be worn during rituals should not be worn as everyday jewelry. Reserve a few pieces as "special."

Here's what you'll need:

- 16–18 large gold or silver safety pins

- A variety of small beads (You can make them all in one color family—different shades of blue, for example—or make them a rainbow of colors; make certain they have holes big enough to thread onto the pins.)

- Elastic string

- Scissors

- Pliers

1. Open a safety pin and thread on beads until it is full but you can still close it. Think about the overall pattern of your bracelet. For example, if one pin starts with two blue beads, then three green beads, and then two more blue beads, you might want to reverse the pattern for the next pin. Be creative!

2. Pinch the flat part of the safety pin closed with the pliers so that the pin doesn't accidentally pop open.

3. Repeat steps 1 and 2 until you have enough beaded safety pins to make your bracelet. You can always add more or take away a few to make it fit.

4. Cut two lengths of elastic string. Thread the elastic string through the "top" of one pin and through the "bottom" of the next pin. Keep alternating the directions the pins face so they don't get too bulky on one side.

5. Thread the second elastic string through the other ends of the pins.

6. Once you have enough beaded safety pins on the elastic that it wraps around your wrist, tie the two ends together.

Make several bracelets in a variety of colors and use beads that are different sizes to add interest. Some sewing stores also carry colored safety pins which can be used to add more zip to your bracelet.

Simple Shawl

Throwing a ceremonial shawl over your shoulders is sometimes just the thing, especially for simple indoor rituals. This one is easy to knit.

Your individual choices in yarn and needle size will affect the finished size and thickness of the shawl, but there isn't one "right" way. If you aren't looking for warmth, using very fine yarn and large knitting needles produces a lovely spider-web look. Adding fringe is optional.

Here's what you'll need:

- Three or four skeins in the color and weight of your choice
- Size 10.5 (6.5mm) inches through 15 (10mm) knitting needles

Cast on 63 stitches or any multiple of three, such as 54, 57, or 60. For the first row, knit three purl three to the end of the row. For the second row, knit the purl stitches and purl the knit stitches.

Repeat the pattern until your shawl is the size you want it to be. An average size is approximately 24 by 60 inches.

The Least You Need to Know

- A magick robe isn't a necessity, but wearing one when you cast spells or attend a ceremony can help put you in the proper mood.
- There is no "right" ceremonial outfit—wear what feels good.
- If you aren't a seamstress, ask a friend for help or buy a shawl or cloak to wear.
- Special jewelry that calls upon Goddess or God energy should only be worn during Wiccan rituals.

12

Ritual Tools of the Goddess and God

In This Chapter

- ◆ Sweeping with a magickal witch's broom
- ◆ Goddess bowls and cauldrons for your altar
- ◆ Bells to invoke the goddess
- ◆ Making an athame to use on the spiritual plane
- ◆ Creating a witch's wand

As we've been saying all along, there is nothing inherently magickal in the tools Wiccans use during a ritual. The magick comes from your own spirit and intent. This chapter is not meant to be a complete list of tools, because many of them are included as projects in other chapters. However, in this chapter you'll find the directions for making some of the most commonly used ritual tools. Creating them yourself infuses them with the best magick of all—your own wisdom and essence.

Traditionally, some tools "belong" to the Goddess and some to the God, although like everything else in Wicca, nothing is set in stone. Goddess tools are generally placed on the left side of the altar while tools that represent the God are on the right. (For more suggestions about how to place tools on your altar, see Chapter 7.)

Sweep in a Little Magick

Broom making is a great group activity and could even become a coven moneymaker. All of us need brooms, right? The broom represents woman energy and so must also represent the Goddess: *"As above, so below."*

First you need a broom handle about 4 or 5 feet long and an inch to an inch and a half in diameter. You may choose wood according to your purpose, but any hard wood will do.

Summon and Stir
From early times, people have believed groves of trees are sacred. In the Celtic social system, Druid was a title given to learned men and women possessing "oak knowledge" or "oak wisdom." Some trees are specifically associated with the Lady or Lord. Oak and cedar are obvious examples of symbols for the God. Willow and hazel are Goddess symbols. Some trees, pine and ash, for example, are considered androgynous and also have their place in Wiccan rituals. The symbolism of the wood is very important in the construction of any magickal tool.

Here's what you'll need:

◆ Wide-toothed comb

◆ Some strong jute or hemp twine

◆ 6–8 inches of rawhide thong

◆ Broom straw, broomcorn, or a bunch of branches or rushes 2½ to 3 feet long (scotch broom or sagebrush are perfect choices for this, but make sure you aren't allergic!)

1. With the wide-toothed comb, comb out any seeds, flowers, or leaves from your straw. They may look pretty, but you don't want your broom to litter the area as you sweep.

2. Arrange the straw all the way around your handle, covering about 10 inches up from the bottom.

3. Secure the straw tightly with twine 3 inches from the top of the straw bundle. You can make a thicker bundle of straw by tying on another layer and fastening the twine tight 4 inches from the top.

Tie the reeds onto your handle.

4. Lay your broom on a grassy area. Pour boiling water over the straw and let it sit about 15 minutes to soften.

5. Fold the top straw down over itself and tie tightly with twine. For extra security, tie another length of twine about 1 to 2 inches below the first tie.

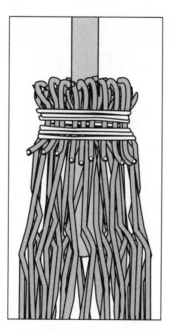

Folding and tying off the reeds.

6. Drill a hole through your broomstick 1 inch down from the top and slip the rawhide thong through it. Tie the ends and hang your broom to dry.

7. When completely dry, you may choose to treat the straw with spray varnish to make it more durable. If you do this, hang it up to dry for a couple more days before you use it.

Make a Smaller Version

Smaller hand brooms can be made using the same type of branches or straw. These can be turned into whisk brooms to sweep negative energy off a small area like an altar.

1. Lay the straw out on the grass or a clean concrete area.

2. Pour boiling water over branches to soften. Let sit 15 minutes.

3. Halfway down the branches, tie the bundle tight with twine, wrapping it several times around the bunch.

4. Slip the bundle onto the handle and tie it on tightly with the twine, wrapping it upward to 1 inch from the top and tie it off. An attractive alternative if the broom material is soft enough is to braid the handle part and tie it off with twine $1/2$ to 1 inch from the top.

5. Hang the broom to dry.

A Sweeping Ceremony to Banish Negativity

Sweeping a sacred space of negative energy and influences is a common practice once a magick circle has been cast. You will want to sweep deosil (clockwise) from the center of the circle to the outside just as though you were sweeping out dust. (Liguana says that if you do happen to pick up a little dust in the process, it's just a bonus!) Remember, however, this is symbolic sweeping. You can sweep on a rug or grassy area as well as on a hard floor.

If you have others inside the circle with you, some Wiccans like to make sure the broom is swept over the toes of all of the participants. This sweeps away any negativity being brought into the circle with them.

As the high priestess sweeps (or as you sweep if you're casting your magick circle alone), have everyone chant softly the negative things they want to see eliminated from the circle. This does not have to be in unison, but each witch murmuring to him or herself, "I banish jealousy. I banish depression. I banish fear. I banish excess spending. I banish procrastination." And so on. Each participant should recite whatever words best apply to him or her, chanting until the circle has been swept clean. Once the entire circle has been swept, the leader might recite something similar to the following:

> *Banish fears and banish woe,*
> *Within this circle, powers grow.*
> *We welcome in what's wise and good,*
> *And make it strong with reed and wood.*

Proceed with whatever spells you intend to cast.

Bowls and Cauldrons for the Goddess

It seems logical that cooking utensils and bowls would be symbols of the Goddess, and they are! Don't limit your idea of what a cauldron is to the image of the huge one the three witches in *Macbeth* were hovering over. Cauldrons can be smaller, symbolic vessels.

Decorate a Cauldron

There are all sizes of ready-made cauldrons you can buy. If you want the cauldron to fit on your altar, it will most likely have to be small. But a slightly bigger cauldron can be placed on the floor to the left of your altar. If you can't find a "traditional" cauldron, a heavy cast-iron pot will work just as well. Copper pots can also be energizing.

Cauldrons can be decorated with paint, but you must make sure the paint is heat resistant if your cauldron is actually going to boil and bubble. If your cauldron is mostly ceremonial, the type of paint you use is less crucial. For example, some rituals call for a spell to be written down, read aloud, and then burned. The paper can be dropped into the cauldron to finish burning.

If you want to add decoration to your cauldron, spirals, pentacles, and round shapes are most appropriate to honor the Goddess. If you want to honor the directions, you can paint symbols representing each one on the four sides of the cauldron: a feather or dandelion seeds for the East, a flame or candle for the South, a shell or fish for the West, a mountain or rock for the North.

Make Your Own Cauldron

If you want to try making your own cauldron, here's a fun project to do outside.

Here's what you'll need:

- Two small buckets or the bottom halves of two milk jugs (these are interchangeable in the directions)
- Sand to fill up bucket or jug to approximately 6 inches
- A hand trowel for mixing
- A small bowl
- A stick approximately 1 inch in diameter (may use a dowel or even a shovel handle)
- Quick-drying ready-mix cement
- A ball smaller than the bowl in diameter

1. Fill one bucket with about 6 inches of sand. Wet the sand enough so it holds a shape, about sand-castle moist.

2. Push the bowl into the sand to create a bowl-shaped indentation.

3. Using the dowel, poke three holes down through the "bowl" of sand to the bottom of the bucket; these will be your cauldron's legs. Angle them out for a broader base of support.

4. Using the hand trowel, mix a small amount of the cement with water so it has a thick consistency but can be poured.

5. Pour the cement into the sand mold, being sure the concrete is well mixed and the sand and gravel at the bottom gets used, too.

6. If you stop here, this makes a wonderful candle holder. For a cauldron, wait a few minutes until the mix begins to thicken and then place the ball in the center of the bowl, working it down halfway.

Craftworking

Liguana says these also make great holders for those oh-so-trendy reflective garden balls. Place one next to a bench or an outdoor altar to further honor the Goddess.

7. Periodically wiggle the ball a little bit so the indentation it makes is larger and so the ball can be removed easily.

8. When the cement is thickened enough to hold the ball shape, take the ball out and allow the cauldron to dry for two days. Then, carefully free your cauldron from the sand and brush it off with a soft paintbrush or cloth.

Paint a Bowl

Small bowls are used for a variety of purposes on a witch's altar. They can hold salt to represent the Earth or water to represent Water. They can even act as a symbolic cauldron when lack of space is an issue. Finding antique bowls at a flea market or an auction is one way to include a special bowl on your altar. If you're feeling more artistic, you can buy and paint your own bowl. Many towns have studios that specialize in selling bowls and statues to paint. But you can also order bisque to paint from a variety of online sources. If you don't own a kiln and neither does anyone in your coven, you must make sure to order bisque, not greenware. Greenware is not ready to paint.

Greenware is what all ceramic pieces are before the piece has ever been fired. It is clay that is bone dry, very brittle, and must be fired to maturity. If you purchase greenware, you will need to clean all the seam lines and any imperfections and add any detail to the item you purchased. After you are finished cleaning your item, you will need to fire it in a kiln. After it has been fired in a kiln, it is bisque and ready to be painted.

The Sound of Bells

Bells not only represent the Goddess, their happy sound draws positive energy into and around the home. Bells can be placed on the altar or worn as a bracelet or an anklet and played in rhythm as the coven chants, Draws Down the Moon, or casts a magick circle.

Bells on the Altar

There are many places to buy decorative bells. Small brass bells work very well on an altar. As we talked about in Chapter 7, altars need to be tended. One nice bit of attention you can give your altar is to buy thin, different-colored ribbons to wind through the top of your bell or bells, depending on the season or on the sabbat. They can match or complement your altar cloth, or they can be directed toward a particular intention you have.

When you change the current ribbon to a new color, cast a simple spell:

> *As seasons change so do your colors,*
> *Bless my altar with your presence.*

String 'Em Along

Another way to use small decorative bells is to string them together using a bright red cord. Just slip a bell onto a cord, knot it in place, add another bell and so on until you have nine bells in place. Tie it to a doorknob or hang it in a window to bring positive energy into the house.

Summon and Stir

In numerology, the number 9 is considered lucky. The ancient Greek pagans held the number 9 sacred because to them 9 symbolized the nine Muses or sister goddesses, daughters of Zeus and Mnenosyne, who were believed to preside over mankind's activities on earth. Their names were Calliope, Clio, Erato, Euterpe, Melpomene, Polyhymnia, Terpsichore, Thalia, and Urania. (Looking for a great pet name?)

Bells to Wear

Making a wrist or ankle bracelet to wear during a ceremony is a way to invoke the Goddess as well as a way to add rhythm and music to a chant or an invocation.

This project is as simple as taking some elastic cord and stringing enough bells together to fit around your wrist or your ankle. These make nice gifts to share with your coven or guests. You should scout around for the right kind of bells. Jingle bells are the right size, but are so strongly associated with winter holidays that they might not seem right for spring and summer celebrations. Small, round Indian bells add a lovely, light sound and can often be purchased at fabric stores. An alternative is to use small brass bells threaded into a circle that coveners carry around the palms of their hands rather than to wear around their wrists. These can be shaken like a tambourine or like, well, a string of bells. You'll know the right bells to use when you find them.

Cutting on a Spiritual Plane

An athame is a God tool and is used, among other things, to cast magickal circles, to trace symbols in the air, and to cut a door in a circle so coveners can leave once it has been cast.

There are lots of places online to purchase an athame, but if you're really ambitious, you can make your own.

You will need a 1-foot length of steel 1 inch wide by $1/8$ inch thick. This is commonly called flat stock. You can get this from any steel supplier, or ask around at metal fabrication, welding, or machine shops. You might also find what is called mild steel or cold-rolled steel. This is just fine for your knife. Don't buy hardened steel. It is tougher to work with and unless you have a backyard forge, you may not be satisfied with the end product.

Craftworking

Metalworking involves risk and requires both creativity and patience. Like magick itself, intent is an important factor. Keep in mind the sacred nature of your task. Many ancient societies had forge gods or goddesses. Seeking divine assistance couldn't hurt.

Shaping the steel can be done in several ways. The easiest way is to use a 4-inch angle grinder. This can be obtained from any hardware store for under $100. The grinding discs are replaceable and it's not a bad idea to buy a few spares. You will also need to buy goggles for eye protection.

Draw the desired blade shape on your steel "blank" with a permanent ink marker. Make the blade the length of your hand from the middle finger tip to your wrist. Be sure to include a "tang" or protrusion at the handle end. This should be around 3 inches long.

Put the blank into a vise and be sure it's tightly held. Wearing proper eye protection and observing all the shop safety rules you know (and if you don't know the proper safety rules for using this kind of equipment, metalworking may not be the project for you ...), use your grinder to remove everything outside your pattern.

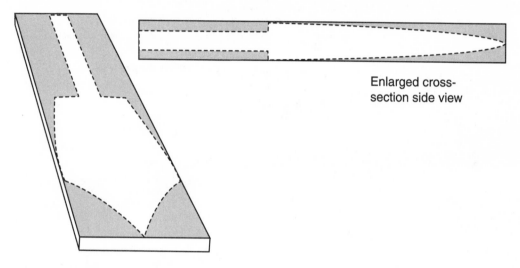

Enlarged cross-section side view

Draw a blade shape onto the blank.

Now you need to create the cutting edges of your blade. This is also done with the grinder. This is finer work and may be a bit tricky to get it the same on both sides. Basically what you are doing is beveling all edges on both sides of the blade. Once you have the shape you want, use a metal file to smooth and further define it, then use a knife stone to finish.

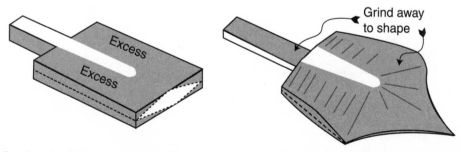

Beveling the blank to make blade edges.

Handles are very important too. Procure bone, antler, or hardwood (we like ebony best) about 1 to 2 inches longer than the width of your hand. Drill a hole down the center as long as and slightly wider than your tang. Seat your blade in the handle and fill the remaining space with epoxy to be sure blade and handle never part company (which is embarrassing in circle and dangerous anyplace else!). When the epoxy has dried you can grind, polish, or wood-burn your handle to suit your tastes.

Glue the blade into your handle.

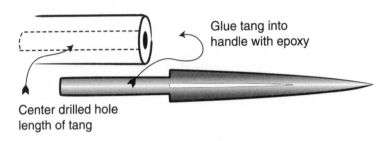

Glue tang into handle with epoxy

Center drilled hole length of tang

Widdershins

The rules of the shop and the forge were written in the blood of other smiths and blademakers. *Never* neglect safety practices: Use eye protection, wear work gloves, don't rush, when using the angle grinder hold it firmly with both hands. In short, please be careful. And if this project is beyond your skill, consider asking someone who is experienced to make the blade for you and concentrate your talents on adding the handle. Safety first, *always!*

Wave a Magick Wand

Making a working wand, also a God tool, is a process involving time, dedication, and a sense of harmony with the Earth as the supplier of your materials. The type of wand we are describing is not the simple priapic wand you made in Chapter 5. This will be a wand you use to channel your own magickal energy. It can be used to represent yourself on any altar you use. It is a strong symbol of your personal connection to the Earth and the Divine. Given all that, it's appropriate to create it over time and with reverence and care.

The first step in wand making is finding and befriending a tree from which your branch will be taken. You may choose a tree suited to your magickal purpose. You may also choose a tree that you already feel close to. In either case, you should be aware of the magickal properties of whatever wood you will use. There are many websites and reference books that can help you determine which type of wood might be most appropriate.

When you have chosen a tree, spend at least a full cycle of the moon, from Full Moon to Full Moon, making regular visits, bringing gifts and generally getting to know your tree. Part of this process will be sitting in silence and meditation nearby. Trees are not known for their chattiness, so be open to the tree's subtle communication. If all goes well, you will begin to understand how your tree thinks and feels. Tell your tree your plans to use one of its branches for a wand. Be sure that some of the gifts you give are fertilizer and water, things trees seem to appreciate a lot.

After a month has passed, you are ready to cut your branch. Only do this at the Waning Moon. This is very important. A plant's vital energies shift up and down with the phase of the moon. Removing a branch at Waxing or Full Moon is more traumatic to the tree, probably more painful as well. (Wiccans and Druids believe trees do feel pain and can withdraw sensation.) Bury a final gift near the tree trunk. Tell your tree your intention and identify the branch you intend to cut by touching it. Ask the tree to withdraw sensation from that branch if it can. Cut a length of branch longer than your forearm. It's fine to use loppers or pruning shears. Just don't tear the branch off. That is definitely traumatic to your tree friend. Once you have your branch, thank the tree. You are now ready to complete your wand.

Decide which end is the point and which is the base. Select a crystal for the point. Many people use quartz points, but other crystals can be used based on the magickal properties desired, and of course it must be of a good size to fit in your wand. Also choose a stone for the base. This will be for balance and better control when directing your energy, so give it careful consideration.

Summon and Stir

When Liguana made her wand many years ago, she wanted to anoint each end with her own blood to make it undeniably hers. She planned to use venous blood on the solar or sending end. Being a bit squeamish, she waited until she accidentally cut herself on a piece of glass. She wanted to anoint the lunar end with menstrual blood. She knew she could finish her wand soon. All she had to do was wait. That's how she found out she was pregnant with her first child. It turns out she had to wait a long time to complete her wand!

Carefully drill an indentation in the point of your wand for the crystal to rest in. The crystal should fit snugly into the hole, so the diameter depends on the width of the wand and of the crystal. Use a hot-glue gun to secure the crystal in the hole. Put the point of the crystal at the end of your longest finger on your dominant hand and measure to your elbow. Mark the branch and cut it to this length. Now you may repeat the embedding process at the base end of your wand with your grounding stone. Some people prefer to put a strand of their own hair or a drop of their own blood under the crystal or the stone before securing it in place. It will be your wand. Do what feels right.

After the wand is tipped with stone and crystal, wrap it in dark cloth and let it rest until the moon is waxing. At this time you can choose to keep the bark on or peel it off. If you peel off the bark, oil your wand with almond oil. You can scent the oil with an appropriate essential oil if that feels right to you.

Now you can decorate your wand with runes or stones, feathers, or lacing. If you like, wrap the handle area with fur or leather. You can even wood-burn designs into your wand. Liguana recommends securing decorations with hot glue—that is, if you are comfortable using synthetic materials on your wand, and if you want a long-lasting creation. Some people drill shallow holes in their wands and melt wax into them, then embed stones and jewels in the wax. If you choose this natural method, be prepared for changing the look of your wand, that is, you'll likely be doing frequent repair work to replace or remount magickal decorations. Wicca is also called The Art. You are the artist. Do whatever feels right and appropriate for you.

> **Summon and Stir**
>
> Liguana has a lot of wand pet peeves. She detests metal in or on wands, as it makes the energy flow erratic and detracts from the natural magick of the wood. She feels the same way about Sculpey and Femo modeling compounds. While they make great dragon and wizard designs, they just don't belong on a wand. And plastic? "AAA-RRRRRGGGGHHHH!!" Get the picture?

Consecrate your wand to your practice of Wicca at the next Full Moon. While waiting for the Full Moon, it can rest on your altar or be kept wrapped in its dark cloth. After it is consecrated, the process is done and you have a wand made in proper, reverent Wiccan fashion.

The Least You Need to Know

♦ Some tools are considered Goddess tools, others are tools of the God.

♦ Creating your own tools infuses them with your personal magick.

♦ When making a tool, don't rush the process. Meditating on your intent before beginning is a good idea.

♦ Tool making can be a good group project. If you make "extras," they can be sold to earn money for your coven.

Tools for Connecting with Our Spiritual Allies

In This Chapter

- ◆ Attracting faeries and songbirds
- ◆ Genie in a bottle
- ◆ Elf in a house …
- ◆ Totem animals, familiars, and animal companions

Everyone can use more friends. In this book we've encouraged you to lean on other members of your coven when they possess a talent you don't have, or to turn some of these projects into group activities so that your family and friends can share talents with each other.

But we shouldn't forget to include our spiritual allies—the deities, faeries, animal guides, and other spirits who can also come to our aid when we ask for help.

Faery Fancy

In some traditions, Wiccans use the Gaelic word *Sidhe* to mean any being of faery or spirit realm except deities and dragons. There seem to be many species of Sidhe, and they can be useful allies, adding their flare and energy to any magick you do. They have their own way of viewing the world and their reactions are sometimes unpredictable.

Dealing with the Sidhe is kind of like herding cats. Don't expect them to always come when you call or do your bidding in the manner you expect or prefer. They are fine with your appreciation but would rather be paid for any effort put forth on your behalf. Tangibly recognizing that you coexist on this Earth with the Sidhe can do a lot toward bringing their benevolent assistance, whether or not you ask for it. Here are a couple of ideas for giving homage or payment to those of the faery realms.

Faery Food and Milk of the Mother

Later in Chapter 19 we'll give you lots of potions for all magickal occasions. Here's one for the faery realm. Warm a cup of whole milk or half and half to almost boiling. Stir in a tablespoon of honey and a few drops of almond or vanilla extract.

Take this warm concoction to an outdoor location and call the Sidhe. Let them know that you have prepared this drink in their honor. Pour a small libation onto the ground and then fill a small cup or bowl to leave out as an offering of goodwill. This is a great use of an outdoor cauldron, by the way. (We gave you a project for making an outdoor cauldron in Chapter 12.)

It's fine for you to drink what may be left over. It's like sharing a beverage with friends. If your coven is in on this, the amount can be increased so everyone can share. If you are out on a cold day to honor the Sidhe, give your libations and then add a pinch of cinnamon and a pinch of cayenne to the portion allocated for human consumption. Should warm you right up! Don't give these spices to the Sidhe lest your relationship heat up more than you planned ….

Here's another recipe that can be shared with the Sidhe folks. Leave a piece of fritter with the hot beverage.

Faery Fritters

- 1 cup cottage cheese
- 1 egg, well beaten
- $1/4$ cup milk
- 1 cup flour

- ◆ 2 tsp. baking powder
- ◆ $\frac{1}{2}$ tsp. salt
- ◆ $\frac{1}{2}$ cup borage, calendula, or elder flowers, well washed
- ◆ Oil for frying
- ◆ Powdered sugar (optional)

Add the cottage cheese to the egg and beat until well blended. Stir in the milk. In another bowl, mix the flour, baking powder, and salt. Add this to the liquid mixture and stir lightly.

Gently fold in the flowers, trying not to tear them.

Drop the fritter dough by spoonful into a deep pot of hot oil or a deep fryer. Fry until brown (2 to 4 minutes). Drain on absorbent paper. Dust them lightly with powdered sugar, if desired.

Faery Bells

If you want to feed the Sidhe to honor them, you need to attract them first. Faeries are especially attracted to music and pretty colors. An easy way to accomplish this is to hang faery bells from a nearby tree or shrub.

Take a length of brightly colored ribbon. Tie a bell on one end and tie the other end to a limb. Or attach several bells to the ribbon, tying each one on at intervals. As the ribbon becomes worn or tattered, change it. Neglecting a faery bell indicates you have no respect for these entities and your luck could take a turn for the worse.

Inviting Spirits to Hang Around

When you create a space dedicated to benevolent helpers from other realms, they will notice. They may even choose to hang around and help out where they can.

Summon and Stir

Liguana warns against stirring up dragons. She reserves this only in times of great distress when she needs mighty allies. Once when she felt in danger, she awoke a dragon with her sword, swinging the sword around over her head and driving it down into the Earth with a roar, saying, "Stand beside me, great one. I am small and unprepared for this confrontation. Grant what protection you may until I feel strong enough to stand alone." It worked, too: The confrontation was delayed until she was ready!

A Genie Bottle

Genies may not really hang out in colorful bottles, but the concept for this next project is a good one. Whether you seek the aid of genies or just want an unusual flower vase, you'll have fun with this easy craft.

Here's what you'll need:

◆ ¹/₂ cup white glue

◆ ¹/₂ cup water

◆ A selection of colorful magazines

◆ Scissors

◆ A bottle or jar (Thrift stores are good places to find unusually shaped old jars and bottles; don't get textured glass, the surface must be smooth.)

◆ Small paintbrush

◆ Shellac (optional)

Make a solution of the white glue and water. Mix well and remember to stir it periodically while you are working.

Cut small, bright pictures from the magazines. Use lots of different shapes and colors. You can choose a theme or just choose pictures that strike your fancy.

Paint a small area of your bottle with the glue solution and apply one of your pictures, pressing it down firmly against the bottle.

Repeat this process with the other pictures, making a collage and covering the outside of your bottle. Don't be afraid to paint over your pictures with the solution. Overlapping the pictures is important. You don't want to be too geometric on this project. It won't all line up perfectly. That's just fine.

When your bottle has dried, wipe off any excess glue with a tissue. For extra hardiness, apply a coat of shellac over the collage.

Dedicate your bottle as a safe place for benevolent beings to stay whenever they're in town and display it somewhere in your home. You'll want to leave the lid off so energy beings and benevolent helpers can get in and out!

Craftworking

If you do this project with a wide-mouthed jar instead of a bottle, it can easily become a beautiful luminary with a votive candle placed inside. A small-mouthed bottle can also be a vase or a candle holder.

Elf Houses

The basic concept for elf houses is the same magickal concept we were working with on the genie bottles. It's the *Field of Dreams*, "If you build it, they will come" idea. If you dedicate and offer an area to benevolent entities, your odds of calling them into your life are much improved. Elves and faeries seem to prefer inhabiting wood and stone. Here is an idea to welcome these beings.

You will need a branch about 2 inches in diameter and 12 inches long. Search for interesting shapes and don't be put off if your stick has smaller branches extending from it. Driftwood is fine for this project, too.

Using a drill with a large bit, make a hole about halfway through the branch. It should be in the center or toward the bottom of your branch, not at the top.

Angling the drill downward into the wood, carve out a little pocket area so you have a doorway with a hollow place below it. This is the simple, basic design. You can also use a chisel for this. As always, be careful. Elves do not require or appreciate blood sacrifice!

Finish your elf house in your own artistic fashion. You may decide to leave bark on or peel it off. You may burn runes or designs into the branch. Soft dry moss tucked into the hollow is a good touch and a small white stone dropped inside is an invitation to faeries. Oiling the wood will make it shiny and preserve it. We don't know how elves and faeries feel about it, but we don't like the idea of using commercial varnishes and paints. You are the witch and the artist. Do what feels right for you.

Publicly invite the elves to take up residence in this cozy new house.

Hang your creation from a ceiling hook in a corner of your home and say out loud that this is for any benevolent entity to inhabit. Invite them in, and they *will* show up.

> **Summon and Stir**
>
> Liguana has an elf house on a shelf in her home. It is a more standard, thatch-roof cabin design. One day her teenaged son had a bunch of friends over for a party. When they asked about the elf house, he told them they shouldn't touch it or put their fingers inside it. Not believing a bit of it, one of the boys reached into the house and wiggled his fingers, asking what the elves were gonna do about it. Just then a small book dislodged itself from an upper shelf and dropped right onto the boy's head. He wasn't hurt because it was a small paperback. He certainly showed a lot more respect after that reprimand, though!

Animal Guides and Companions

Many traditions use animal spirits as guides and allies. Sometimes referred to as totem animals, they are derived from shamanistic practices like that of Native Americans, and in some cases in Druidic and Celtic lore. These spirit guides often take the form of a wild animal—a wolf, fox, owl, or bear, for example. But paying attention to your everyday life will remind you that we have animal spirits all around us.

If you share your house with a pet, you might be living with your familiar. A familiar represents all of the good qualities of that animal. The animal provides a witch with a link to the animal kingdom and the essence of the animal's power as it assists a practitioner in magickal works. Traditionally cats are associated with witches, but other animals such as dogs, rabbits, horses, and snakes can be familiars, too.

Even if you don't have a pet, there are animals in your life all the time like wild birds, squirrels, and—especially if you grow vegetables—your friendly neighborhood rabbits.

> **Summon and Stir**
>
> In addition to several cats, Liguana shares her space with chickens and goats. After an unfortunate run-in with a dog, only four chickens were left: Molly, Keri, Freddy, and Doodle. Doodle survived by passing for a goat. She decided it was safer in the goat barn. She comes out in the morning and eats beside the goats with her head in the

Our live-in animal companions offer us so much in the way of love and entertainment, it's only natural to repay them with some special treats of their own. Here are a couple of ideas.

Cat-Nippy Treats

Keeping your animal companions safe and content is important. Making *catnip* mice for the feline set is an easy treat to get started on. Catnip corresponds magickally to love, happiness, and beauty—all perfect homage to our feline friends and magickal companions.

It's easy to grow your own catnip. Most gardening supply stores sell catnip seeds or starter plants. Follow the directions on the packet for best planting results. Sow catnip seeds in the early spring in your outdoor garden. The plants do best in full sunshine and be sure to plant them where they have room to spread and grow. If you live in a cat-friendly neighborhood, growing catnip outdoors will tend to attract every cat within a four- or five-block radius. If you have a problem with that, opt for a pot of catnip grown indoors in a sunny window. But be forewarned, your own cat will insist on nibbling on it as the catnip grows—if not knocking it to the floor and rolling in it!

Magickal Properties

Catnip is a member of the mint family and is a perennial herb which will grow back each year if the winter is not too severe. Only bring your catnip toys out for special play sessions. If cats are exposed to catnip all the time, they will become immune to it and enjoy it less. Keep the toys in the freezer in between play times to keep the catnip fresh.

Seeds will not germinate for a couple of weeks, or longer. You will need to be patient. Once they start growing, thin the plants to one plant every 15 inches. Let plants grow until they just start to show signs of flowering. Then cut all the stems off to about 6 to 8 inches above the ground. You should be able to get two to three cuttings each season.

Most commercial catnip you buy contains the whole stalk ground up—both stems and leaves. We're going to use only the leaves, which are easier to dry and where the most aromatic oils are.

To dry, strip off the leaves and spread them on a tray or cookie sheet. They do not have to be in a single layer, but don't layer them more than 4 inches deep. Set the trays somewhere where they will get good air circulation (and somewhere out of cat reach!). Once or twice a day, "stir" the leaves with your hands.

After a couple of weeks, depending on room temperature and moisture conditions, the leaves should start to get brittle and crumble. They should get to the point that you can take a handful and roll them between your palms, making flakes. After they are flaked, store in a jar or plastic bag.

When the catnip is ready to use, make your catnip mice. Using the following mouse pattern, cut out two mouse shapes. Be sure the material you're using isn't too porous or you'll end up with catnip flakes all over. A soft cotton fleece is nice because it makes the mice fuzzy, which cats enjoy. If you want to add a tail, cut a length of twine or cotton cord.

Sew the two shapes together, making sure the tail runs inside about half the length of the mouse as well as outside and is double-stitched so it won't pull out easily. Leave the mouse's nose end open.

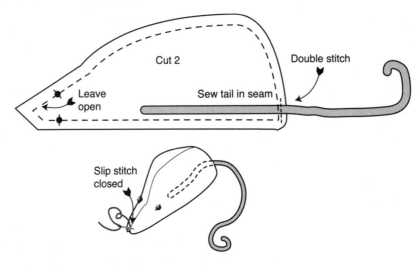

Make sure to double-stitch over the mouse tail.

Turn the mouse right side out and fill it with dried catnip. Stitch the mouse closed using small stitches very close together.

Widdershins _____

Although you might be tempted to add cute features to your mouse, like felt ears or whiskers or button eyes, they can be dangerous. If kitty chews one off, he or she could choke or require surgery to have it removed. Keep the mice simple. After all, it's the catnip that cats like, not the shape.

If you're having mice problems in your house, the catnip mouse can be used as a magickal poppet. Introduce the poppet to your cat with these words:

This poppet takes a mouse's form,
now catch the ones alive and warm.

If you have a soft spot for all animals, instead of letting your cat kill the mouse, you can catch the mouse once your cat has cornered it by putting a glass or jar over it. Slip a heavy piece of paper or cardboard underneath the glass and take the mouse outside to let him go. However, don't be surprised if you see him back inside in a day or two.

Doggie Treats

If your animal companion is a dog, make him some fresh dog biscuits as a treat. Because so many store-bought treats include preservatives and artificial color, you'll know your treats are healthier. Just remember, these are meant to be used as an occasional treat. You don't want to contribute to an overweight dog.

- 1¹/₂ cups whole-wheat flour
- 1 cup all-purpose flour
- 1 cup skimmed milk powder
- ¹/₃ cup melted fat (beef, lamb, bacon)
- 1 egg, slightly beaten
- 1 cup cold water
- 2 tsp. thyme (for courage, happiness, and determination)

Craftworking

You can buy dog bone–shaped cookie cutters several places online and in some pet stores. Of course, just like the catnip mouse, the shape doesn't matter. Use any cookie cutter shape you like.

In a mixing bowl, combine the whole wheat and all-purpose flours and the milk powder. Drizzle with melted fat. Add the beaten egg, water, and thyme and mix well. Gather dough into a ball.

On a lightly floured surface, roll out the dough to ¹/₂ inch. Cut into dog-bone shapes. Bake on ungreased baking sheets in a 350°F oven for 40 to 50 minutes or until dark and crispy. Makes about three dozen dog biscuits.

Feeding the Winged Ones

Attracting songbirds to your outside altar is a delightful way to honor their guiding spirits. They add music and movement and color. (Hmmm. Sounds like they might also be helpful in attracting faeries.)

Although we always think of feeding the birds during the winter, it's equally important to feed them in the spring during nesting season and in the fall before migrating season. Let's face it, once you've started feeding them, you should keep it up all year around.

The following directions are for making a simple bird feeder for your backyard.

Here's what you'll need:

- A post large enough in diameter to screw a light shade to (see the following items)
- Paint

- An extra-large flower pot (the size you plant trees in)
- Fill dirt
- A screw and a thin rubber washer
- Shallow glass light shade made for an overhead fixture
- Birdseed

Paint the post and let dry. Drill a small hole in the top for the screw. Bury the other end into the flower pot with the fill dirt (or directly into the ground).

Place the rubber washer over the screw hole you drilled, place the glass shade on top of that, and screw in place. Fill with seed.

You will want to place the feeder next to some shrubbery to provide cover for the birds. Place several of them next to each other at different heights to make a pretty and functional garden sculpture.

Asking for Allies' Help

As with anything else in magick, asking allies for help must be done with knowledge and reverence. Learn the power of the totem animal you are invoking; reward the faeries as you seek their favors; ask your familiar for wisdom and guidance. Allies are all around you. Using them can be as simple as lighting a candle and sending a wish skyward with a flock of birds.

Remember to thank your allies by honoring them every day. Feed them, groom the ones you can, meditate on the ones whose power and talents you want to borrow. They are vital components in the practice of Wicca.

The Least You Need to Know

- Call on benevolent spirits as allies when you need a little extra help.
- When a spiritual ally helps you, be sure to thank it either with food or a special ritual.
- Honor the animal spirits you see in your everyday life, whether they're a pet or just sharing the world with you.
- Approach allies with reverence—don't demand their help, request it.

Part 5

Get "Crafty" and Make Magick

Harnessing the power of some of Wicca's favorite traditions: incense, candle, mirror, poppet, cord, paper, flower, and divination, you'll find projects that help you learn how to maximize magickal energy and potential for your spellworking and ritual celebrations. You'll also find ways to dispel negative energy and ward off evil intentions. Add the special influence of stones and crystals and deepen your personal connection to Wicca's nature-based practice.

Chapter 14

Incense, Candle, and Mirror Magick

In This Chapter

- The strength of magickal portals
- The fragrant magickal power of incense
- Make your own magickal candles
- Wiccan mirrors for scrying

This chapter touches on a few more Wiccan tools to make and use. Although incense and candles are easy and inexpensive to purchase, it can be very satisfying to make them yourself. Incense, candles, and mirrors provide powerful gateways to connecting with and raising magickal energy. Infusing these tools with your personal energy and intent by creating them by your own hand can enhance the strength of these magickal portals, making them deeper, wider, and rich with possibilities.

Although all of the projects in this chapter can be done alone or in a group, with the exception of the incense burner, they are not child-friendly. Candle making can be especially dangerous for young children. Please consider this chapter *Adults only*.

Interesting Incense

Often used to represent the element of Air on an altar, incense can also be used in purification rituals, to help you relax, or just to set the mood before you cast a spell. There are many theories about what fragrance to use when casting a particular spell and it is fine to follow other people's advice in these matters, but mostly you should use incense that has a fragrance you find appealing.

The most common way to buy incense is in a long joss stick or in a cone shape. Either one is fine to use.

An Incense Burner for Your Altar

Securing incense by placing it into sand not only keeps it from tipping over, but ensures you won't be leaving burn marks on your altar. This incense burner is attractive and easy to make as well as functional.

Here's what you'll need:

- Small clay pot
- Primer and paint
- Paintbrushes
- Modeling clay
- Sand

Cover your work space with newspapers. You can paint the whole pot or just the rim. Painting just the rim leaves the earthy clay color of the pot visible, which can be an attractive look on an altar.

Craftworking

Although you can buy sand at craft stores, this project warrants a trip to the beach if you live close to one. Just make sure the sand is clean and not full of twigs or large stones. If you don't live near a beach, a trip to a gravel pit can be an adventure, too.

Begin by painting on a white primer coat. Let dry thoroughly. Next, paint on the top color. You will want to use two coats, letting each one dry thoroughly.

Add whatever figures or decorations you'd like in a contrasting color.

Once the pot is completely dry, plug the hole in the bottom with the modeling clay. Fill the pot with sand up to the rim. Cone incense can be placed directly on top of the sand and lit. Push the thin end of stick incense deep into the sand before lighting it.

Add a decorative border.

An Outdoor Incense Burner

You can use the same principle to make an incense burner to use outdoors. The difference is size and weight, because you'll want to make sure it won't blow over or be knocked over easily.

Here's what you'll need:

◆ An empty coffee can or other large-sized can, rinsed and dried

◆ Paint designed to be used on metal

◆ Sand

Paint and decorate the can in any way that appeals to you. Fill it three quarters full of sand and use it to hold your incense.

These also make excellent candle holders for pillar candles. Stir up the sand to loosen it and twist the candle's base into the sand about 2 inches. Make several and set them out to light up a sidewalk or to point the way to an altar.

Make Your Own Incense

It is possible to make your own incense, but the ingredients may be somewhat difficult to find. There are several places online where you can order the supplies if none of your local stores carry what you need.

The basic instructions for making incense are to mix powdered fragrances with a water-soluble binder and some warm water. This dough is kneaded together and formed into cones. Once they've been shaped, they are set aside to dry for 10 days to two weeks.

The tricky part is using the right amount of each ingredient so that the incense burns steadily without being too smoky or going out completely. Some fragrances, like sandalwood, burn easily; others, like frankincense, are more difficult to burn and must be used sparingly or your incense won't light.

Here's a starting incense recipe, but if this is an activity that appeals to you, experiment with your own fragrance combinations.

> **Magickal Properties**
>
> **Makko** is a common natural binding agent. It comes from the bark of a tree that grows in Southeast Asia, the Machillus Thunbergii tree. It is sometimes marketed under the name Tabu no ki. This powder is adhesive, odorless, and burns readily, which makes it the perfect incense ingredient.

Mix together two parts *Makko*, one part sandalwood powder, one part cedar powder, and a half part clove powder.

Add a few drops of warm water to create a soft dough. Be careful not to add too much or the dough won't hold together and the cones will take too long to dry out. It's also best to make a small sample batch to see if you've got the right proportion of each ingredient before you make a larger batch.

Knead the dough until it is well mixed and holds a shape. Form small cones and set them aside to dry out of direct sunlight. If they dry out too fast they will lose their fragrance.

A pleasant thing to do on a warm late summer evening is to gather pine or cedar resin. It is yellow or light orange and clings to the evergreen tree. Only gather what has hardened. Liquid tree sap does not burn well on charcoal and it is terribly sticky! Liguana likes to send her kids hunting up resins to burn on scented charcoal in her cauldron. These are good for smudging an outdoor ritual space. They are smoky and heady, and seem to keep the mosquitoes at bay.

Using Your Incense

Incense is often used on an altar to represent the element of Air. As you call down the elements, light your incense and think of the properties of Air that will help you in your endeavors—mental clarity and alertness. Incense can also be used to purify a sacred space (see Chapter 18). There is no "correct" fragrance to use; pick a scent that appeals to you. Or use a fragrance that reminds you of the season, such as pine during Yule or gardenia at Beltane.

Light a Creative Candle

Flaming candles are at the heart of almost every Wiccan ritual. They are used both to draw in positive energy and to dispel negativity. They also are generally used on an altar to represent the element of Fire.

There are many sources available both online and in books that will suggest what color candles to use for particular spells. Use them as a guideline but listen to your own intuition. And keep in mind, you can never go wrong with white. White candles symbolize, among other things, pure intentions. So, no matter what intentions you bring to your ritual, your purpose can be strengthened using white candles.

An Easy Beeswax Taper

Beeswax candles have a pleasant honey scent and are often used in magickal ritual because of their natural ingredients and their association with the bee, which symbolizes creativity, self-sufficiency, and creating order out of chaos.

Many hobby shops sell square sheets of beeswax. Making candles with one of these is easy. Turn your wax so it looks like a diamond shape or a square turned sideways. Lay a length of wick string across one corner of your wax square and roll the square tightly from corner to corner. It should become soft as you work on it with your warm hands.

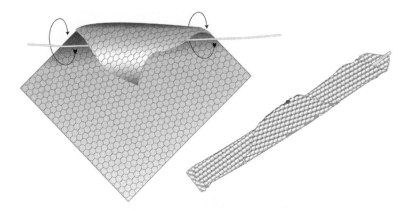

Roll the wick inside the beeswax taper.

You can drop dried lavender flowers or rose petals on your wax and roll them up inside. Be sure before you start that your wick is longer than your wax when measured corner to corner. Squeeze the candle base tight and fold the pointed flap over to seal in flowers and wick. It's just nasty to pick up your candle and have the wick fall out the bottom! Roll this candle between your hands until you are sure the wax is clinging to itself. Now you have a simple beeswax taper.

Melting the Wax

If you're serious about candle making, you will want to invest in a few basic supplies. With a little precaution, candle making can be safe and fun. However, using the wrong equipment or guessing at temperatures can quickly escalate into disaster. Melted wax has properties similar to hot oil and can be dangerous if not watched carefully. In addition, hot wax on skin can cause serious burns.

> **CAUTION**
>
> ### Widdershins
>
> Never try to put out a wax fire with water. If the wax reaches its flash point—300°F or hotter—the vapors are extremely flammable and should be treated like an oil fire. Smother small fires with a pot lid. Know how to use your fire extinguisher and make sure it hasn't exceeded its expiration date! Also, never heat wax hotter than 250°F or leave melting wax unattended, even for a moment.

Here's a list of the basic supplies you'll need to have on hand:

- An old, large pot big enough to hold your pouring pot.

- An aluminum pouring pot (available online at www.peakcandle.com).

- A thermometer. This is vital!

- An electric hot plate. This is optional, but it's safer to melt wax on an electric burner than on a gas burner. And you won't ruin your stove if you accidentally spill hot wax.

- A working fire extinguisher. Hey, better safe than sorry!

Use the large pot as the bottom of your homemade double boiler. Add 2 to 3 inches of water and place the pouring pot inside. Bring the water to a simmer, not to a rolling boil, and melt the wax until it is the right temperature for the wax you are using.

Making Pillar Candles

These wide-base candles are stable and won't knock over easily. You can make them in a variety of colors, fragrances, and shapes, and they make great gifts. Buying candle molds online or at a hobby shop is one way to get started. Or you can make do with some "homemade" molds to see if you like candle making before you invest too much money. You'll also find wax, dyes, fragrances, and wicks at hobby shops.

Here's what you'll need:

- Wax

- Dye and fragrance (optional)

- A purchased mold or an empty cardboard milk carton, rinsed and dried

◆ A wick

◆ One or more small flat metal washers

◆ Pencil or chopstick

Melt the wax in your double boiler to the temperature recommended on the package. One more reminder—tend to your melting wax carefully!

Use an old wooden spoon to stir in dye and fragrance, if desired.

While the wax is melting, set up your mold. If you've purchased a mold, follow the directions included with the mold. If you're being adventurous, here's what you do.

Cut the top off the milk carton to slightly taller than you want your finished candle to be.

Tie one end of the wick around the washer. This will weigh down your wick so it won't float as you pour your hot wax into the mold. (You might want to use two or three to be sure.)

Tie the other end around the pencil or chopstick, making sure the stick is long enough to lie across the top of your milk carton. This is the top of your wick and should be pulled tight so the wick hangs straight.

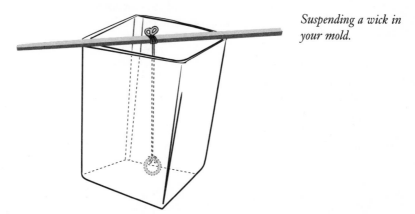

Suspending a wick in your mold.

Pour the melted wax into the mold carefully so as not to create air bubbles, wearing gloves to protect your hands and arms from splatters. Don't use all the wax, and take it off the heat. Reposition the wick if necessary.

Allow the candle to cool a bit until a surface forms on top. Take another pencil or stick of some kind and poke four or five relief holes into the candle to stop the natural shrinkage that will occur as the wax cools. The holes should be positioned around the wick and poked to about 1 inch less than the depth of the candle. Without these venting holes, the candle may look deformed when unmolded. If the holes start to close up, poke them again to make sure the vent stays open. Allow the candle to cool completely.

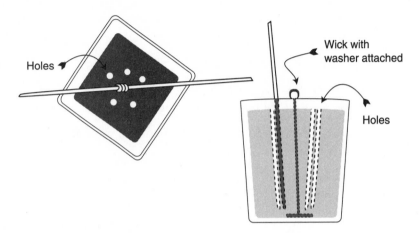

Poking relief holes makes a smoother candle.

Remelt the leftover wax to a temperature that's about 10 degrees hotter than your original temperature. This helps the two layers to adhere. Pour the wax into the holes just below the level of your first filling.

Let the candle cool thoroughly and remove it from the mold. Trim the wick before lighting.

A More Decorative Candle

Follow the basic directions for making a pillar candle but replace the wick with a thin taper placed in the center. Before pouring the melted wax into the mold, loosely pack crushed ice around the taper, centering it as you add the ice. The key to success here is to fill the mold to the top with ice, but to keep it loose enough to allow room for the wax to be poured in.

This requires you to pour quickly because the wax will start to solidify as soon as it hits the ice. No relief holes are required. As the ice melts, you will produce a candle with lacelike holes.

Let the candle cool, remove it from the mold, and trim the wick.

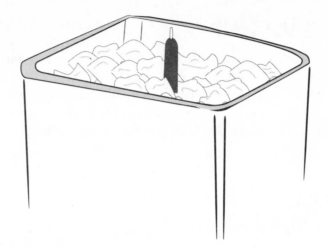

Center the taper and add crushed ice.

Container Candles

If you want to make a candle inside a container, you must make sure the container is heatproof and won't crack when you pour in the hot wax. Recycle containers that you purchased with a candle in them already. Or look for heatproof containers.

Follow the same basic instructions for placing the wick and melting and pouring the wax. Once the candle cools you might notice an indentation in the top. Reheat the reserved wax to 10° hotter than the temperature of the original wax and top off the candle until it is level.

Once it's completely cooled, trim the wick to about ¼ inch.

Widdershins

Do not use a clay pot as a container for a candle. Clay acts as a wick itself and can cause a small blaze once it's lit.

Practicing Candle Magick

Candles can be charged to strengthen a spell when they are lit. Let's say you want to cast a spell for prosperity. Carve a money symbol into a green candle and as you light the candle say, *"With this flame I draw money and good fortune into my life."* Remember that money coming into your life may not mean winning the lottery; it may come to you through a new job opportunity. If your desire is to take a trip, cut out a picture of the place you want to visit, carve the rune symbol of journey (*Raido*) into a yellow candle and set the candle on top of the picture. Visualize yourself on vacation as you light the wick. Candle rituals are limited only by your own imagination.

Mirror, Mirror, on the Wall

We talk about using mirrors to Draw Down the Moon (see Chapter 4) and to conse-crate a tool (see Chapter 18). Wiccan mirrors can also be used to predict the future, answer questions, and find solutions to problems. This is called *scrying* and is often accomplished through a special scrying mirror. These mirrors are best made during a Waxing Moon (when it is possible to see more and more every night …) and should be consecrated like any other tool.

Here's what you'll need:

- ◆ An oval picture frame with a glass insert, 8–12 inches long

- ◆ Glossy black acrylic paint

- ◆ A paintbrush

Magickal Properties

The term **scrying** comes from the English word *descry*, which means to make out dimly or to reveal. In addition to a mirror, you can scry using a dark bowl full of water or a crystal. The best efforts come from staring into a shiny surface.

Take the picture frame apart and clean the inside of the glass insert very well with a mixture of vinegar and water and a soft cotton cloth. (Or use a commercial window cleaner). Make sure it is completely dry.

Paint the inside of the glass with the black paint. Use three coats and let each one dry thoroughly.

Decorate the frame if you desire. Or buy a frame that already appeals to you.

Reassemble the frame, being careful not to scratch the paint. Clean the front side of the glass so no fingerprints remain.

Using Your Scrying Mirror

Scrying takes quite a lot of practice, so don't be discouraged if you aren't successful right away. Stick with it and you will eventually be rewarded.

Scrying is best done at night by candlelight or full moonlight. Place your candle (handmade from a project earlier in this chapter!) so that it illuminates the mirror but isn't shining directly into it. To get results you will need to spend anywhere from 20 minutes to an hour concentrating, so be sure you're in a comfortable position. Light some incense you like. Take several deep breaths and look deeply into your mirror. State your intent aloud and be clear about what visions you are trying to see.

If you stare intently your eyes will start to water. Rather, you want to unfocus your eyes a little and let the images start to come to you. As you first begin this process the images may not be clear or make sense to you. Don't be critical. Relax and let your mind free-flow with the possibilities. Above all, don't give up. Spend some time every day practicing the art and the images will sharpen and make more sense. When you become good at it, ask your mirror a specific question and it will provide you with an answer.

Another Scrying Tool or Two

If you enjoy your newfound scrying power, here's another scrying tool to use. Find a shallow, antique bowl and paint the inside of it glossy black. Once it's dry, fill it with spring water. Drop a silver coin in the bottom to represent the Full Moon. Real silver is best. Using candlelight or moonlight, gaze into your scrying bowl as you would your mirror.

You can also try scrying by using a crystal, but this is a more advanced skill despite the gypsy cliché of reading a crystal ball. Black surfaces are best for beginners.

Putting It All Together

These three simple tools—incense, candles, and mirrors—have been used in the Craft for hundreds of years. They are simple to use to draw in or dispel energy and can be left out in the open even if you're living with people who might be suspicious of your religion.

Use the magickal power of your handmade incense, candle, and mirror to see with deeper vision.

The Least You Need to Know

◆ When considering an incense fragrance, choose one that you find pleasing so the smell doesn't distract you.

◆ Pick candle colors that further your intentions, but if you have limited funds, keep a supply of white candles to fall back on.

◆ Take every precaution when working with hot wax. Safety first is crucial.

◆ Scrying takes time and patience to perfect. Do you have the personality for it?

Poppet, Cord, Paper, and Flower Magick

In This Chapter

- ◆ Communicate your magickal intent with poppets
- ◆ Hold magickal energy with knot magick
- ◆ Send a message with paper magick
- ◆ Blossom with nature's magickal unfolding

This chapter offers you some more crafty ideas to incorporate into your Wiccan rituals. Whether you're looking for group activities or solitary ones, easy or challenging, there is something here for everyone.

Wiccans use mundane objects to bring about magickal results. Sometimes the everyday items around us might escape our attention, but bits of yarn, dried flowers, and plain old paper can be used to invoke your desires and make your wishes come true.

Make a Magick Poppet

People who are afraid of witchcraft might look at these dolls as "voodoo" dolls meant to cause harm. But as we all know, witches do not set out to harm someone, for fear it will come back threefold (the Wiccan Law of Three) ... not to mention the fact that having evil intentions is a horribly negative way to walk through the world.

Wiccans use poppets to promote healing, encourage wisdom, improve communication, and support good luck. In creating a poppet, you must be sure your intentions are pure. You cannot use a poppet to force someone else to behave in a certain way. Use poppets to encourage, not to manipulate.

A Yarn Poppet

This is a perfect way to use up extra yarn from knitting or crocheting projects. You can make them in a variety of sizes and colors and in both genders.

Here's what you'll need:

 ◆ A piece of cardboard 4 inches long or longer, depending on how tall you want your poppet to be (the width doesn't matter; keep it small enough to slip the yarn off easily)

 ◆ Yarn in two contrasting colors

 ◆ Scissors

Wrap the yarn lengthwise around the cardboard 20 to 30 times. The more times you wrap it, the fuller your poppet will be. The number of times you will want to wrap it also depends on the weight of the yarn you're using. Wrap it loosely enough so that you can slide the yarn off the cardboard.

Slide the yarn off the cardboard, keeping it in a loop. Tie the yarn together at one end with a small piece of yarn. This will become the top of the poppet's head. Next, tie another piece of yard about an inch below this around the poppet's "neck" to form the head.

Using a contrasting color of yarn, wrap it lengthwise around the piece of cardboard 15 to 20 times. This will form the arms and hands. Slide the yarn off the cardboard and tie a small piece of yarn around each end where the poppet's wrists would be. Slide this loop through the first loop of yarn just below the neck and tie another piece of yarn below it, forming the waist and holding the arms in place.

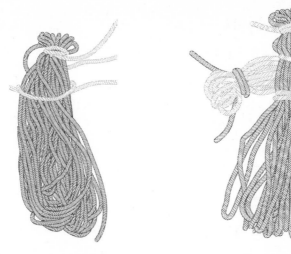

Forming the poppet's head.   *Adding the poppet's arms.*

At this point, you can cut open the bottom loop to form the poppet's skirt. If you want the figure to represent a male, divide the skirt into two bundles and tie each one into pants at the poppet's ankles.

Two finished poppets.

Now you're ready to use the poppet magickally. Breathe life into the poppet and name it by saying, "I name you (person's name for whom you made the poppet)." Then continue the spell or charm. Ask the Lady and Lord for guidance and state your intention. Place the poppet on your altar until you've gotten the desired effect. It's a good idea to disassemble the figure once it has served its magickal purpose. For more on performing spells with poppets and for destroying them once the spell is done, you'll want to read *The Complete Idiot's Guide to Spells and Spellcraft*, written by Liguana's good friend and fellow Wiccan Aurora Greenbough, and Cathy Jewell (Alpha Books, 2004).

A Slightly Different Version

Using a cloth poppet enables you to add symbols to the figure to assist you in giving it an identity and in naming your intention. Add a lock of the person's hair, for example (and, of course, with his or her permission), or embroider his or her astrological symbol onto the doll.

Use the following pattern to cut out two figures. You will want to use cotton cloth. It can be plain or in a color that corresponds to the type of magick you want to use. Stitch the two figures together, leaving a hole to add the stuffing. Turn right side out and stuff the doll with cotton batting. Before you finish closing the last seam, add any herbs or crystals that support your intention. You can also add a piece of paper written in the person's handwriting or a photo of the person (again, with his or her permission). Follow your magickal instincts.

Use this pattern to make a cloth poppet.

If you don't want to spend money on cotton batting, stuffing your poppet with old cotton underwear works, too. Make sure it is clean and dry. Cut off any elastic bands, then tear or cut the soft cotton into small strips to avoid having the stuffing bunch up. A little recycling magick!

Knot a Creative Cord

As we pointed out in Chapter 10, knots and crosses and braids are symbolic holding places for magickal energy. This means many simple spells can be cast just by knotting a cord or two.

Summon and Stir

The use of knots in magick has been widely practiced throughout the world for many reasons. It is quick, simple, and discreet, but very powerful. Especially in Celtic lands where, it was believed, the faery folk could not be held in any knot, the skill of tying knots was a faery gift. In times gone by, knot-tying would have been a basic skill all Wiccan practitioners would know.

Take a Magick Moment

Prepare yourself to cast a spell in whatever way makes sense to you. Take a ritual bath, cast a circle, light a candle, take up a cord in a color that supports your intentions.

State your desire in positive terms. Then, tie a series of knots, saying something like the following with each knot you tie:

> *Knot number one, the spell's begun.*
> *Knot number two, to see it through.*
> *Knot number three, so mote it be.*
> *Knot number four, let wishes soar.*
> *Knot number five, the spell's alive.*
> *Knot number six, the spell is fixed.*
> *Knot number seven provides balance even.*
> *Knot number eight, will set it straight.*
> *Knot number nine, will make it mine.*
> *The spell is cast, the knotting done,*
> *This witch's charm is now begun.*

Place the string of knots on your altar and repeat the spell daily, touching each knot as you do so. Repeat this until your intention has been realized.

Handfasting

Handfasting is when two people in love decide to make their feelings known publicly. Traditionally, in a meaningful ceremony or ritual, the couple declares their choice to live together for a year and a day. At the end of the year and a day, they can repeat their declarations publicly again, go their own ways, or get married legally. There are as many versions of a handfasting ceremony as there are couples.

Magickal Properties

Handfasting has its origins in shaking hands to close a deal. This ritual is also where we get the cliché of "tying the knot" to signify marriage because the couple's hands are bound together with a silk cord to physically acknowledge their spiritual union.

Handfasting ceremonies begin much like traditional Christian weddings. The bride and groom are escorted to an altar, where they exchange vows before a priestess or priest. Once the vows are exchanged, the couple joins hands—right hand to right hand, left hand to left hand, in an infinity symbol.

At this point the priestess takes a silken cord and binds the couple's hands together. (White, gold, silver, or red are all good color choices for the cord because these colors symbolize purity, the God, the Goddess, and passion, respectively.) The couple might say something like the following:

Heart to heart, body to body
Freely together our lives we entwine.
Before the Lord and before the Lady
Blessed be this sacred bind.

Working Paper Magick

Paper magick doesn't have to be as complicated as origami folds or papermaking. Some paper magick is as easy as knot-tying magick. Buy decorative paper to make the spell seem special or use ordinary tablet paper. The power of the spell is in your focus and intent, not the cost of the paper.

A Paper Chain of Blessings

Most of us remember making red-and-green paper chains when we were children to hang on a Christmas tree or to decorate a window in a classroom. This project is a take-off on that theme, updated to use throughout the year and for magickal purposes, not just for decoration.

This is definitely a group project. Prior to your get-together, cut strips of paper about 7 inches long and 1 inch wide. Origami paper and wrapping paper are both good to use for this because they're usually decorated on one side and white on the other. However, construction paper works well, too.

Give each participant a handful of paper strips and some colored pens. Have everyone write a wish, a blessing, or a positive affirmation on 10 (or more) paper strips. Loop them together randomly to make a paper chain using tape or rubber cement.

Creating a paper chain.

Once the chain is complete, cast a magick circle and purify the chain by passing it through the smoke from a candle or incense. Say something like the following:

> *May all the good within this chain*
> *be with you till we meet again.*

Use the chain to decorate your group altar, putting it safely away at the end of each ceremony. Offer participants the chance to add more rings to the chain as they think of new ideas or have new blessings come into their lives.

A "Stained-Glass" Lampshade

It's easy to set a sabbat mood in your home with just a little effort. This project creates a stained-glass effect with designs and colors appropriate for every season.

Take a large sheet of white paper, at least 3 feet by 3 feet. (You might have to go to a print shop to find a sheet big enough.) Buy tissue paper in a variety of colors. Think about the season—pastels for spring, natural colors for summer, earth tones for autumn, bright colors for winter.

Make a lampshade out of the white paper that is big enough to slip over your current lampshade. Lay the paper flat.

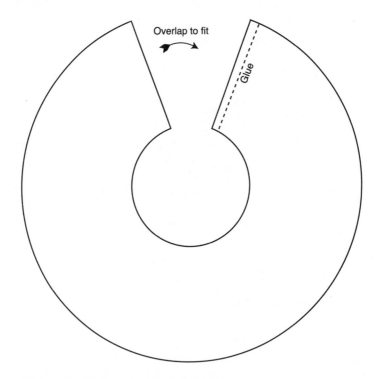

This is the shape of your lampshade laid flat.

Tear (do not cut) small squares of tissue paper. Don't try to make them perfect; the odd shapes add to the appeal. Lay the squares out on the white paper close enough together to completely cover the lampshade. Once you have a pattern you like, use clear-drying white glue to paste each square to your lampshade.

Let the paper dry completely, then glue together the back seam of the lampshade. Slip the homemade shade over your current one and turn on the lamp for a stained-glass look.

The torn-paper pattern can be random, or you can incorporate an astrological symbol, your coven's sigil, or a rune into the pattern.

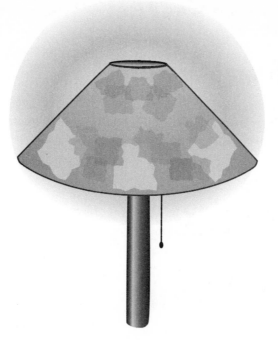

Your finished lampshade casts a magickal glow!

Homemade Cards for All Occasions

Sending someone a greeting card lets them know how special they are to you. It not only strengthens the fellowship you might have with other Wiccans and friends, but on a practical level, it's an ideal way to announce sabbat festivals and Wiccan gatherings. Sending a card you made yourself makes the card even more special.

Whether you plan to hand draw the card or use a computer card-making program, it's best to start with blank card paper. Almost every office supply store sells blank card stock in a variety of sizes. This type of paper is the weight of a purchased card but blank on both sides and scored down the middle to fold easily. (Card stock is different from the cards you can buy in a store that have a picture on the cover but are blank on the inside, although those work, too.) This is an opportunity to use your creativity to its fullest. Decorate your card with any symbols or pictures that seem appropriate for the occasion.

Craftworking

Browse through the card sections in stores and then adapt the ideas you see to create your own designs and sentiments.

Computer greeting-card programs do most of the work for you, but you can rewrite the verses to make the card unique. Don't send cards just on traditional holidays. It's more fun to receive a card unexpectedly in amongst the phone bill and the offer for a new credit card.

Bring a Little Nature Indoors

Because Wicca is a nature-based religion, it's important to bring a touch of nature indoors throughout the year. Live plants, dried flowers, seed pods, or anything that reminds you that we live on a growing planet, is appropriate.

Pinecones and Beads

Pine is sacred to the Lord and silver beads and pearls can symbolize the Lady, so this centerpiece makes a nice Yule decoration for your table.

Here's what you'll need:

- A large plate (any kind)
- Artificial moss
- Pine oil
- Two large pinecones
- Small beads and pearls
- Hot-glue gun
- Tweezers

Cover the plate with the artificial moss. Sprinkle the moss with a few drops of pine oil.

Hot-glue one bead or one pearl on the end of each "petal" of the pinecone. Use a tweezers to place the bead onto the dollop of hot glue so you don't burn your fingers. Vary the colors or make each pinecone a uniform color. One filled with silver beads and one with pearls evokes the Moon and the Goddess.

Let the pinecones dry thoroughly. Place them on one half of the moss-covered plate. Add a large red bow to the other side and use the plate as a centerpiece for a Yule table.

Ring Around a Heart of Roses

Roses and romance just naturally go together. Displaying dried roses in a heart-shaped container invites love and companionship into your home. This can be placed on a

bedroom vanity or on an end table as potpourri. The colors of fresh roses change
as you dry them but that doesn't change
their magickal intentions. Reds for passion
turn to burgundy, yellows for friendship
turn creamy, pinks for innocent love turn
lavender—experiment with combinations.

> **Craftworking**
>
> Silica gel turns pink as it
> absorbs moisture and blue
> as it dries. If the roses are
> left in the gel too long they
> may become brittle. The gel
> may be reused once it's dry.

Here's what you'll need:

- ◆ Roses
- ◆ Silica gel (available in floral shops and craft stores)
- ◆ Casserole dish with lid
- ◆ Soft paintbrush
- ◆ Floral wire
- ◆ A heart-shaped mold
- ◆ Floral foam cut into a heart shape to fit the mold
- ◆ Rose oil (optional)

For the best results, use roses that are half-opened. Cut the rose stems, leaving
$1/2$ inch below the heads. Pour about 2 inches of silica gel into the casserole dish.

Insert the rose stems into the silica gel. Fit the flowers closely together without
crushing them. Pour more silica around and over the roses, filling all the spaces.
Cover the dish and place it in a warm, dry place.

When the roses are dry—in about five to seven days—gently remove them from the
gel. Brush them gently with a soft paintbrush to remove any lingering traces of gel.

If any stems have broken off, insert a piece of floral wire into the flower head.

Put the foam inside the heart-shaped mold. Insert the rose stems very close together
into the floral foam. Sprinkle the petals with rose oil, if desired.

Down-Home Magickal Traditions

It isn't necessary to spend a lot of money to make magickal objects. As this chapter
has pointed out, using the bits and pieces around your house can produce powerful
outcomes. A Wiccan tradition is to "waste not, want not." Or, in other words, "Use it

up, wear it out, make it do, or do without." You can accomplish this by making poppets out of leftover yarn, blessing chains out of paper scraps, and potpourri out of dried flowers.

In the next chapter, we'll show you how to recycle and create objects to use for divination purposes.

The Least You Need to Know

◆ A poppet should only be used for beneficial purposes, not to manipulate another person.

◆ Knots and braids are symbolic holding places for magick—use them often.

◆ Paper magick can be an inexpensive way to bring joy and positive affirmations into the lives of your friends.

◆ No matter what the season, keep a touch of nature indoors to remind you of the Lord and Lady.

Chapter 16

Make Divination Magick

In This Chapter

- ◆ Handcrafting symbols that carry magickal messages
- ◆ Rune talismans, magickal Ouija boards, and pentagram oracles
- ◆ Crystal pendulums answer yes, no, and more
- ◆ Brew a cup of tea, cut a deck of cards, read the future

There are several things to keep in mind when working with divination tools in the context of your practice of Wicca. First of all, the future is *never* set in stone. "Predicting the future" should be done with caution, especially if you are doing a reading for someone else. Remember that what you are seeing is a set of possible outcomes that you or another person can use to guide their everyday choices.

If, in your divination, you see the potential for difficult situations, particularly for an accident, illness, death, or other dire consequences, avoid announcing a tragic outcome. In these cases, more than ever, predicting does *not* make it so. Instead you might work with the person you are reading for to understand and explore the circumstances surrounding his or her situation so that together you can suggest lifestyle changes or other courses of action that may lead away from trouble and toward a more beneficial outcome.

Divination can be a powerful magickal tool to help direct and focus your spellcasting. Working with divination tools can also deepen your intuition and connect you more powerfully to the flow of natural energy from the All, the Lady, and the Lord. The more you can understand and can see or intuit about a situation, the more specific and resonant the intent and effect of your spells will become.

Make Your Own Tools for Seeing

Divination tools are serious magickal tools—avoid the impulse to "play" with them, as you would play a parlor game. And don't "test" a tool by asking the same question three times in a row to see if you get the same answer. Whether you're using I Ching, runes, or Tarot cards, the vehicle for divination should be treated with reverence and respect. Treat divination tools lightly or with disrespect and they will stop working for you.

A Set of Runes

When consulting the runes, you are consulting an Oracle rather than having your fortune told. An Oracle does not give you instructions for what to do next or predict your future. Instead, the runes put you in touch with your own inner guidance—the part of you that knows everything you need to know for your life now. They remind us that when you take a spiritual journey, you're always at the beginning.

Making your own set of runes helps to connect their energy to yours. Runes can be made out of almost anything. Try seashells, clay (dried or fired), glass, stones, wood, river pebbles, twigs, card stock, leather, ceramic, nuts, or bottle caps, for example.

The following directions are for a simple set of wooden runes, but let your imagination go when it comes to making your own set.

Here's what you'll need:

- ◆ A wooden dowel, 1 inch in diameter (or any scrap wood that will yield small round or square pieces of wood)
- ◆ Fine-bladed handsaw
- ◆ Sandpaper
- ◆ Wood-burning tool (or paint and a fine paintbrush)
- ◆ Varnish (optional)

Using the handsaw, slice the dowel into 25 rounds about ³/₈ inch thick. Smooth off any rough spots with the sandpaper.

Lightly sketch the rune symbols onto the wooden rounds with a pencil.

Starting with the first rune, burn a runic symbol into one of the rounds. Continue with each piece of wood until all 24 are done. (The 25th one will be blank.) Or paint the symbols onto the wood with a thin paintbrush and black paint or ink. Finish with a thin coat of clear varnish or shellac if desired.

The rune symbols and their meanings. Use this template to carve or paint your own set of runes as powerful talismans for divination in your spellwork.

Craftworking

Take time with each rune as you make it. Repeat its name out loud several times and take a moment to meditate on its meaning. You might want to start a journal, taking note of anything that comes to you during this creative process. Eventually you will turn this into your "rune-reading" journal.

Once your rune set is complete, purify it within a magick circle (see Chapter 18). You will want to buy or make a drawstring bag to carry your runes in. The bag will need to be large enough to insert your hand so you can pull a rune out of it easily. (You can adapt the directions for the talisman bag in Chapter 10.)

Carry the runes with you for the first week or so. Some people like to sleep with them under their pillow. Keeping them close to you further connects your energy to theirs. If you want to study rune reading, a good source is *Empowering Your Life with Runes* by Jean Marie Stine (Alpha Books, 2004).

Talking Boards

Although it's easy to buy a talking board such as Ouija board or find an animated board on the Internet (a great website is www.museumoftalkingboards.com), making your own is more satisfying. Though it may look like a game, a talking board is an intense spiritual gateway that must be highly respected. When given magickal uses, the talking board takes on even more serious purpose and power.

Here is a creative approach to making your own talking board and customizing it for your magickal intent. Create a board layout that is unique and compelling to *you*. Decorate it with magickal symbols, rune symbols, whatever deeply resonates for you in your practice of Wicca and spellcraft. The template we include in the directions for this project uses characters from the English language standard alphabet, but you can adapt this to use Theban script or some other magickal alphabet on your board if you like. Make more than one board!

Here's what you'll need:

♦ Pencil

♦ Heavy sheet of white paper

♦ Calligraphy pen and permanent ink

♦ Wide, soft paintbrush

♦ A cup of strong black tea (or coffee)

♦ Square antique frame, large enough to hold the paper

♦ Paint or varnish, if needed for frame

- Glass cleaner

- A small rune, crystal, or other special talisman

Planning the talking board's layout will be the most challenging part of this project. You will want to adapt the standard layout, or create a whole new layout, and this will require some strategy. You will want to take some basic measurements: the distance between letters, the shape of the arc, the height and width of the letters. You'll want to plan out on graph paper or in a sketchbook (or on the computer!) exactly how you'll want the letters, numbers, and words on your board laid out. As in all projects, don't strive for perfection. Some imperfections add to the charm of the finished board.

A talking board template. This is only one idea; create your own!

Using a pencil, lightly sketch the template onto the paper. Once you have it laid out, use your calligraphy pen to draw the letters, numbers, and symbols on using permanent ink. Let the paper dry for 24 hours.

Brew an extra strong cup of tea (or coffee). Dip the paint brush into the tea and gently swipe the mixture over the paper to create an aged parchment look. Laying a tea bag directly onto the paper creates an interesting blotchy pattern. Let the paper dry completely.

Widdershins

Before aging the final talking board paper that you've spent hours laying out and drawing—experiment! Use the same type of paper and ink and paint on some tea to make certain the letters won't smear. If they do, consider aging the paper before painting in the letters.

If the antique frame needs refinishing, do that next. Use paint or varnish and add any symbols that seem appropriate to you. If it's an attractive, ornate frame by itself, leave it alone.

Using vinegar and water or a commercial glass cleaner, clean the inside of the glass thoroughly. Make sure it is completely dry and that no smudges or fingerprints remain.

Lay the talking paper inside the frame. Use the rune stone, crystal, or other small talisman you've selected as your talking pointer. Be sure to purify the board and dedicate it to the Lord and Lady for good use only!

Divination Made Easy

Casting stones and scrying with a pentagram or pentacle are both easy ways to venture into the art of divination. Be on the lookout for crystals and stones that attract you.

Pentagram Oracle

Although you can make gathering up stones part of this project, because you need stones of specific colors, you might want to go to a New Age or metaphysical shop and buy them. However, found stones are just as effective.

Here's what you'll need:

- A 1-by-1-foot square of black cloth, preferably soft cotton or velvet
- White or silver textile paint

- Several stones of different colors depending on what areas of your life you want to explore:
  - Pink for affection and compassion
  - Brown for honesty and stability
  - Green for prosperity, employment, and luck
  - Black for absorbing negative energy
  - Orange for courage
  - White for intelligence and communication, insight, growth, and success

With textile paint, create a pentagram or pentacle in the center of your cloth. (For a pentagram, paint a five-pointed star; for a pentacle, paint a circle around the star.) It should be about half the size of your cloth. Label each of the five points of the star with the areas of your life: Home, Health, Work, Family, Relationships. If you have another area of your life that you know needs your attention, you can substitute it. Always keep your stones or crystals wrapped up in this cloth when not in use. Congratulations, you've made an oracle.

Purify the stones using saltwater, smoke, or moonlight, as described in Chapter 18.

> **Summon and Stir**
>
> Stones are especially sensitive to the energy of anyone who touches them. You will want to cleanse your divination stones often. Some witches prefer not to let anyone but themselves touch their stones or runes.

To use the oracle for divination, hold the stones in your right hand, feeling them and hearing them and concentrating on receiving whatever message the Goddess sends. Turn your hand down, facing the cloth and open it to let the stones fall. First look at any stones that fall in the middle. These are things that you need to manifest right now to avert difficulties in the near future. Any area the black stone lands on needs your special attention because the black stone warns of a place that has troubled or difficult energy. If a stone lands on the crossed juncture between two areas, apply it to both. Let the Goddess guide you in your interpretation.

The project we've given you creates a very simple oracle. For more sophisticated divination, you need to access your own magickal intuition and feel the deeper meanings to the stones and the pentacle points as they speak to the circumstances surrounding your life, your situation, and your magickal intent.

Pendulum Magick

Pendulums are simple to use and easy to make. Anything with a little weight to it, dangling from a thread, can be used as a pendulum. Some of the simplest designs are a threaded carpet needle or a heavy button on a string. The magick in this is what you and the Divine put into it, not the materials used. Even so, buttons and needles may seem a bit commonplace and dull. Here is an idea for making a pendulum you can impress your friends with.

Procure a small stone or crystal. Using three colors of Femo modeling compound, make three small ropes about 6 inches long. Pinch them together at one end and braid up about an inch. Anchor your stone into the braid and lay each rope alongside of your stone so that it is caged by the ropes. Begin braiding again until you have about 3 inches of braid from the top of your stone. Fold this braided line back onto itself to form a loop.

Forming a braided loop.

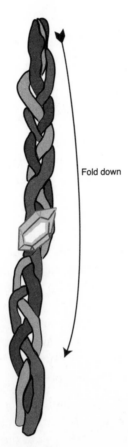

Fold down

Gently work with this loop to center it over your stone so that when suspended from a cord your pendulum hangs straight down. Now just follow the package directions for baking Femo. When it's baked hard, string your pendulum onto a soft cord the length that feels right to you.

Pendulums are easy to use. Slip the cord loop over your middle finger. You should use your dominant hand, right if you are right-handed, left if you are a lefty. Let the pendulum dangle free while holding your hand still with fingers extended. Ask the pendulum to show you what means yes. This may be a back and forth motion or it may be a circular clockwise motion. Also clarify what movement means no (this might be a circular counterclockwise motion), and what means unable to answer at this time. You can test this understanding between you and your pendulum by asking a simple question like, "Do I have a sister?" Once you and your pendulum are communicating well, you're ready to move on to other, more meaningful questions.

Craftworking

You can also use scrying with a pendulum to find lost objects. Make a layout of your house and state what it is you're looking for. Let the pendulum swing over the blueprint until it "lands" on a spot. Check in that area of your house for those missing car keys.

When asking a question for someone else, it is good to hold the pendulum over their hand which should be down-turned and resting on a flat surface. Begin with simple questions that can be answered yes, no, or unable to answer at this time.

Eventually you can move on to more complicated questions, but you'll have to communicate with your pendulum ahead of time. For example, you can get a time frame from a pendulum but you'll have to "agree" as to what each movement means: back and forth might mean "this month," circular rotation might mean "within the year." Or, if you're torn between two jobs, you and your pendulum can agree that one direction means one job and another direction means a second job. Just state your intentions and the "rules" out loud before you begin. These kinds of questions require you to be highly attuned to your pendulum. Practice is essential.

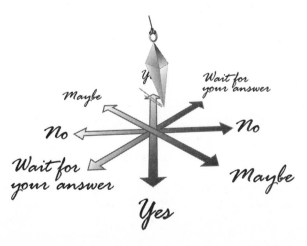

Magickal answers are available with the swing of a pendulum.

Tea Leaves and Tarots

Divination can be even easier than anything we've given you so far in this chapter. Rather than making a magickal divination tool, buy a set of Tarot cards or pour some tea. Either of these techniques is effective. And, remember, you can also make your own set of Tarot images, customized to the Wiccan symbols and images that speak most directly to you.

We've created our own High Priestess Tarot card to honor the Goddess energy of deep intuition and magickal insight.

A Tea Party with a Twist

Reading tea leaves is a simple and entertaining form of divination. It allows a great use of imagination and hunches. The reader has to interpret the shapes and forms that are made by tea leaves that remain after the tea has been drunk.

Use a cup that is white inside or any undecorated pastel teacup. The cup should be very wide at the top, the sides should slant, and the bottom shouldn't be too small. You might want to buy a special tea cup and saucer that you use only for divination purposes. Antique cups bring a lot of old energy and wisdom along with them. Look around until you find one you like.

Magickal Properties

A **tisane** is a beverage made by steeping tea or herbs in hot water. In France, a tisane was often made for medicinal purposes.

Use China tea or a very good grade of tea that has a minimum of tea dust. Make a *tisane* by brewing the loose tea in a teapot without a strainer so there are enough leaves in the cup for a reading.

The person whose fortune is to be read should drink the tea, leaving a little in the bottom of the cup. With the left hand, the reader should take hold of the handle and slowly swirl the cup around deosil (clockwise) three times. This should distribute the tea leaves around the sides of the cup, sometimes reaching the rim, and still have a few on the bottom. Turn the cup over onto the saucer to slowly dump out the last bit of tea. Study the shapes and position of the leaves that remain in the cup.

The timeline of events is determined by the parts of the cup. The rim represents the present or things that may happen within a few days or weeks. The sides predict the future. The bottom predicts the very distant future.

The handle of the cup represents the house or surroundings of the consultant; therefore the closer a symbol is in relation to the handle, the sooner the event may take place.

Numbers represent time such as minutes, hours, days, or weeks, depending upon the relationship to other symbols. Letters of the alphabet indicate people such as relatives, friends, or associates. The closer to the handle, the more important they are.

Wavy lines mean uncertainty. Straight lines mean plans will follow a pattern or definite course. Stars and triangles represent good fortune. Circles mean success. Squares represent protective energy.

Reading tea leaves, like any other divination, requires patience and practice and a lot of intuition. With time, the tea leaves will give up their secrets.

Group Tarot

Although traditional Tarot readings are meant to be given for one individual, throw a Tarot party and change the rules. Cast a circle, light a white candle and some incense. Shuffle the deck while everyone thinks of a question they want to ask the cards.

Have each covener pull a Tarot card and meditate on its meaning. Next, let each person in turn explain the symbolic meaning of the card, relate it to his or her own life, and choose an animal spirit that relates to the card.

This is a good way for everyone to become more familiar with the cards and their meanings.

> **Summon and Stir**
>
> Tarot cards are divided into Major Arcana cards (cards of karmic energy and intent) and Minor Arcana cards (cards of everyday endeavor in the mundane world). Tarot suits include Cups for emotion, creativity, and love; Wands for enterprise and wisdom; Swords for action and intellectual thought; and Pentacles for abundance.

Divination and Your Wiccan Ways

Although everyone would love to know what the future holds, it's important to remember that we can't know for certain. Wiccan tools like the ones described in this chapter can give you glimpses into the future, but they can't provide definitive answers. Let your intuition guide your readings. Divination is a combination of physical tools and spiritual insight and we should always leave open the possibility of change.

The Least You Need to Know

- Making your own divination tools helps charge them with your spirit.

- The future is not set in stone. Reading the future simply means looking at a series of possibilities.

- Don't make dire predictions about the future. Try to present the reading as positive actions to take.

- Treat your divination tools with respect and not as parlor games to entertain your friends.

Add the Power of Stones and Crystals

In This Chapter

- ◆ Drawing positive magick through crystal energy
- ◆ Ancient magickal wisdom through stones
- ◆ A mosaic box to hold magickal tools
- ◆ Wicca meets Zen!

As a general rule, stones stabilize while crystals energize. Stones and crystals communicate in subtle ways. Because they are so old, their energy is very slow. You might want to spend some time holding them and meditating until you feel as though they are communicating with you.

Working with stones and crystals in your practice of Wicca should be a very rich sensory experience. Remember to enjoy the feel and sound as well as the look of the rocks and gems you use in your Craft. Try to understand the spirit of a stone before using it.

Crystal Energy

Adding crystals to your house, altar, or magickal tools is a way to give added energy to your spells and rituals. Crystals keep positive energy in while repelling or banishing negative energy. Purify your crystals often using smoke, incense, saltwater, or moonlight. Purifying the crystals keeps their positive energy flowing.

Energize Your Household with a Crystal Mobile

This eye-catching mobile is great to hang in a window or outside on a tree branch. The combination of wood and crystal is soothing and energizing at the same time. Driftwood is a good choice for this project; or use a saw and cut your discs from a branch 3 to 4 inches in diameter. The discs should be $1/2$ inch thick.

Here's what you'll need:

- Four disclike pieces of wood approximately 3 inches in diameter and $1/2$ inch thick
- Drill
- Hot-glue gun and glue
- Six glass or clay beads
- Four clear, smooth stones or crystals such as rose quartz or carnelian
- Jute twine
- A branch or dowel 1 inch in diameter and 12 inches long

Craftworking

Remember to ask the tree's permission before you take a branch or use one already on the ground. Thank the tree for its gift.

Using your drill, put two holes in each disc of wood, one slightly larger than the diameter of the stone to fit into it, the other hole just large enough to thread twine through.

Run a line of hot glue around the perimeter of the larger hole and carefully seat your stone inside. Repeat this with each wooden disk.

Drill six small holes in your dowel with the holes at the ends being 1 inch in from the end of the dowel. The other holes should be evenly spaced along the dowel.

Take 2 feet of twine and put one end through one of the end holes on the dowel. Tie one of your beads onto the end of twine to secure the line on the dowel. Do the same thing with the other end. You now have a stick with a line to hang it with.

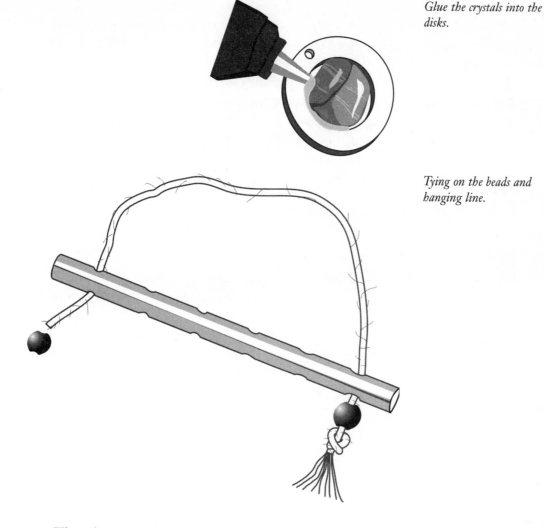

Glue the crystals into the disks.

Tying on the beads and hanging line.

Thread a piece of twine through the small hole of each wooden disc and tie securely. The other end of the twine should be threaded through the dowel holes and secured with beads.

You may want to experiment with different lengths of twine for each disc. The heaviest stone and wood discs should be toward the outside for better balance.

Add Some Crystal Magick to a Tool

Although we've given you lots of suggestions for making tools, we haven't said too much about adding appropriate crystals to them for extra energy.

Take the broom you made in Chapter 12. Once you have it completed, chisel a hole in the very top of the handle wide enough to seat a crystal inside. Using your hot-glue gun, glue the crystal firmly in place. For this tool, onyx works well, giving the broom an "eye" that provides protection from all negativity, magickal or otherwise. For other tools, use whatever crystal seems appropriate.

As always, use your own intuition about what stones or gems to use. Here is a partial list of stones and their magickal properties that will give you some general suggestions. Add them to your tools as it strikes your fancy.

Stones and Their Magickal Correspondences

Stone	Magickal Correspondence
Amethyst	Draws peace of mind, justice, wisdom, and calm
Coral	Draws love, romance, and protection
Emerald	Draws health, happiness, and joy
Jade	Draws wealth, wisdom, and courage; it also repels negative energies
Jasper	Protects against troubles of the mind and unpleasant entities from any realm
Lapis lazuli	Draws protection, psychic power, and clairvoyance
Malachite	Acts as a bridge between the worlds; a great healing stone
Moonstone	Draws peace of mind and banishes fear
Obsidian	Grants vision and aids in directing magickal energies
Onyx	Protection from all negativity, magickal or otherwise
Quartz	Grants clarity and understanding
Turquoise	Grants protection and health; draws wealth and happiness

As we've said, it doesn't matter whether you purchase your stones or find them in the wild, or use a mixture of both. Be sure to clean any rocks you find outside very well with soap and water before using them in a project and before purifying them for magickal use.

Stone-Cold Magick

The energy in stones is "quieter" than in many crystals. Use them to ground and stabilize an object.

A Mosaic Box

Make a box with a mosaic of stones glued to the top of the lid. This box is the perfect place to store your Tarot cards in between use. Just make sure you measure your deck of cards so they fit inside easily once you've completed the box. Of course, you can store any ritual or magickal tool of importance to you in this special place.

All of the wood used in this project is $1/4$ inch thick.

Here's what you'll need:

- Hot-glue gun and glue
- Two pieces of wood $3^3/4$ by $1^1/2$ inches (box ends)
- Two pieces of wood 6 by $1^1/2$ inches (box sides)
- Two pieces of wood $3^3/4$ by $3/4$ inches (box lid ends)
- Two pieces of wood 6 by $3/4$ inches (box lid sides)
- Two pieces of wood 6 by 4 inches (box bottom and lid top)
- Two pieces of wood $1/8$ inch thick, 4 by $3/4$ inches (stops for lid)
- Paint and a small paintbrush
- Felt to line the box lid (optional)
- A variety of stones and crystals—look for ones that are somewhat flat or have at least one flat side

Using the hot-glue gun, run a line of glue around all four edges of the box bottom. Set the box ends in place first. Run another strip of glue down the side edges. Press the box sides into place.

Repeat this same procedure for the box lid. Once the lid has dried, turn it upside down and glue the wooden stops flat against the inside of the box lid's ends. This produces a small ridge at either end so the lid can't slide off.

Let the glue dry thoroughly. Paint the box a color that appeals to you and let it dry 24 hours. Line the box lid by gluing a piece of felt to the inside top if desired.

CAUTION

Widdershins

It's best not to start gluing until you have all of the stones in place. Once you fix them permanently, you're stuck—no pun intended. In fact, it's a good idea to live with your final pattern for a day or two before you glue. This gives you some time to change your mind.

Now, the fun begins—laying out your stones and crystals. Taking your lid top, begin to make a pattern with your stones. Don't become locked into a plan. Remember to let the stones find their own places on the lid. When you have a design you like—there will always be some of the lid's top showing through—glue them into place using your hot-glue gun.

If you plan to use this box to hold your Tarot cards, wrap the cards in a piece of silk, which helps keep negativity and harmful energy out and also keeps your cards psychically clean. Put the lid on and place the box on your altar.

An Indoor Rock Garden

A Zen garden is not traditionally Wiccan, but it is a great way to display stones or crystals that have meaning for you and to bring their energies into your living space. Simplicity is the keyword when creating a Zen garden. Remember not to overdo it.

Here's what you'll need:

+ A large shallow bowl (Traditional Zen bowls are square or rectangular, but round bowls are more Wiccan; choose a shape that suits you.)

+ Enough sand to fill the bowl half to three quarters full (White sand is traditional, but if you live near a beach, local sand helps you better connect with your own environment.)

+ A collection of stones and crystals you have found or otherwise acquired; these should be of different shapes and sizes, but all small enough to fit into the palm of your hand

+ A fork, a spoon, and a small paintbrush

Craftworking

If you aren't familiar with Zen gardens, you might want to investigate them before choosing a bowl. Shallow is key here. Learn the technique before you commit to a bowl.

Fill the bowl with sand and smooth it out as much as possible with the spoon, trying not to leave any lines in the sand at all.

One by one, hold each stone or crystal in your hand, meditating on its magickal correspondences and its meaning for you. Choose which stones you will use but try not to have more than five or six. These can be stones you've found on a hike or ones that you've purchased that are already polished and clean. Carefully place the stones in a pattern that feels right for you. Brush excess sand from the base of the stones with your paintbrush. You can use the fork for making decorations in the sand like a rake.

Remember, this is a meditative process. Take your time. If you aren't satisfied, just remove the stones and start over. Change your design often, using different stones and different patterns. Your garden is a metaphor for your life, physical and spiritual. Use stones that represent what you want to manifest. Don't clutter your garden with too many rocks, and let change and flow be a part of your gardening process.

An example of a Zen pattern.

An Easier Display

Another way to display stones that are meaningful to you is to buy a small bowl, pile your stones into a pleasing pattern and place them on your altar to represent Earth or north.

Just like in the Zen garden, meditate on each stone as you place it into the bowl and rotate them often. As we said in Chapter 7, altars need to be tended lovingly. Don't allow the stones to become dust-covered. And make spiritually cleansing them part of your regular routine.

> **CAUTION**
>
> **Widdershins**
>
> If you have small children or cats, a Zen garden may not be the best project for you unless you have a closed display cabinet to keep it in. Otherwise, it's a tempting sandbox!

The Least You Need to Know

◆ Crystals provide added energy, while stones generally provide a stabilizing influence. Use your own intuition when choosing them, as usual.

◆ Stone and crystal energy is slow. Great patience is needed to strike up a communication with this energy.

◆ Purifying crystals and stones often keeps their positive energy flowing and keeps negative energy out.

◆ Stones and crystals can be found objects or purchased at a store.

Part 6

Witches' Brew: Notions, Potions, and Powders

Are you picturing a trio of witches bent over a bubbling cauldron? It's oh, so much easier. Learn how to purify and cleanse, consecrate and dedicate your ritual tools, including your most important, unique, and special tool for working magick: *you!* We'll give you recipes to create soothing and energizing baths, potions to celebrate the Wheel of the Year, herb combinations to honor specific deities, lotions to attract positive energy, and scents to purify your living space.

Chapter 18

Cleansing and Purifying

In This Chapter

- ◆ Ritual baths for your body temple
- ◆ Chakra alignment to promote harmonic resonance
- ◆ Making tools and sacred spaces ready for ritual
- ◆ Charging a tool to give it extra magickal power

Removing negative energy and replacing it with positive vibes is at the heart of the Wiccan religion. Cleansing means to purify, and cleansing makes a person, place, or object free of negative feelings and energies. There are probably as many ways to cleanse magickal objects and rooms as there are magickal practitioners.

If these cleansing and purifying rituals don't seem quite right to you, feel free to make up your own. Remember, it's the intent that counts, not the words you say. Let's begin by looking at ways to cleanse and purify your most important magickal tool: *you!*

First Cleanse the Body

A person takes a ritual bath for one of two reasons: to cleanse away negative energy and emotion or to prepare for a specific magickal working. When a cleansing bath is needed, the practitioner should set up the bath area with symbols, scents, and colors that call in tranquility and self-love.

Take a Ritual Bath

Begin by lighting candles. The candles should be pink for love and affection, white for protection and health, or light blue for peace and calm as well as for increasing the psychic energy flow. A clear piece of quartz and a rose quartz crystal should be placed in the tub, preferably one at either end. Clear quartz is for clarity of vision and purpose as well as to increase the magickal vibrations. Rose quartz is for self-love and developing inner strength in general.

If you find music soothing, put on a CD or tape. Just make certain the music isn't jangling your nerves.

Add a tablespoon or two of prepared bath salts, an herbal sachet, and plenty of positive affirmations. Here's a suggestion for some fragrant bath salts that will dispel negative energy.

- ♦ $^1/_2$ cup of sea salt
- ♦ 4 drops of myrrh oil
- ♦ 6 drops of lavender oil
- ♦ 9 drops of food coloring (5 blue, 4 green)

Mix all ingredients well and let sit in the bathroom near or in the tub for three hours before using.

You can also make an herbal sachet for the bath. Putting herbs directly into the bath water, though aesthetically pleasing, makes cleanup more difficult and can cause big plumbing problems. It's better to place the herbs in an old, clean knee-high stocking, a nylon stocking, or one of those cotton tea bags found at tea shops or health-food stores. In your bag or stocking put any combination of the following herbs or flowers:

Herb	Significance
Hyssop	Repels negativity and purifies
Lavender blossoms	Draws love and lifts spirits and calms
Mugwort	Cleanses and grants prophetic dreams
Rose petals	Encourages love of self and others
Sage	Provides protection and wisdom

Herb	Significance
Spearmint	Provides mental acuity
Valerian	Encourages protection and calm
Vervain	Dispels bad energy and evil spirits
Vetiver	Attracts material wealth and fortune
Willow	Attracts love and health, dispels evil
Wintergreen	Provides protection and removes hexes

Floating just a few rose petals on the top of the water is very luxurious and won't take too much cleanup. Just make sure you take them out of the water before you empty the tub.

Shower Away Your Troubles

If you don't have a bathtub or don't like taking baths, you can still do a ritual cleansing. Set the stage with candles and soft music as suggested for the ritual bath. Pick a luxurious soap that you save only to use for this ritual shower. Make sure the fragrance is one that is soothing to you—lavender is a good choice. Starting at your shoulders, sweep down your arms with a loofah or natural sponge, then down your body, down your legs until you get to your toes. Picture all the negative things causing stress in your life rinsing off your body and floating down the drain. Stand for an extra minute while the water rinses over you. Take deep breaths and let yourself relax. Now you're ready to ground yourself for magick making.

Grounding by Cleansing Your Chakras

Because it's not a good idea to try spellcasting or performing rituals while you're feeling listless or out of sorts, it's important to cleanse your spirit as well as your body. Keeping your energy centers or *chakras* in balance is one way to promote the flow of positive magickal energy through your body, mind, and spirit.

Chakras are the openings for life energy to flow into and out of our aura. They help to vitalize the physical body and to bring about the development of our self-consciousness.

Magickal Properties

The word **chakra** is derived from the Sanskrit word meaning "wheel." If we were able to see the seven major chakras (as many psychics, in fact, do), we would see wheels of energy continuously rotating.

The seven chakra energy centers channel magickal energy through your body.

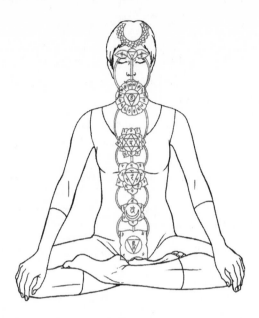

Lie down in a comfortable place—beds are good, or a patch of soft grass works if you want to perform this ritual outdoors. Or sit in meditative pose like the woman in our chakra illustration. Breathe deeply and evenly throughout the meditation. Begin by closing your eyes and visualizing a red light entering into the base of your spine. This is your root chakra, which helps you connect to the earth. It brings your spiritual body in alignment with your physical body. If you're feeling "spaced out," it might be that this chakra is out of balance.

Next, visualize an orange light entering your navel. This is your sacral chakra that helps you to maintain a healthy yin-yang existence and to keep balance in your life.

The solar plexus chakra is associated with the color yellow. Picture a soft yellow light entering your solar plexus. This intuitive chakra defines your self-esteem and is where you get your "gut-level" feelings to do something or to not do something.

Next picture a green light entering your heart. The heart chakra is, not surprisingly, the love center of the human energy system. Learning to love yourself as well as others is a healing power for this chakra.

The throat chakra is associated with the color sky blue. This chakra is your will center. We have all experienced that "lump in our throats" when we are at a crossroads of not knowing how to speak the right words in any given situation, perhaps even stuffing our own emotions. A challenge of the throat chakra is to express yourself in the most truthful manner and to seek out the truth.

By now you should feel very relaxed. Picture an indigo light entering your forehead. This is your brow chakra or your third eye. Your ability to separate reality from fantasy depends on this chakra. Balance in this chakra helps you avoid small-mindedness.

Finally, picture a violet light entering the crown of your head. The crown chakra allows you to communicate with your spiritual nature. It is from this chakra that the life force comes out of the universe into the other six chakras.

Once you have visualized the light from all seven chakras entering your body, picture a bright white light streaming down through the top of your head and into the ground from your feet. Say something like the following:

> *Dissolve all negativity, restore my balance, improve my energy, and open my chakras. Allow me to be compassionate, understanding, and loving to myself and others. May I speak with truth and be open to the natural positive energy of the universe, of the All.*

Purifying Tools for Rituals

Once you've cleansed your spiritual and physical body, it's time to purify the tools you will be using, many of which you will have made using the projects in this book! Again, take these rituals as suggestions for consecrating any tool you plan on using, but make them your own by adding language or magickal ingredients that are meaningful or appropriate to your purpose and intent.

Consecrating an Athame

An athame may be consecrated using thistles, nettles, hawthorne, or holly. Note the prickly nature of all of these plants. There are a couple of reasons for using them. The first reason is these plants are sacred to the God and in their sharpness represent his horns and the ability to cut a doorway from one reality to another. The second reason is that these plants have for centuries symbolized chastity, purity, and faithfulness. Given that a knife has a high potential for becoming a weapon and your athame is *not* a weapon, these plants evoke faithfulness to one's magickal mission for his or her blade.

> **CAUTION Widdershins**
>
> Be sure to wear gloves when dealing with these prickly plants. They can cause very uncomfortable rashes in addition to embedding sharp thorns in a thumb.

Make an *infusion* of nettle or thistle to anoint your athame. You may wash it all over while concentrating on your intent to purify and consecrate it. Burn a little bit of

Magickal Properties

An **infusion** is basically a tea. When making an infusion of wood or roots, the plant material should steep for at least 10 minutes. Leaves and stems can steep for five minutes. Let the liquid cool to a safe temperature before using it to cleanse your tools.

holly or hawthorne and pass your blade through the sacred smoke, bathing it in this energy as well. Say your words of dedication:

> *Gift of the God, I consecrate this athame and dedicate its blade to the Lord and Lady and in my service to the Lord and the Lady.*

Once the leaves have burned completely, extinguish your flame. Dry the athame blade carefully with a natural-fiber cloth and place it on your altar or sheathe it until you are ready to use it magickally.

Dispelling Negative Energy

Let's say a person you don't particularly like gave you a pentagram ring that you *do* like. You want the ring to be cleansed of negative energy, dedicated to Craft service (presuming you want to wear it while doing Wicca work), and charged with extra zing to make it a working magickal tool. We use this example here, but you can use these steps to prepare *any* magickal tool for spellcraft or ritual use.

The first step requires no more of you than a plot of land, a hand spade, and a clear sandwich bag with a zipper-type seal. Go to your bit of land, seal your ring (or whatever tool you desire) in the bag and bury it in the earth for three days. Say these words as you bury the tool and again three days later when you dig it up:

> *Into the tomb,*
> *then from the mother's womb,*
> *bring forth the Divine.*
> *Leave negatives behind.*

Pretty simple, eh?

Dedicating an Object to the Lady and Lord

Now you want to dedicate your ring (or whatever tool you desire) to make it a meaningful part of your Wiccan practice. Cast a sacred circle or in some other way create your sacred space. Take a moment to sit and feel the energy of the Earth and of your own body. Feel yourself empowered, because you are. Touch your ring (or other tool) to your heart area, then your forehead, and then hold it to the sky with both hands and say:

Gift of the Goddess, gift of the Earth, ring of power (or _____ *of power,* whatever the object is), *I dedicate you to the work of the Lord and the Lady, and to my service in the practice of Wicca.*

Abracadabra, the thing is done, or in Wicca words, *as above, so below, so mote it be!*

Charging Your Ritual Tool for an Added Zing

The only thing left to do before you can use your ring (or other ritual tool) for mag-ick is to charge it. Charging a magickal tool is giving it a jolt of energy to enliven it and ready it for your work together. It's a psychic boost. A common practice is to charge an object by setting it out on a mirror on a raised surface to soak in the Full Moon's light and energy. Another quick way is to hold your magick tool up to the sun and reflect the sunlight into your eye, holding it there until you feel it is well and truly charged. The method you chose depends on the nature and future use of the rit-ual tool you want to charge.

Let's go back to your magickal pentagram ring. On the night of the Full Moon, take your ring outside and cast a circle to create sacred space. Hold your ring in your right hand and lift it up so you look at the ring with the moon as a backdrop. Lower your left hand so your palm is facing forward and your fingers are extended toward the ground. Say to yourself and your ring:

> *I am a channel of energy pulsing up from the Earth and down from the sky. Let this ring be filled and charged from the Earth, from the sky, from my hand, and by my will. So mote it be.*

Be sure to take the time to feel empowered. Don't rush. When you feel the time is right, thank the Goddess and God, put your ring on your finger, open your circle, and go inside where it is warm and cozy.

Summon and Stir

When Liguana got her first athame she cleansed it but didn't dedicate it. She planned to participate in a Summer Solstice ritual but a priest stopped her and told her no blade could be brought into circle unless it was dedicated and charged. She drew her athame out of her belt and held it to her mouth. "I charge you with the holy breath of a priestess of Wicca," she said. "And I dedicate you to the work of Lady and Lord and to my practice of Wicca." She held the blade up to the sun. Into circle she went with her new cleansed, dedicated, and charged ritual tool.

Purifying a Ritual Space

So, you've cleansed yourself and your tools, now you might want to cleanse a room, a house, a backyard, or just a small corner space.

A Simple Cleansing Ritual

Whether you want to purify a room or an entire house, it can be as easy as using the broom you made in Chapter 12. Sweep widdershins (counterclockwise) from the center of the room outward in a circle while chanting:

> *Sweep, sweep, sweep the floor.*
> *Sweep the badness out the door.*

Purifying with the Elements

State your intention of cleansing and blessing your home or a particular room. You may wish to invoke the powers of whatever god, goddess, or other divine beings you work with to assist you in your efforts.

Begin by lighting a white candle and going to your front door if purifying your entire house, or to the door of the particular room you are concentrating on. Meditate on the purifying quality of the element of Fire and move deosil (clockwise) from the door around the inside perimeter of the house, moving room to room deosil. As you move, visualize the flame transforming and purifying any negative energy in a positive and life-affirming way.

When you reach a stairway, proceed to that floor and again move in a deosil direction. Continue to move deosil through the home until you return to your front door. Take a bowl or chalice of water which has been combined with sea salt. Start again at the front door. Sprinkle the water-salt mixture lightly while meditating on the positive qualities of the elements of Earth and Water—stability and intuition. Proceed again in a deosil manner throughout the house until you return again to the front door.

Now proceed in the same manner beginning at the front door with burning incense—sandalwood is a good choice of fragrances. Meditate on the positive qualities of the Air element—mental clarity, alertness, and clear communication—as you move clockwise through the home.

Your home has now been cleansed and balanced through the use of the four elements. You may wish to further protect your home by psychically tracing a protective

pentagram with your athame at any openings like doors or windows. You may meditate on the idea that any energy that enters your home will be transformed through
the symbol into a positive force within your space.

Smudge Away Negativity

Smudging is a purification technique with Native American origins. It has been
embraced by other Earth-honoring spiritual paths and basically is the burning of specific sacred plants for their cleansing and purifying properties. The most common
herb to use is sage, but cedar, pine, juniper, sweetgrass, and lavender are also sometimes used.

Though as we said, smudge sticks are not traditionally Wiccan, many American
Wiccans use them in their practice. Here is an easy method of making one for yourself.

Here's what you'll need:

 ◆ Any or all of the following: cedar, wild sage (*not* culinary sage), juniper, rosemary,
   lavender, sweetgrass

 ◆ Embroidery thread

Make a bundle of your chosen plants about 1 to 2 inches thick and 6 to 8 inches long.
If using lavender, put it in the center surrounded by the other herbs. You don't want
tiny purple flowers to dust your floor while trying to cleanse the place!

Take a long piece of embroidery thread and use one end of it to tie your stems
together. Wrap the thread around your bundle several times at the base, then spiral
the thread upward around the herbs. When you get to the top, spiral back to the
stem end and tie the thread off securely. Repeat this process with another piece of
embroidery thread to secure your bundle extra well. Trim off excess stems and foliage
to make it neat; just don't cut your thread.

Craftworking

Red and white seem to be common thread colors when making a ritual smudge
stick. Wiccans choose colors based on magickal properties, or on what feels
right at the time, or for the specific magickal purpose. As you are wrapping your
smudge stick, remember that knots and crosses draw in and hold energy. Your
threads will cross each other many times. A smudge stick is a very powerful tool!

Choose embroidery thread for your smudge stick that resonates to your magickal purpose.

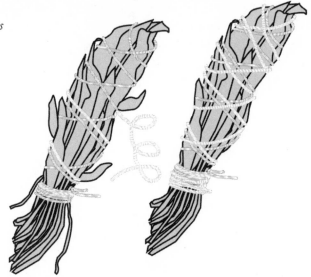

Smudging is as simple as lighting the bundle and letting the smoke drift over the object, person, or space to be cleansed A smudging fan or broom can be used to help direct the smoke throughout an area or over the body to prepare for ritual work or the cleansing of a sacred space.

Cleansing and purifying objects and spaces is an important part of Wiccan ritual. Whether you use smoke, incense, water, or moonlight, consecrating your tools and dedicating them to the Lady and Lord produce more powerful magick.

The Least You Need to Know

♦ The most vital, magickal ritual tool you possess is *you!* Take time to cleanse and purify your body, mind, and spirit before doing magickal workings.

♦ In doing group ritual, some priests and priestesses require all magickal tools to be properly cleansed, dedicated, and charged before they can be used for magick.

♦ When cleansing and purifying, choose magickal ingredients such as incense, herbs, crystals, and colors that are appropriate, but that also have special significance and personal meaning to you.

♦ Smudge sticks are powerful magickal tools for cleansing and purifying anything from your own body to magickal tools to sacred spaces.

Chapter 19

Potable Potions

In This Chapter

- ◆ Potions for every season in the Wheel of the Year
- ◆ Natural energy boosters to enhance Goddess power
- ◆ Giving thanks to the God
- ◆ Celebrate with special concoctions

The interesting magick about mixing and brewing potable potions is this: You can drink them. The magick becomes a part of *you*.

This chapter will give you lots of recipes for potable potions. Any of these potions can be used during ritual to salute the Lord and Lady or to begin or end a ceremony. They are also just fun to serve at a coven gathering or an esbat or sabbat celebration—perfect to serve while reveling at a Beltane spring fling or to enjoy before Mabon's hearty harvest fire.

Chilled Potions for Warm-Weather Celebrations

There's nothing better on a warm day than kicking back in a shady spot and enjoying an ice-cold drink served in a frosty glass. During the spring and summer while fresh fruits and vegetables are plentiful, they provide the basis for some lovely chilled potions for summer coven gatherings and summer solstice celebrations. Remember that using fresh ingredients enhances the magickal properties of your potion and is highly preferable.

A Fancy Ostara Cocktail

Special occasions call for spectacular libations. When done correctly, this is a lovely layered drink—very festive-looking and yummy, too. This is the perfect potion to raise the magickal energies of an Ostara spring equinox celebration. The following recipe makes one drink.

◆ Nonalcoholic grenadine

◆ 1 whole pink grapefruit

◆ 1 lime

◆ Tonic water

◆ Lemon wedge and maraschino cherry for garnish (optional)

Craftworking

Prior to serving, rinse your 8-ounce glasses in cold water and, without drying them, place them in a freezer. Within a half an hour you will have frosty, chilled glasses in which to serve drinks to your guests.

Widdershins

Some grenadines contain low amounts of alcohol; check the label and choose a nonalcoholic brand if there will be children or teens in the group, or if members of your group don't drink alcohol. It's not a good idea to mix alcohol and magickal workings; you want to be focused and clear if you intend to do rituals or perform spellcraft at your Ostara celebration.

Pour a shot of nonalcoholic grenadine into an 8-ounce glass. Add four ice cubes.

Juice both halves of the grapefruit. Holding the glass at a slant, slowly add the juice.

Cut the lime in half. Cut one half into four wedges to use as garnish. With a zester, scrape the peel from the uncut half into fine strips. Sprinkle them into the glass. Squeeze the juice from the lime half and slowly pour it into the glass.

Tilt the glass and fill it to the top with tonic. Garnish with a wedge of lime, a wedge of lemon, and a maraschino cherry if desired.

The key to this drink is to pour slowly so you serve the drink in layers. Let the guests stir the layers together before they drink this delightful Ostara potion.

Elderberry Flower Syrup for the Goddess

A lovely way to save summer's bounty is to preserve its flowers in a syrup. Elderberry shrubs bloom with fragrant white blossoms in early summer and when steeped in sugar and lemon juice create a tart, refreshing syrup. The elderberry tree is very sacred to the Goddess. It is said to attract faeries and it's considered bad luck to cut an elderberry tree down. This recipe makes approximately two cups of syrup.

- 2½ cups water

- 1 cup sugar

- 6 clusters of elderberry flowers

- 2 lemons

- 2 tsp. citric acid (sold in the canning or kosher section of the grocery store; also called sour salt)

Craftworking

To gather the elderberry flowers, look for clusters where all of the blooms have opened. Pick them in the early morning. If you don't know anyone who has an elderberry bush, the blossoms can sometimes be purchased in gourmet food stores or floral shops.

Make a simple syrup by combining the water and sugar in a heavy saucepan. Bring it to a boil, stirring frequently to dissolve the sugar.

Wash the flowers and pat them dry with paper towels. Add them to the syrup and boil gently for 10 minutes. Remove from the heat.

Using a vegetable peeler, peel the lemons in a spiral, cutting only the yellow peel and avoiding the white, bitter pith. Add the peel to the syrup and let it steep along with the flowers for five hours.

Squeeze the juice from the two lemons and set it aside. Once the syrup has steeped for five hours, strain the syrup through a fine sieve. Press the flowers and the peels with the back of a spoon to remove all of the liquid.

Strain the lemon juice to remove any pulp and mix in the citric acid. Whisk the mixture into the syrup until well blended.

Pour the syrup into a decorative bottle and, if desired, add a fresh cluster of flowers. Refrigerate and use within four weeks.

Use the syrup to make a refreshing Midsummer solstice potion. Mix a half-glass of orange juice, half-glass of club soda, and elderberry syrup to taste. Pour over ice. Or use some of the syrup to sweeten fresh lemonade. Garnish with a wedge of lemon or lime. This syrup can also be used over ice cream or pancakes, to marinate fish, or in a fruit compote. Use it anywhere you need a little magickal summer sweetness.

Nature's Bounty: Fruit Smoothies to Boost Your Magickal Energy

As the summer days drift by, fruit trees give up their bounty until there's almost more of nature's magick available for your potable potions than you know what to do with.

Whipping up a cold fruit smoothie makes a nutritious potion loaded with vitamins and natural magickal power that connects you to nurturing Earth energy and the Goddess. This recipe makes one pitcher.

- 1 lb. of very ripe fruit (try peaches, nectarines, apricots, melons, or a combination)

- ²/₃ cup coconut milk (*not* cream of coconut)

- 2 cups buttermilk

- 1–2 TB. sugar to taste, if desired

Wash and cube the fruit and place in a blender. Add the coconut milk, buttermilk, and sugar if you're using it. Blend until smooth.

Strain the mixture into a pitcher and refrigerate until chilled. Stir well before serving.

Fruit drinks are an excellent choice to use in honoring the Goddess because it is through her that the Earth element feeds us. Cast a magick circle outdoors (see Chapter 8). Have everyone inside the circle lay a symbol of themselves on the altar. Then, raise a glass as the priestess says:

> *Honored Lady, we thank you for the earth's bounty;*
> *may we remember to use it wisely, share it generously,*
> *and protect it fiercely.*

Remember to thank the Goddess and God for attending.

Warm Potions to Chase Away the Chill

If your idea of a hot beverage is a cup of coffee or some powdered "just-add-water" cocoa, try one of these chill chasers instead. Imbibing warm brews adds spark to cold-weather coven gatherings, rituals, and sabbat celebrations.

Hot Buttered Cider

There are as many hot cider recipes as there are fall leaves. When the Samhain bonfires have died down, bring the crowd indoors for this delicious holiday potion. Cinnamon corresponds magickally to success and prosperity; nutmeg to fidelity, luck, and psychic intuition; and cloves to protection and strength. There's a reason this drink is appropriate to the season—you'll want a little success, foresight, and strength as you prepare for winter!

For the spice mixture:

♦ $\frac{1}{4}$ cup unsalted butter

♦ 2 cups light brown sugar

♦ $\frac{1}{4}$ tsp. each ground cinnamon, nutmeg, allspice, and cloves

♦ 1 cup apple cider per person

♦ Cinnamon stick, optional for garnish

Before the party, cream together the butter, brown sugar, and spices. Refrigerate. (This mixture keeps almost indefinitely—not that you'll need to worry about that once people taste how good it is!)

To make the drinks, heat the apple cider just to the boiling point, but don't allow it to boil. For each serving, put 1 rounded tablespoon of the butter mixture, or to taste, in a mug. Pour in hot apple cider and stir well. Garnish with a cinnamon stick, if desired.

Gingered Citrus Tea

There's nothing like a hot cup of tea among friends on a cold afternoon. Or throw a tea party for the children in your life. Add little tea cakes, some pretty china dishes, and finish up with one of the child-friendly projects from this book. Ginger corresponds to love, power, and success. That'll wake up your winter magick!

Wash and peel one orange and one lemon. Cut the peel into very small pieces and place on a cookie sheet. Next, cut about 1 teaspoon of fresh ginger slivers. Add them to the cookie sheet and place the peels and the ginger in a 250°F oven until dried. This will take one or two hours. Mix the citrus and ginger with 4 ounces of any loose-leaf black tea.

> **Craftworking**
>
> At Yule time, this blend of tea makes a nice gift for any tea drinkers. Buy a pretty tea cup and saucer, put a transparent bag of tea inside, tie a tea ball to the handle with a bow, and presto! A gift of magickal love.

Transfer the mixture to transparent bags and tie with ribbon. To use, pour boiling water over 1 teaspoon of the blend and let steep for three to five minutes.

Cocoa with a Magickal Kick

In those dark February days when spring still seems like a long way away, sweeten up a Candlemas celebration with some hot chocolate. The cinnamon brings healing, prosperity, love, intuition, and success. This makes approximately four mugs of cocoa.

- ¼ cup unsweetened cocoa powder
- ¼ cup sugar
- ½ tsp. ground cinnamon
- ⅛ teaspoon salt
- ½ cup water
- 3½ cups milk
- 1½ tsp. vanilla extract
- 4 sticks cinnamon

In a saucepan over moderate heat, add the cocoa, sugar, ground cinnamon, salt, and water. Cook five minutes or until mixture is smooth.

Pour in the milk, reduce heat to low, and simmer for five minutes or until hot. Stir in the vanilla extract.

Using a hand blender or mixer, whip the hot chocolate until foamy. Place a cinnamon stick in each mug and pour in the hot chocolate.

More Potent Brews

For adult-only social get-togethers and holiday celebrations, a touch of wine or liqueur can be a festive addition. Try one of these more potent potables to end ritual celebrations with the traditional cakes and wine. Once again, remember that your magickal workings should be done with clarity of mind, body, and spirit. Save alcoholic beverages for *after* your magick is done. You want your rituals and spellcraft to actually *work*, right?

Spiced Wine

Wine and rum—nectar of the God. This is just the beverage to use to toast the God after ritual, too. Or plan a Candlemas (Imbolc) gathering with a pitcher of warm wine as the centerpiece. This recipe makes one pitcher.

- Peel from half of a lemon and half of an orange
- Fresh ginger, about the size of a half dollar and peeled
- 1 cinnamon stick
- 5 cloves

- ◆ 2 star anise

- ◆ 1 bottle of red wine

- ◆ ½ cup water

- ◆ ½ cup sugar

Widdershins

Do not substitute ground spices for whole or fresh spices when a recipe calls for them. They will not provide the same flavor and you will wind up with spice residue in the bottom of your glasses.

Put the lemon and orange peel and all of the spices into the center of a square of cheesecloth and tie it into a small bag. Pour the wine, water, and sugar into a pan and hang the bag over the side. Heat slowly over very low heat. Do not boil!

Before serving, remove the bag. Serve warm. If you have any left over, which isn't likely, refrigerate and use it within two weeks.

Earlier in this chapter we toasted the Lady; now we need to give equal time to the Lord. Build a bonfire, cast your circle, perform your ritual, and once the ritual and spellwork is done but before pulling down the circle, have each guest pour a mug of wine. Raise your glasses while the priestess says:

> *Honored Lord, we thank you for bringing into our circle your strength and your wisdom. May we use both to choose the right, to speak the truth, and to protect our family and our friends.*

Cherry Cordial for Cakes and Wine

Witches operate under nature's bountiful "waste not, want not" principle. Have you ever found yourself with a cherry tree loaded with fruit and no time to use them in complicated recipes? Cherries attract love and friendship. Turn them into a tasty liqueur.

Cherry *cordial* is easy to make but it requires planning ahead. You'll want to let it age for at least two months. The longer it ages, the smoother and more flavorful it becomes. If you can wait even longer, you will be well rewarded.

Pick or buy enough sour cherries to fill about half to three quarters of a wide-mouthed gallon jar. If you're lucky enough to own your own

Magickal Properties

Cordials are sweet, syrupy alcoholic beverages often made with brandy. They can be flavored with fruit, spices, herbs, or a combination of all three. Serve them in very small glasses as an after-ritual potion.

cherry tree, you might double or triple this recipe. It keeps indefinitely and, decanted into pretty bottles, the liqueur makes a lovely gift.

Wash the cherries. It isn't necessary to pit them, which makes this a really easy recipe, but do remove any stems.

Put the cherries into the jar with 5 to 6 cups of sugar. This may sound like a lot, but remember, cordials are meant to be sweet. Pour in 100-proof vodka, enough to completely cover the cherries. Store in a dark, cool place. Once a week you should shake or stir the mixture. You'll know it's ready when the sugar has completely dissolved. Taste it to see if it's sweet enough. If not, add more sugar and let it continue to steep.

When you're ready to decant it, strain the liquid into bottles and discard the cherries.

After a ritual, share a sip of cordial with your friends. Pour it into 2-ounce cordial glasses as you say the following:

> *Let love enter*
> *Let friendship stay*
> *Let peace abide*
> *In every day.*

You can use this recipe to make almost any fruit cordial. You will have to experiment with how much sugar to use depending on the sweetness of the fruit. Blueberry cordial, raspberry, strawberry, peach, apple—the possibilities are endless. Use brandy or cognac in place of the vodka, if desired. If you're using fruit without pits, save the marinated fruit and use it as a topping for your post-ritual cake.

Magickal Punches for All Occasions

If you're hosting a sabbat celebration with a large number of celebrants attending, the easiest way to provide enough potion for everyone is to make a punch. That way, all of the preparation happens before your guests arrive and they can serve themselves. Just remember to keep an eye on the punch bowl and replenish as needed.

Peach Melba Punch

Just like the cherry cordial recipe, you can choose the fruit you want to use. We're using peaches and raspberries, but experiment with different combinations.

Use 2 pounds of peaches and 1 pint of raspberries. Wash and peel peaches and cut into slices. Wash the raspberries. Place the fruit into a large glass punch bowl. Add one pitcher of raspberry-flavored Kool-Aid and 16 ounces of peach-flavored juice. Chill at least one hour.

Just before serving, stir in one 32-ounce bottle of chilled peach-flavored sparkling water or a bottle of club soda. Put a whole raspberry into each glass and fill with punch.

Peaches are a Goddess fruit that encourage prosperity. Drink this punch in late summer to guarantee a bountiful table all winter long.

Simmering Fruit Punch

We often think of punch as a cold beverage, but this warm punch can brighten up a winter buffet while adding a hint of the warm weather to come. This recipe makes about three quarts.

- ◆ 5–6 tangerines
- ◆ $1/2$ cup whole cloves
- ◆ 3 quarts unsweetened cranberry juice
- ◆ 2 cups sugar, or to taste

Cut tangerines crosswise into $1/4$-inch-thick rounds and remove the seeds. Stud the rind of each tangerine round with four or five cloves.

In a large covered saucepan, simmer the cranberry juice, tangerine rounds, and sugar for five minutes. Do not bring to a boil. Remove from heat.

Keep the punch warm by placing it on a warming tray or over a candle. If possible, serve in glass mugs; this makes a punch as pretty to look at as it is good to drink. Cranberries can bring newfound prosperity into your life. Serve this punch at the start of a new year to encourage money and good fortune to flow your way.

Punch Fit for a Goddess

Adding roses to a lovely wine punch will attract guests even before they taste it. This is a sophisticated punch, whether you serve it for an all adults-only holiday brunch, lunch, or dinner. Add sweet woodruff for a May wine to celebrate Beltane.

- ◆ 8 roses
- ◆ 5 TB. sugar
- ◆ 2 chilled bottles of white wine
- ◆ 1 chilled bottle of champagne

Rinse six of the roses under cool water and pull off the petals.

> **CAUTION**
>
> **Widdershins** _____
>
> In any recipe that calls for edible flowers or herbs, make certain that they were grown without the use of pesticides. Better to err on the side of caution. Either grow your own, borrow them from your garden witch friend, or don't use them.

Add the sugar and wine to the rose petals. Cover and steep for five hours.

Strain the liquid through a sieve into a punch bowl, pressing the petals with the back of a spoon to extract all the liquid.

Rinse the remaining two roses. Sprinkle their petals into the punch bowl. Set the bowl into a larger bowl or a tray filled with crushed ice to keep the punch chilled without diluting it.

Immediately before serving add the champagne. Stir gently.

Freshly Brewed Potions

Making and serving beverages for group gatherings not only provides an opportunity to show off your culinary skills, but can also be used for magickal purposes. Choose herbs and ingredients that help further your intentions. Although there are lists that can guide you as you select ingredients, state your intention out loud and ask the Goddess to use the fruits or herbs you have on hand for the good of all and for your stated purpose. Be sure to serve alcoholic beverages sparingly and only after rituals are completed.

The Least You Need to Know

- ◆ You can almost always substitute your favorite fruit in any potion recipe. You might have to adjust for sweetness.

- ◆ Potions add an easy festive touch to any sabbat gathering. Choose ingredients that further your magickal intentions.

- ◆ Alcoholic beverages are for adults only and should only be consumed after all ritual and spellwork is completed.

- ◆ Ingredients are not automatically magickal; your intentions as you combine them create the spell.

Chapter 20

Herbs, Oils, and Other Ingredients

In This Chapter

- Creams for anointing your body before ritual
- Formulas for stress-free magick from head to toe
- Mixing up some kitchen magick
- Powders to consecrate magickal workings

Sometimes homemade potions just help you feel good about yourself, which is always magickal. Herbs can invigorate, relax, inspire, soothe, or inflame. Choosing herbs and oils carefully will ensure that the outcome of your magickal working is the one you expected, whether you are creating a ritual bath oil, a cleansing hand cream, an herbal remedy, or a cooking oil for kitchen magick.

Making your own potions is not only economical, it assures you that the ingredients are all natural and fresh, enhancing their magickal properties. Many of these potions can be given as sabbat gifts to Wiccan friends and relatives. Share the magick!

Hand and Body Creams

Creams not only add wonderful fragrances to your life, they are soothing for those of us who live in cold, dry weather. Smooth one on after a ritual bath while your skin is still damp to keep your skin moisturized and healthy.

Bewitching Hand Cream

This is a sumptuous hand cream laced with the beautiful fragrance of rose water and oil of roses or, if you prefer, with lavender water and lavender oil. Beeswax and lanolin make it a soothing, rich lotion. This is an all-natural indulgence you can whip up in very little time to treat yourself or to delight a friend. The cream nourishes even the driest hands and the scent of flowers invokes the Goddess. Either of these would make a soothing fragrance to use before a purification ceremony. Lavender corresponds to harmony, love, prosperity, and protection; rose corresponds to love, of course, and to beauty and the intuition of the priestess. This makes about ³/₄ cup of hand cream.

- 2 tsp. beeswax pastilles or granules (available in most health-food stores)
- 2 TB. lanolin (also available in health-food stores)
- ¹/₂ cup wheat-germ oil
- ¹/₃ cup rose or lavender water
- 5 drops of oil of roses or lavender oil

Craftworking

You can make almost any magickal fragrance you want using this basic hand-cream recipe. If you can't find the right fragrant water, use spring water and add in a few extra drops of whatever essential oil you've chosen. You might have to experiment with the amounts of oil and water to get the right consistency.

Using a double boiler or a heatproof glass measuring cup set in a pan of simmering water, melt the beeswax and lanolin over low heat, stirring constantly.

Pour in a slow stream of the wheat-germ oil, stirring well.

Using a candy thermometer, heat the mixture to 160°F.

Slowly add the fragrant water a little at a time until the mixture thickens. Keep stirring!

Take the mixture off the heat and let it cool to 105°F. Add the rose or lavender oil and stir well.

As the cream thickens and cools, it will become smooth and white.

While the cream is still lukewarm, pour it into clean jars. Stored in a cool place, your bewitching hand cream will last up to three months.

Honey-and-Herb Skin Cream

Why buy an expensive cream made with ingredients that sound as if they come from a pharmacy? This all-natural skin cream disinfects, moisturizes, and calms skin that tends to break out. Honey is associated with the Goddess and so is a soothing balm to use before dedicating yourself or a ritual tool to the Goddess. Sage is a purifying herb; rosemary is soothing and magickally healing; mint is stimulating, so this cream is perfect to smooth on before you cast a spell or perform a ritual to help ground, ready, and energize yourself. This makes about $1/2$ cup of skin cream.

- ◆ 2 tsp. each dried mint, sage, and rosemary
- ◆ $1/2$ cup boiling water
- ◆ 2 tsp. beeswax
- ◆ 2 TB. lanolin
- ◆ $1/2$ cup wheat-germ oil
- ◆ 1 tsp. honey

Combine the herbs in a clean bowl, pot, or cauldron. Pour $1/2$ cup of boiling water over them and steep for 10 minutes as though making tea.

Strain through cheesecloth or a very fine sieve, collecting the liquid in a bowl or a glass measuring cup. Discard the herbs and set the liquid aside to cool.

Using a double boiler or a heatproof glass measuring cup set in a pan of simmering water, melt the beeswax and lanolin to 160°F.

Add the wheat-germ oil slowly, stirring constantly. Add the herbal water by teaspoonful, stirring until well blended.

Remove from heat and let cool. Stir in the honey until blended. Cool thoroughly.

Stir the cream well once it has cooled and spoon it into small jars. Store it in a cool place and use within three months.

Peppermint Hand Cream

Peppermint has many relaxing, cooling, and healing properties. If you're Drawing Down the Moon or casting a magick circle, this is a lovely potion to use before you begin the ritual. This makes about $1/4$ cup of hand cream.

- 1 tsp. lanolin

- 2 TB. plus 1 tsp. petroleum jelly

- ½ tsp. rubbing alcohol

- 1 generous tsp. of jojoba oil

- ¼ cup spring water

- 4–6 tsp. fresh peppermint leaves

- 6–8 drops peppermint oil

Craftworking

Buy fresh peppermint at the grocery store or grow your own. Mint grows easily and spreads quickly. Using dried peppermint will produce a disappointing result. (Spearmint is also an interesting fragrance to infuse.) Likewise, use 100 percent pure peppermint oil; synthetic flavorings do not have the same effect.

Using a double boiler or a heatproof glass measuring cup set in a pan of simmering water, melt the lanolin, petroleum jelly, rubbing alcohol, and jojoba oil until it reaches a temperature of 160°F. Set aside to cool.

Bring the spring water to a rolling boil and pour it over the mint leaves. Let steep at least 10 minutes.

Strain the infusion into a clean bowl. Cool to 100°F. Measure out 2 tablespoons plus 1 teaspoon of water and stir it gradually into the alcohol-oil mixture.

Stir the mixture slowly until it forms into a cream. Add the peppermint oil and mix thoroughly.

Transfer the cream into a jar with a tight-fitting lid. Store in a cool, dark place up to three months.

Soothing a Tired Witch

Some days, the best thing you can do for your spiritual and mental health is to relax! Here are a few lovely potions you can use to indulge yourself. Remember, *you* are your most valuable vehicle for making magick. Use these potions to refresh and revitalize. Invite some friends over and make it a witches' spa day.

Purifying Chamomile Facial

Chamomile has long been regarded as a remedy for sleeplessness, stress, anxiety, and minor skin irritations, and magickally corresponds to purification and harmony. As we talked about in Chapter 18, purifying yourself prior to performing rituals is vital. This chamomile facial can be a nice alternative to a ritual bath for this purpose.

Growing and drying your own chamomile blossoms ensures that they are free of pesticides. Gently wash the flowers and pluck or cut them from their stems. Lay the blossoms out on a towel or on paper towels and let them dry for several days out of direct sunlight. Dried chamomile can also be purchased in flower stores, or buy chamomile tea at your grocery store.

For your facial, pour about 2 cups of boiling water over 4 or 5 tablespoons of dried chamomile blossoms. Cover your head with a towel, lean over the steam and let it penetrate your pores. After a few minutes, splash your face with cool water and moisturize with a lanolin-rich face cream.

Don't Forget Your Feet

If you've been running around all day—getting children off to school, going to work, grocery shopping, cooking dinner, meeting with your coven—your feet deserve special care. Every day you shove them into sweaty tennis shoes, high heels, or shoes with heels worn down on one side. When was the last time you really pampered your feet? Prepare a soothing herbal foot bath that can help recharge your spirit after a demanding and stressful day, and reconnect you to your inner Goddess energy.

- ♦ 6 fresh red roses for energy—homegrown are best

- ♦ 12 rosemary stalks

- ♦ 12 lavender sprigs

- ♦ 2 lbs. Epsom salts

- ♦ 12 drops lavender oil

Gently strip the petals from the roses. Remove the rosemary leaves and lavender blossoms from their stalks.

Put the Epsom salts into a large nonmetallic bowl. Sprinkle the rose petals, rosemary leaves, and lavender blossoms on top. Drip the lavender oil over the mixture.

Using a plastic or wooden spoon, carefully mix the ingredients. Make sure it's all distributed evenly. To use, put 3 heaping tablespoons into 1 quart of very warm water. Soak until you feel relaxed and sleepy. Refrigerate unused portion and use within three or four weeks.

Widdershins

When a recipe calls for an essential oil, don't use wooden spoons or bowls. Wood will absorb the oil, ruining both the recipe and the utensils.

When the Day Gives You a Headache

Some days, no matter how positive the witch, the stress and anxieties of everyday life in the mundane world seem overwhelming. Negative energy can build up and before you know it your head is pounding. Maybe you just feel out of sorts and a little tired. Gently massaging a bit of this potion on your temples will revive your spirit and relieve the physical pain as well. If you are going to do a chakra meditation (see Chapter 18), this balm will help clear your head and facilitate the flow of healing magickal energy through your body.

- 1½ TB. cocoa butter

- 2 tsp. lanolin

- 1 tsp. olive or almond oil

- 1 tsp. cinnamon

- 20 drops camphor oil

- 20 drops peppermint oil

- 10 drops pine oil

- 10 drops eucalyptus oil

- 2 drops clove oil

> **Summon and Stir**
>
> When Liguana's partner has had an especially trying day, she rubs his temples or shoulders in a gentle massage using some of the headache remedy and then brews a cup of chamomile tea to top it off. Very relaxing!

Using a double boiler or a heatproof glass measuring cup set in a pan of simmering water, melt the cocoa butter. Add the lanolin and the olive or almond oil and let melt, stirring until blended.

Remove from the heat and whisk in the cinnamon and essential oils. Trying rubbing a little of the mixture on the back of your hand. It should feel both warm and cooling.

Pour into a small clean jar and let it set. You might have to stir it gently before using. This also works as a massage cream on tired, aching muscles. Use within six to eight weeks.

Herbs and Oils

Combining the right amounts of herbs and oils can produce everything from a soothing bath to a tasty salad or stir-fry. It depends mostly on the type of oil you use and what additional ingredients you toss in.

Use these recipes as a starting point for inspiration to make your own individual concoctions. Browse flea markets and auctions to find pretty bottles and jars to recycle as containers for your oil. Add a decorative ribbon and you have a sabbat gift to give to a friend.

Mystic Bath Oil

This recipe uses jojoba (pronounced *ho-HO–buh*) oil, which is rich in vitamin E and minerals much like the body's own natural oils. Jojoba has a long shelf life, doesn't turn rancid, and its light texture and lack of scent makes it an ideal base oil. Most health-food stores carry jojoba oil.

For this recipe, you can choose any essential oil that appeals to you or resonates to your magickal purpose and intent. Experiment with different oil combinations: lavender and lemon balm; lemon, lime, and grapefruit; rose and carnation; cinnamon and clove; ginger and white hibiscus. Or use just one favorite scent. The only limit is your imagination—the magickal possibilities are endless!

These make sumptuous oils to add to ritual baths, to give to coveners for the holidays, or to comfort a friend who needs a little TLC.

- 1 cup jojoba oil

- 5 tsp. *emulsifier* (optional)

- Approximately 20 drops of your favorite essential oil, or a combination of oils

Magickal Properties

An **emulsifier** is added to prevent the ingredients from separating. Two good choices are melted beeswax or stearic acid, both of which should be available at most health-food stores. Ask your friendly neighborhood store clerk to make other suggestions. If you choose not to use an emulsifier, you will have to shake the bottle well before using.

Pour the jojoba oil into a glass measuring cup. Pour slowly or you'll create unwanted air bubbles.

If you're using an emulsifier, add it slowly.

Add the essential oil(s) you've chosen. You will need approximately 20 drops (2¹/₂ to 3 teaspoons total), but you will want to experiment. Better to start out by adding less and increasing the amount until you have the fragrance you want.

Using a funnel, pour the oil into a decorative glass bottle. It will last for several months out of direct sunlight.

Garlic–Red Pepper Oil

One magickal ingredient in any kitchen witch's pantry is flavored oil. Just like the bath oil, you are limited only by your own imagination. Oils infused with herbs and spices can be used to make a vinaigrette, enhance a stir-fry, or marinade a steak. Garlic and rosemary are magickally associated with healing and protection. Use this oil in a meal served after a group ritual, or any time you want a little feisty flavor for protection.

- ◆ 1 red pepper
- ◆ 1 large sprig of fresh rosemary
- ◆ 1 tsp. red or black peppercorns to add intensity
- ◆ 1 cup red wine vinegar or salad vinegar
- ◆ 3 large garlic cloves
- ◆ 2 cups extra-virgin olive oil

Cut the pepper in half and remove the seeds. Place the cut sides down and place under the broiler until the skin blisters. Place them in a brown paper bag for a few minutes, then remove skin. Set aside.

Place the rosemary sprig and peppercorns into a bowl. Heat the vinegar—do not boil. Pour it over the seasonings and let steep for at least five minutes. Remove and reserve seasonings. Discard the vinegar.

Peel and halve the garlic cloves. Cut the pepper into small strips. Place the garlic, pepper strips, peppercorns, and the rosemary sprig into a 1-pint sterilized wide-mouthed bottle with a tight-fighting lid.

Pour the olive oil into the bottle, covering seasonings completely. Seal well and let steep for one week in a cool, dark place, shaking occasionally.

You can vary the flavor by varying ingredients. Try a garlic-tarragon combination or dried tomato and basil. If the seasonings fall apart while the oil is steeping, you might have to strain it through cheesecloth before using it. This oil lasts for several months if kept in a cool, dark place.

Fiery Cooking Oil

If you would like more spice in your life, this is the oil for you. Use it to make a meal to enflame a lover's passion or to energize yourself for a special ritual.

Drizzle this oil over pasta, mix it with vinegar for a salad dressing, brush it over meat on the grill, or use it for a spicy shrimp stir-fry.

- 1–2 tsp. black peppercorns, depending on how hot you want the oil to be

- 1 sprig each of fresh rosemary and thyme

- 3 garlic cloves

- 1–3 hot chili peppers, again depending on your tolerance for spicy

- 2 cups olive oil

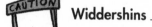

Widdershins

Do not substitute finely ground black pepper for the peppercorns. It will be difficult to strain out and it won't add the same quality of zip to the oil.

Grind the peppercorns coarsely using a spice grinder or a mortar and pestle. (Another choice is to buy coarsely ground black pepper, but this will most likely require you to strain the final product and the results won't be as pleasing as grinding your own.)

Rinse off the fresh herbs and gently crush them to release their fragrance. Peel and halve the garlic cloves.

Pierce the chili peppers a few times with a fork. Fill a 1-pint sterilized wide-mouthed bottle with a tight-fighting lid halfway with the olive oil. Add the peppercorns, garlic, herbs, and chili peppers. Finish filling the jar with oil, making sure the seasonings are completely covered.

Let the mixture stand for two weeks in a cool, dark place, shaking occasionally. Strain the oil if desired and insert fresh herbs. This oil will last several months if stored in a cool, dark place.

Walnut Vinaigrette

This recipe is meant to be made and used immediately. It makes enough to serve four small salads or two large salads. Walnuts are associated with strong mental powers and the walnut tree is most often associated with the God. This makes a delicious dressing for a light salad luncheon in the early fall or to celebrate the autumnal equinox.

- ¼ cup chopped walnuts
- 2 TB. salad vinegar
- ¼ cup walnut oil
- 1 tsp. salt
- 1 tsp. sugar
- Freshly ground pepper

Put the walnuts onto a cookie sheet and toast them in a 350°F oven until lightly browned. They burn quickly, so keep an eye on them.

In a glass bowl briskly whisk vinegar, oil, salt, sugar, and pepper until slightly thickened and salt and sugar are dissolved. It is important to use a wire whisk to produce a creamy consistency. Stir in the toasted walnuts.

Choose a variety of fresh greens: spinach, radicchio, arugula, red lettuce. You can also add mandarin oranges and cubes of chicken if you want a heartier salad. Spoon the vinaigrette over the salad and top with croutons.

Powerful Powders

Wiccan powders are often nothing more than finely ground herbs mixed together and used to cast a magick circle, to consecrate a tool or a crystal, or to sprinkle on your altar. Of course, there are also cosmetic powders to pat on after a ritual bath or at the beginning of a long, hot day.

Soothing/Invigorating Powder

If you're making this powder to evoke soothing, healing magickal energy, you will want a soothing fragrance—passionflower, sandalwood, or lilac, for example. If your magickal purpose needs invigorating, centering energy, you might want to use a more invigorating scent—ginger, citrus, or peppermint, perhaps. You can use this powder on your body after a ritual bath or when starting your day with a ritual shower.

- 1 cup base powder—arrowroot, cornstarch, rice flour, or talc, for example
- 1 cup baking soda
- 10–15 drops of essential oil(s) of your choice

Mix together the base powder and the baking soda in a glass bowl. Next add the essential oils, one drop at a time, into the base. Finally, mix well and store in an airtight container.

Powders to Cook With

Grinding your own herbs to create cooking powders allows you to adjust the combination to suit your family's taste.

If required, you can use a spice grinder or a mortar and pestle, although that will produce a coarser powder. Both of these powders are spicy kitchen magick, designed to add passion and zest to a meal, or add spark to your magickal purpose. Use them liberally.

Chili Powder

- 4 garlic cloves or 2 tsp. garlic powder
- 1½ tsp. cumin seeds
- 1 tsp. paprika
- 1 tsp. cayenne pepper
- 1 tsp. oregano

If you're using fresh garlic, chop and dry it in a low oven for 20 hours. Check often. Grind the garlic and the cumin seeds to a fine powder. Stir in paprika, cayenne pepper, and oregano. Store in a dry place out of direct sunlight.

Curry Powder

- 2 TB. black peppercorns
- 2 TB. cumin seeds
- 1 tsp. whole allspice
- 1–2 bay leaves
- 1 tsp. cayenne pepper
- 2 tsp. hot chili powder
- 4 tsp. coriander
- 2 tsp. fenugreek (an herb with seeds that are roasted and ground and used to flavor curry; available in most spice sections)
- 4 tsp. garlic powder

- 2 tsp. paprika
- 2 TB. salt
- 4 tsp. turmeric

Grind the peppercorns, cumin seeds, and allspice to a fine powder. Mix with the crumbled bay leaves, cayenne pepper, chili powder, coriander, fenugreek, garlic powder, paprika, salt, and turmeric and store in a cool, dry place.

Herbs, Oils and Magick

Whether you're infusing oil and herbs to create a soothing lotion or to add flavor to a favorite dish, you're creating potion magick. Experiment with herbs, not only for their magickal properties but for the fragrance and flavors they bring to your table or bath. Use our recipes as suggestions but feel free to substitute ingredients as your inner self dictates.

The Least You Need to Know

- Use the recipes in this chapter as a jumping-off point for your own magickal creations.
- Infused herbs and oils can be used for everything from kitchen magick to ritual bath oils.
- Different herbs have different "powers" or magickal correspondences. Check to see if an herb you've chosen is soothing, invigorating, or somewhere in between.
- Making your own potions and powders ensures that they are fresh and all natural.

Chapter 21

Enhance Your Magickal (and Mundane) Energy

In This Chapter

♦ Potions to boost magickal power

♦ The perfect perfume to begin any ritual with clarity and focus

♦ Powders for protection and dispelling negativity

♦ Trust your own magickal intuition

Not surprisingly, potions that draw in positive energy are often made with fresh fruits and vegetables. Drinks that nourish your body and raise your physical energy level also raise your spiritual energy because the two are so closely tied together. Those energy-inducing potions that aren't drinkable usually use a soothing fragrance to encourage your spirit to relax and soar. The best Craftworking is done when you're feeling upbeat and strong.

Spells to banish negative energy often use potions or powders designed to purify an area or to put up a barrier so evil intentions can't enter.

Cast spells meant to attract energy during Waxing Moons and spells meant to dispel energy during Waning Moons. Or use the cord energy you created if the moon isn't in the right aspect (see Chapter 15).

Energizing Brews for Mind and Body

As we've discussed throughout this book, before performing a spell or ritual you will want to prepare yourself. We've already talked about taking a ritual bath, casting a magick circle, and sweeping out negative energy. But you should also consider drinking a healthy potion. Spellcasting can require a truly intense mental and physical (and spiritual!) effort if you're really focused and concentrating. Not to mention it's hard to concentrate if your stomach is growling. A light energy brew is just the way to begin. (For more potable potions for specific occasions and magickal purposes, refer to Chapter 19.)

A Veggie Delight

If you're a gardener, chances are at some point during the growing season you have more tomatoes and zucchini than you know what to do with. You might want to consider investing in a vegetable juicer. The surplus vegetables can be juiced and the juice frozen for later use. The following recipe makes two drinks.

Craftworking

Pour some of any drink you're making into an ice cube tray and freeze. Use them instead of regular ice cubes so you won't dilute the drink.

- 2 or 3 ripe tomatoes

- 1 sweet red pepper

- 1 lb. of carrots

- 1 garlic clove, peeled

- Fresh basil, green olives, celery stalks for garnish; dash of Tabasco (optional)

Carefully wash the tomatoes, pepper, and carrots, scrubbing but not peeling them. Halve the pepper, removing the stem and seeds.

Cut all of the vegetables into chunks—remember, you're going to be juicing them so they don't have to be pretty!—and place in an electric juicer along with the garlic clove. Following the instructions that came with the juicer, slowly press the vegetables through.

Pour the juice into two tall glasses and, if desired, garnish with fresh basil. For a spicier drink, sprinkle in some cracked black pepper, a dash of Tabasco, and garnish with green olives and a celery stalk.

The vegetables in this beverage are naturally sweet, but be sure to experiment with other vegetable combinations.

Garlic and basil add magickal touches to this drink. Garlic provides protection and has been known to alleviate headaches and high blood pressure. Basil attracts love and friendship. In addition, black pepper and Tabasco sauce make the potion fiery, which might add some extra zip to your spells. As you drink, you might say something like the following:

Energize me through this drink,
give me power that I may think clearly
as I cast this spell,
keep my friends and loved ones well.

Melon-Mango Smoothie

This makes a delicious, light, refreshing summer energy drink. Treat your guests to this lovely brew before casting an outdoor circle at the end of the summer. To strengthen the positive energy of this all-natural drink, stir it three times deosil (clockwise) before serving to enhance its power threefold! As you stir, chant:

Power times three
Grant it to me.

This makes one pitcherful of drinks. You might have to blend two separate batches.

- ◆ 1 honeydew melon or cantaloupe (or a combination of both)
- ◆ 1 mango
- ◆ Honey, to taste
- ◆ Fresh fruit for garnish (optional)

Cut the melon, cantaloupe, and mango into small chunks and place in a blender along with their juice. Blend the fruit mixture until smooth. Stir in honey, taste, and adjust sweetness. Pour over crushed ice. Thread a variety of fresh fruit onto a bamboo skewer as a garnish. Try using kiwi, strawberries, or raspberries.

Any combination of fruit can make a tasty smoothie. Don't hesitate to try your own concoction.

Spicy Potent Perfume

The smell of aromatic spices and essential oils makes an invigorating perfumed potion that clears your head and focuses your natural energy on the magickal task at hand.

Dab some on your wrists before starting a ritual to add a little extra zip to your spell. This makes about ¹/₂ cup of perfume.

Here's what you'll need:

♦ 1 golf ball–size piece of fresh ginger

♦ 4 cardamom pods

♦ 4 whole cloves

♦ 1 stick cinnamon (don't use ground cinnamon)

♦ ¹/₂ cup 100-proof vodka (you can substitute rubbing alcohol, but vodka is a superior alcohol base for perfume because it is odorless)

♦ Essential oils: ylang-ylang, orange blossom, rosewood, sandalwood, patchouli

♦ Plastic or glass stirrer, or old wooden spoon

♦ 2 jars with tight-fitting lids

♦ A coffee filter

♦ ²/₃ cup rose water

♦ Funnel

> **Widdershins**
>
> Remember, if you use a wooden spoon it will absorb the fragrance of the essential oils and ruin it for cooking. Likewise, you don't want to stir perfume with a spoon that smells of garlic. Keep one wooden spoon on hand especially for your aromatic potions, or use a plastic or glass stirrer.

Peel and chop the ginger into fine pieces. Using a mortar and pestle, grind the ginger, cardamom, cloves, and cinnamon stick.

Pour the ground spices into a sterilized glass jar. Pour in ¹/₄ cup of vodka and shake well.

To the remaining ¹/₄ cup vodka, add 5 drops of ylang-ylang, 6 drops of orange blossom, 15 drops each of rosewood and sandalwood, and 2 drops of patchouli. (Adjust essential oil amounts to suit your own tastes.) Shake well and add the mixture to the spiced vodka. Stir together well. Seal the jar tightly and let the mixture steep in a cool, dark place for one week.

Strain the mixture through the coffee filter into another sterilized jar. Add the rose water and shake well. Using the funnel, pour the perfume into a dark-colored glass bottle with a tight-fitting lid. Store it in a cool, dark place. It will keep for several months.

The magickal correspondences of the ingredients of this energy perfume are many and various—a little bit of anything and everything! This is an all-occasion staple. Of course, we just like the way it smells … a wonderful fragrance for magick.

Magickal Correspondences for Spice-Potent Perfume

Ingredient	Correspondence
Cardamom	Love, nurturing, warmth
Cinnamon	Abundance, psychic sight, well-being
Cloves	Protection, purity, strength
Ginger	Love, power, success
Orange blossom	Beauty and love
Patchouli	Fertility, protection, sensual pleasure
Rose water	Beauty, intuition, love, luck
Rosewood	Protection, purity, love, innocence
Sandalwood	Healing, intelligence, purity, safety
Ylang-ylang	Love, soothing

Potent Powders

Scattering herbs and powders is a common way of using the influence of the herbs to achieve your magickal intent. You can dust your workplace to improve sales, scatter some in your bedroom to spark passion, sprinkle over people to bless or protect them, dust some onto your altar, sprinkle a ritual object, or blow a bit into the air to spread their magickal influence through a room or place.

Powders can be a single herb or a mixture of herbs. You want to make sure the herbs are really ground to a fine powder so there are no large chunks. Use the powder sparingly— you don't want to leave unsightly green trails throughout your house.

If you are blending powders to give to friends, make sure none of them are allergic. This is especially important if you plan to sprinkle the powder directly on them, on their belongings, or in their houses or cars.

CAUTION **Widdershins**

Some ingredients can stain material—turmeric, dragon's blood, and saffron, for example. And some herbs leave a sticky residue, like pine. These mixtures should be reserved for outdoor use or only used on surfaces that can't be affected.

Protective Powder

This powder can be dusted lightly throughout a house to keep the occupants protected, sprinkled directly onto a person to keep him or her safe during the day, or blown into your car before taking a trip.

Grind together equal parts of basil, chamomile, barley, and ash leaves.

Make sure you dust the powder over windowsills and door jambs. As you dust the space you want to protect, say something like the following:

> *Day after day and through the night,*
> *Keep safe this space and make it right.*
> *For everyone who lives within*
> *Bring joy and health and luck again.*

If you're dusting yourself or another person, try this:

> *This powder has but good intent,*
> *Protect me well and be not spent.*
> *Keep me safe from harm and woe*
> *As onward through the day I go.*

You can replace the word *me* with a person's name and *I* with the pronoun *he* or *she*.

This protective powder can also be spread around when you cast a magick circle to keep out any bad vibes or negative energy. As you do so, say:

> *The circle's cast, the spell begun,*
> *Let each who entered one by one*
> *With perfect love and perfect trust*
> *Be protected by this dust.*

Scatter a Little Love

Toss a little of this powder around your bedroom to invoke passion and deepen love. Remember that you can't make someone fall in love with you. This beneficial powder can only heighten feelings that already exist.

Grind together equal parts of basil, rose petals, lavender, vertiver, cinnamon, and witch grass.

 **Craftworking** _____

Don't worry if you can't find some of these ingredients. Use these "recipes" as suggestions. Feel free to substitute similar herbs for each other (rosemary for basil, for example, since they are both sweet, fragrant plants). Or eliminate an herb completely. Just remember that spicy ingredients like cinnamon and cayenne add fire to a spell. Use them cautiously.

Remember to scatter this powder lightly! You certainly don't want to end up sleeping on crumbly sheets. Try this incantation as you dust:

> *Within this room let passion grow,*
> *The love we reap again we sow.*
> *Let seasons change while we together*
> *Hand in hand go on forever.*

Prosperity, Money, and Wealth

If becoming wealthy was as easy as sprinkling powder around your place of business, there would be no poor witches! (Ask Liguana how many millionaire witches she knows.) This powder helps attract money, but you have to put in good old-fashioned, mundane work as well.

Blend together an equal amount of cinnamon, ginger, dried orange peel, and sandalwood. Dust it lightly over a cash register, into a purse or billfold, or just into the corners of the office or room you work in. As you do so, say:

> *Aid me in my daily work,*
> *Let me not my duties shirk.*
> *Through it find prosperity*
> *And share my wealth, so mote it be.*

Another way to create magickal powders is to mix essential oils into unscented talcum powder or cornstarch. Again, dust lightly so it doesn't look like a snowstorm has taken place inside your house!

Repelling Negativity

As much as we would all like people to like us, it is human nature that sometimes people direct negative feelings toward us—jealousy, envy, anger, or general ill will.

While protection spells keep us from being harmed, we also want the negative energy dissipated.

Jasmine Iced Tea

One way to eliminate bad feelings is to sit down with the person who is feeling out of sorts with you and share a glass of tea. This assumes, of course, that it's a minor irritation and not a full-blown hatred. Jasmine is a strong floral tea meant to be soothing. It also invokes the Goddess and encourages friendship. Add sparkling water to lighten the brew and the mood. This recipe makes one pitcher of tea.

> **CAUTION**
> **Widdershins**
> Avoid indulging in alcoholic beverages prior to casting a spell or performing a ritual. You want to be "pure" in both body and spirit. Although alcohol has its place and certainly isn't forbidden (see our spiced wine toast to the God in Chapter 19), it should be reserved for celebrations or post-spellworking occasions.

- 4 TB. brown sugar
- 3 $1/4$ cup water
- 3 TB. loose jasmine tea or 8 tea bags
- 2 lemons
- 1 cinnamon stick
- Sparkling water
- Fresh mint

Boil the brown sugar with $1/4$ cup water over low heat until it forms a thick syrup. Set aside to cool.

Bring 3 cups of water to a boil and pour over the tea. Let steep for seven minutes. Strain tea or remove teabags.

Pour the tea into a pitcher along with the syrup. Squeeze the juice from one lemon. Add it to the tea along with the second lemon cut into thin slices and the cinnamon stick.

Serve by filling each glass about half or three quarters full with tea poured over crushed ice. Top it off with the sparkling water and a sprig of mint.

As you make the tea, think only positive thoughts about the person who is sending you negative vibrations. When you serve the tea, try to talk honestly with that person—there is nothing more magickal than honesty and airing out feelings. Toast your guest with good health and fortune even if you haven't convinced him or her to give up those bad feelings. You'll feel better for it.

A Stronger Remedy

If the negativity being directed at you is really frightening, you will want to use a stronger potion or powder. Here's one to try.

Grind together a fine powder of basil, frankincense, rosemary, yarrow, and rue. Add in just one drop of vinegar. Sprinkle it liberally around the outside of your house in a large circle. (If you live in an apartment, sprinkle the powder on your inside window ledges and outside doorsills, including the main doorsill to the complex or the house.) Cast this spell during a Waning Moon and say the following:

> *Magick powder may you last,*
> *Protective arms around me cast.*
> *Encircle me and mine with charms*
> *To keep us safe from evil harm.*

This is not meant to be used to send out your own negative vibrations, only to protect you from someone else's negativity.

A Final Word About Using Magick

Throughout this book we have been giving you "directions" as though we were providing you with the one and only way to build an altar, cast a circle, or brew a potion. Although we've been saying this all along, it bears repeating: *Listen to your own intuition and use your own creativity; the magick lives there. We know of no Wiccan instruction book set in stone anywhere.*

When you undertake a spiritual journey, you need to trust your own instincts. Wicca's nature-based religion encourages you to tap into the energy and power in your own nature as well as with the natural world around you. You are connecting with the Divine, not staging a show or dealing with pageantry. In the end, it doesn't matter what you wear or what you say but only that your intentions are pure and benevolent. Remember the Wiccan Rede: "An harm ye none, do what ye will." If your intentions are to honor the Lord and Lady and to dedicate yourself to that goal, you will be a true Wiccan.

The Least You Need to Know

♦ Waxing Moons are best for casting spells to attract positive energy, Waning Moons are best for spells to repel negative energy.

♦ Any healthy beverage can be magickal because it keeps you both physically and spiritually fit.

♦ Dust potent powders sparingly. You don't need to be able to see them piled onto windowsills for them to work.

♦ In the end, the most magickal ritual and the most effective tools are the ones you create yourself.

Appendix A

Glossary

amulet   From the Latin word *amuletum*, meaning, well, amulet. An amulet is a small object used for protection and keeping negative energy at bay. Many Wiccans use the terms *amulet* and *talisman* interchangeably. *See also* talisman.

annuals   Plants that require replanting each season.

athame (pronounced *A-tha-may*)   A two-edged knife, usually with a wooden or silver handle, used both as a symbol of God and in various rituals (for example, casting a circle). An athame cuts on a spiritual plane, not on a physical one.

Beltane   May 1, this is the last of the three spring fertility rituals. It is the time when the sun is fully released from his bondage of winter and able to rule over summer and life once again.

besom   A broom meant to be used on a spiritual plane to eliminate negative energy.

boline   Traditionally a white-handled knife used for cutting in the physical world, as opposed to your athame, which cuts on the spiritual plane. Use it to cut wands; chop herbs or vegetables; inscribe symbols onto candles, wood, clay, or wax; and in cutting string or cords used in magick.

Book of Shadows   A witch's diary that contains personal revelations as well as a record of what has worked in the practice of Wicca.

burlap   A loosely woven coarse material used, among other things, to wrap tree roots prior to planting.

Candlemas   February 2, also called Imbolc (which means "in the belly"), this festival refers to all of the animals just beginning to start the cycle of life over again. Most specifically, sheep are usually carrying young at this time.

catnip   A member of the mint family and a perennial herb which will grow back each year if the winter is not too severe.

centering (grounding)   Preparing for a ritual by clearing out any doubts or wandering thoughts. Center yourself by slowly bringing your awareness inward.

chakras   Derived from the Sanskrit word meaning "wheel." They are the seven openings for life energy to flow into and out of our aura. They help to vitalize the physical body and to bring about the development of our self-consciousness.

cordial   A sweet, syrupy alcoholic beverage often made with brandy. It can be flavored with fruit, spices, herbs, or a combination of all three.

cosmology   The study of the order of the universe. In a religious context, it means the hierarchy of Gods and Goddesses in a given religious system.

crystal   A stone with a particular regular molecular structure most often used to draw in or send out energy.

Cups   In the Tarot, the suit of emotions and spiritual experience. Cups are associated with the element Water and describe inner states, feelings, and relationship patterns.

decoupage   A French word which literally means "cutting up." The technique first became popular in Europe during the seventeenth and eighteenth centuries, inspired by the elaborately decorated lacquered furniture imported from China and Japan.

dedication ceremony   A ceremony, either formal or informal, in which a witch dedicates herself or himself to the Lady and the practice of the Craft.

emulsifier   An ingredient added to prevent the ingredients in a potion from separating. Two good choices are melted beeswax or stearic acid, both of which should be available at most health-food stores.

esbat   The monthly celebration of the Full Moon. When a Full Moon occurs twice in one month, the second one is called "a Blue Moon."

font   A set of letters, numerals, symbols, and punctuation marks all the same style and size. For example, all of the letters on your keyboard make up a font.

Grimoire   Often a section of your Book of Shadows, a Grimoire is a step-by-step record of spellcrafting.

handfasting   A formal ceremony joining two people together in the name of the Goddess and God; the Wiccan equivalent of a religious marriage ceremony.

infusion   Basically, a tea; anything steeped in hot water to create a brew.

journaling   Adding words to your Book of Shadows. Be sure to include not just spells, recipes, and incantations, but personal history and observations on the day.

Lady   Also called the Goddess, she embodies the female aspects of Maiden, Mother, and Crone in the Wiccan religion.

Lammas   August 1, also called the Festival of Light or Lughnasadh, this sabbat falls midway between the Summer Solstice and the Fall Equinox and is the first of the harvest festivals.

lignin   The material that holds wood fibers together as a tree grows. If lignin remains in paper, it will become yellow and brittle over time.

Lord   Also called the God, he represents the masculine aspects of the sun in the Wiccan religion and appears as the Lady's son and consort.

Mabon (Fall Equinox)   September 21, the second harvest festival, the days and nights are equal once again and gardens are in full bloom. Now is the time to start preparing for the coming winter months.

magick   Magick with a *k* is the spiritual kind of magick that Wiccans work. Magic is slight of hand left to magicians who perform on stage.

magick circle   Wiccans often create a sacred space by casting a magick circle with a wand or an athame and calling down the four corners.

makko   A natural, common binding agent that comes from the bark of a tree that grows in Southeast Asia, the Machillus Thunbergii tree. In powder form, it is sometimes marketed under the name Tabu no ki.

Midsummer (Summer Solstice)   June 21, "solstice" is Latin for "sun stands still" (sol "sun" and sistere "to stand"). Summer Solstice is the time of year when the sun is at its most powerful.

mulled   To heat a beverage and add spices. Adding cinnamon, nutmeg, cloves, and lemons and oranges to red wine that has been slowly heated makes a soothing beverage.

Ostara (Spring Equinox)   March 21, also called the Spring Equinox, this is the first true day of Springtide. The days and nights are now equal in length and we begin to see shoots of new growth and swelling buds on the trees.

pantheon   A group of deities worshiped by a certain people. For example, the Hindu Pantheon includes Shiva, Vishnu, Ganesh, and many others. Hindu people may worship all or some of the deities in this pantheon.

Pentacles   In the Tarot, the suit of practicality, security, and material concerns. Pentacles are associated with the element Earth and celebrate the beauty of nature, our interactions with plants and animals, and our physical experiences in the body. Pentacles also represent prosperity and wealth. A pentacle is also a five-pointed star within a circle, a powerful and ancient Wiccan symbol.

pentagram   A five-pointed star that is not enclosed in a circle.

perennials   Plants that come up every year, either through their original roots or by self-seeding and spread easily.

poppet   A small doll used during a magickal ceremony to represent a person.

priapic   Literally, phallic; a symbol (such as a wand) representing the God.

quarters   Also called the elements of nature, the corners, Watchtowers, elements, or elementals. They each have a correspondence to the direction.

quinoa   One of the most sacred foods of the ancient Incas of South America (pronounced *KEEN-wa*), a plant so nourishing, delicious, and vital they called it *chesiya mama*, the Mother Grain.

sabbat   The eight major Wiccan holidays: Samhain, Winter Solstice, Candlemas, Spring Equinox, Beltane, Summer Solstice, Lammas, and Fall Equinox.

Samhain   October 31, the last harvest festival and the Wiccan New Year, this is the time of reflection, the time to honor the ancestors who have crossed into the otherworld before us, and the time of divination. As we contemplate the Wheel of the Year, we come to recognize our own part in the eternal cycle of life.

scrying   From the English word *descry*, which means to make out dimly or to reveal. Wiccans use this technique to see visions of the future and to answer questions.

sigil   A magickal sign or symbol.

still rooms   A room that was used to dry the harvest of flowers and herbs to ready them for future use as scented waters, tonics, salves, teas, tincture, and what we know today as potpourri.

Swords   In the Tarot, the suit of intellect, thought, and reason. Swords are associated with the element of Air and are concerned with justice, truth, and ethical principles. This suit is also associated with states that lead to disharmony and unhappiness.

talisman From the ancient Greek word *teleo*, meaning to consecrate or magickally charge. A talisman is an object created and infused with magickal intent to create a specific effect. Talismans often contain an inherent magickal energy of their own. *See also* amulet.

Tarot A deck of 78 cards with 22 Major Arcana, or destiny, cards and 56 Minor Arcana cards that deal with activity in mundane, everyday experience. The Tarot deck contains four suits: Cups, Pentacles, Swords, and Wands (*see* individual listings).

tisane A beverage made by steeping tea or herbs in hot water. In France a tisane was often made for medicinal purposes.

vasilopita A cake of Greek origin traditionally served on New Year's Eve.

Wands In the Tarot, the suit of creativity, action, and movement. Wands are associated with the element of Fire and celebrate such qualities as enthusiasm, adventure, risk-taking, confidence, and passionate involvement.

Wicca A nature-based religion which honors a Lord and a Lady and celebrates based on the phases of the Moon and the change of seasons.

Yule (Winter Solstice) December 22, Yule is the time of greatest darkness and the longest night of the year. Since the Sun represents the male Divinity in many pagan traditions, this time is celebrated as the "return of the Sun God" where he is reborn of the Goddess.

Zen a school of thought that believes enlightenment can be attained through meditation, self-contemplation, and intuition rather than through didactic instructions.

Appendix B

Resources

Here's a list of books on Wicca and also on the Craft (and crafts!) you've learned about in this book. Let your curiosity, piqued by the projects you've been doing here, take you down any magickal path of interest. As your Craftworking knowledge deepens and matures, may your pathworking lead you ever closer to harmony with the Lady and the Lord, the blessed source of All.

Beyeral, Rev. Paul V. *The Master Book of Herbalism*. Washington, D.C.: Phoenix Publishing Inc., 1984.

Cabot, Laurie. *Power of the Witch*. New York: Dell Publishing, 1989.

Chase, Pamela Louise, and Jonathan Pawlik. *The Newcastle Guide to Healing with Gemstones*. North Hollywood, CA: Newcastle Publishing Co., Inc., 1989.

Christopher, Tom, and Marty Asher. *The 20-Minute Gardener*. New York: Random House, Inc., 1997.

Conway, D. J. *Moon Magick*. St. Paul, MN: Llewellyn Publications, 1998.

Cunningham, Scott. *Encyclopedia of Magical Herbs*. St. Paul, MN: Llewellyn Publications, 1990.

———. *Wicca: A Guide for the Solitary Practitioner*. St. Paul, MN: Llewellyn Publications, 1988.

Fennimore, Flora. *The Art of the Handmade Book.* Chicago: Chicago Review Press, 1992.

Ferguson, Diana. *The Magickal Year.* New York: Quality Paperback Book Club, 1996.

Green, Marian. *A Witch Alone.* London: HarperCollins Publishers, 1991.

Greenbough, Aurora, and Cathy Jewell. *The Complete Idiot's Guide to Spells and Spellcraft.* Indianapolis, IN: Alpha Books, 2004.

K., Amber. *Covencraft: Witchcraft for Three or More.* St. Paul, MN: Llewellyn Publications, 1998.

Morwyn. *Secrets of a Witch's Coven.* West Chester, PA: Whitford Press, 1988.

Ravenwolf, Silver. *To Light a Sacred Flame: Practical Witchcraft for the Millennium.* St. Paul, MN: Llewellyn Publications, 1999.

———. *To Ride a Silver Broomstick: New Generation Witchcraft.* St. Paul, MN: Llewellyn Publications, 1999.

Ritchie, Judy, and Jamie Kilmartin. *Great Rubber Stamping.* Westport, CT: Hugh Lauter Levin Associates, Inc., 2001.

Scott, Laura, and Mary Kay Linge. *The Complete Idiot's Guide to Divining the Future.* Indianapolis, IN: Alpha Books, 2003.

Shannon, Faith. *The Art and Craft of Paper.* San Francisco: Chronicle Books, 1994.

Simms, Maria Kay. *The Witch's Circle: Ritual and Craft of the Cosmic Muse.* St. Paul, MN: Llewellyn Publications, 1994.

Sjoo, Monica, and Barbara Mor. *The Great Cosmic Mother: Rediscovering the Religion of the Earth.* New York: HarperCollins Publishers, 1987.

Starhawk. *The Spiral Dance.* New York: Harper & Row, 1979.

Walker, Barbara G. *The Woman's Encyclopedia of Myths and Secrets.* New York: HarperCollins Publishers, Inc., 1983.

———. *The Women's Dictionary of Symbols & Sacred Objects.* New York: HarperCollins Publishers Ltd., 1988.

———. *Women's Rituals.* New York: Harper & Row, 1990.

Wilson, Jim. *Landscaping with Herbs.* New York: Houghton Mifflin Company, 1994.

Zimmermann, Denise, and Katherine A. Gleason. *The Complete Idiot's Guide to Wicca and Witchcraft, Second Edition.* Indianapolis, IN: Alpha Books, 2003.

Index

Check Out These
Best-Selling
COMPLETE IDIOT'S GUIDES®

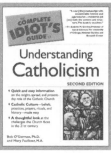

Understanding Catholicism
SECOND EDITION

- Quick and easy information on the origins, spread, and present-day role of the Catholic Church
- Catholic Culture—beliefs, practices, prayers, rituals, and history—made easy
- A thoughtful look at the challenges the Church faces in the 21st century

Bob O'Gorman, Ph.D. and Mary Faulkner, M.A.

1-59257-085-2
$18.95

Learning Spanish
THIRD EDITION

- Easy explanations of Spanish grammar and pronunciation
- Key phrases for travel, hotels, airports, shopping, business, and more
- New and expanded vocabulary lists with English/Spanish and Spanish/English translations

Gail Stein

0-02-864451-4
$18.95

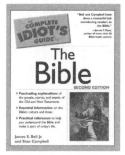

The Bible
SECOND EDITION

- Fascinating explanations of the people, stories, and events of the Old and New Testaments
- Essential information on the Bible's culture and times
- Practical references to help you understand the Bible and make it part of today's life.

James S. Bell Jr. and Stan Campbell

0-02-864382-8
$18.95

Being a Groom
SECOND EDITION

- Top 10 things to remember on the big day
- Brand-new ideas on has honeymoon destinations
- Idiot-proof advice on breaking the ice between the in-laws

Jennifer Lata Rung and Mark Rung

0-02-864456-5
$9.95

Grammar and Style
SECOND EDITION

- Easy-to-understand instructions on writing and speaking
- Perfect punctuation, from the apostrophe to the semi-colon
- Rights and wrongs of sentence structure, word usage, spelling, and much, much more

Laurie E. Buzakis, Ph.D.

1-59257-115-8
$16.95

Playing the Guitar
SECOND EDITION

- Tips and tricks to get you playing your own tunes in no time
- Easy-to-follow steps for learning to read music
- Words of wisdom from a professional musician and instructor

Frederick Noad

0-02-864244-9
$21.95 w/CD

Personal Finance in Your 20s & 30s
SECOND EDITION

- Savvy advice on getting—and staying—out of debt
- Idiot-proof tips on saving money for the future and still having money to spend
- Down-to-earth advice on making wise investments—especially when you're on a budget

Sarah Young Fisher and Susan Shelly

0-02-864374-7
$19.95

Knitting and Crocheting
SECOND EDITION
Illustrated

- An all-new selection of easy-to-follow patterns with step-by-step illustrated instructions
- Crafty tips on choosing the right yarn for your project
- Simple advice for going beyond the basics to create more advanced projects

Barbara Breiter and Gail Diven

1-59257-089-5
$16.95

The Perfect Resume
THIRD EDITION

- Winning resume techniques that will convince an employer to call you for an interview
- Expert advice on solving sticky resume issues such as layoffs, employment gaps, and career changes
- More than 100 up-to-date samples of successful resumes and cover letters

Susan Ireland

0-02-864440-9
$14.95

Buying and Selling a Home
FOURTH EDITION

- What to expect when you buy or sell a home—with or without a broker
- Updated coverage of financing options for buyers, including mortgages and refinancing
- Idiot-proof tips on getting the best possible price when you sell

Shelley O'Hara and Nancy D. Lewis

1-59257-120-4
$18.95

Low-Carb Meals

- Idiot-proof tips on planning great-tasting meals for the whole family
- More than 325 easy-to-prepare recipes for everything from main dishes to desserts—including bread
- A grocery list of foods every low-carb pantry should contain

Lucy Beale and Sandy G. Couvillon, M.S., L.D.N., R.D.

1-59257-180-8
$18.95

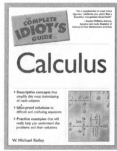

Calculus

- Descriptive concepts that simplify this most intimidating of math subjects
- Idiot-proof solutions to difficult and confusing equations
- Practice examples that really help you understand the problems and their solutions

W. Michael Kelley

0-02-864365-8
$18.95

More than *450* titles in *30* different categories
Available at booksellers everywhere

ALPHA